INDIA'S DEFENCE PREPAREDNESS

INDIA'S DEFENCE PREPAREDNESS

Editor

Shrikant Paranjpe

PENTAGON PRESS

India's Defence Preparedness

Editor: Shrikant Paranjpe

ISBN 978-81-8274-901-6

First Published in 2016

Published by
PENTAGON PRESS
206, Peacock Lane, Shahpur Jat,
New Delhi-110049
Phones: 011-64706243, 26491568
Telefax: 011-26490600
email: rajan@pentagonpress.in
website: www.pentagonpress.in

Printed at Aegean Offset Printers, Greater Noida, U.P.

CONTENTS

FOREWORD

The importance of India's defence preparedness can never be overstated. Its neighbourhood is hostile and two of its neighbours, with whom it has serious issues of discord, are not only armed with nuclear weapons but have close ties with each other. The obvious question in view of such a geopolitical situation is whether India is well prepared to defend itself at two fronts simultaneously.

Modern warfare is technology driven and India depends entirely on imports for weapon systems at enormous cost. To sustain a full-fledged war, it is imperative that India must have an indigenous arms industry capable of producing world-class weapon systems and keeping pace with the advanced nations of the world in research and development in the field of defence equipment. Though serious intent is there, self-sufficiency is still far away.

Another lacuna is the absence of institutionalized co-ordination between Indian political leadership and the armed forces. What could be the mechanism to fill this void? It may be argued that the Cabinet Committee on Security is there for co-ordination. The fact, however, is that the dialogue between the top political leadership and the armed forces chiefs is not what it ought to be. It is therefore necessary to have a better system which provides for inputs from the armed forces in the formulation of the country's defence policy and planning for eventualities they will have to handle.

Nehru Centre examined these issues in a series of seminars in which experts on defence issues participated. The papers presented at the seminars have been compiled in this book which will be useful to policy makers and students of defence studies as well.

SHARAD PAWAR
Chairman
Nehru Centre

INTRODUCTION

Shrikant Paranjpe

The Estimates Committee of the Indian Parliament, in its Nineteenth Report on the Ministry of Defence,[1] raised some crucial questions about India's defence policy. The Ministry of Defence, in its statement to the Estimates Committee, stated that India's defence policy has basically been a policy to defend the territory, sovereignty, and freedom of the country. The Estimates Committee considered this a needless oversimplification of the concerned policy. It felt that India should have a national security doctrine which not only takes a long-term view of the country's security requirements but also looks into problems of internal security. The importance of India's defence preparedness can never be overstated. Its neighbourhood is hostile and two of its neighbours, with whom it has serious issues, are not only armed with nuclear weapons but have close ties with each other. Besides the external threats India faces conflict within. There is left-wing extremism and insurgency coupled with political instability and indecision.

The Context

The services of the Indian military were first requisitioned in the immediate aftermath of Indian Independence. The success of the Indian army in stalling the onslaught of the Pakistani forces into Srinagar indicated India's military preparedness. The 1962 debacle in Sela Bomdila was more a product of the failure of the political and army leaderships, and the lack of a combined services planning.[2] The Henderson Brooks report, only the summary of which was placed before Parliament,[3] had been critical of the collection and processing of intelligence. Indian security policy during the Nehru years—almost until the debacle of 1962 rested on his model of development and the policy of defence through development. In essence, this approach accepted the logic of defence through diplomacy and developed a security framework that had its roots in politico-diplomatic activities and the process of modernization through industrial development. The key to security then was a long-term strategy of self-reliance through development. The 1962 war brought about a change in these perceptions. Prime Minister Shastri sought to have direct linkage between defence (military) capability and political role. The Reports of the Ministry of Defence in the post-1962 years reflect this change.

The late 1960s brought in several changes in the Asian security scene. Pakistan sought to reassert itself by moving closer to China and also through conflict with India, first in the Rann of Kutch and later on in Kashmir in 1965. Richard Nixon's Guam doctrine (1969) and Henry Kissinger's Four Power Balance doctrine spelt out the American position vis-à-vis India. As against this, came the Brezhnev Plan for Collective Security in Asia, the Kosygin Plan for Economic Co-operation (1969) and a series of bilateral treaty initiatives, one of which later culminated in the Indo-Soviet treaty of Peace, Friendship and Co-operation of 1971. This period also saw the beginning of Soviet arms aid to India. By the early 1970s, a new thinking set in. This was the post-Bangladesh era and there was certain degree of credibility about India's position in South Asia. This period saw some serious efforts being made to develop Indian military capability; both consolidation and modernization of the armed forces were undertaken. Unlike with the Soviet Union, India's security relationship with the United States was of limited nature. The American decision to arm Pakistan, taken in the face of Indian opposition, and the Pakistani decision to join the American alliances had strained the Indo-US security relationship. It was only in the 1980s that positive changes became visible. Indo-US dialogue on defence matters began obliquely during the tenure of Mrs. Gandhi and continued through the Rajiv Gandhi years. Of relevance were the Kickleighter proposals that were put forward in the post-Soviet phase of Indo-US relations.

India's 'exclusivity' in Indo-Soviet relations started to end with Gorbachev's 'New Thinking'—opening up a dialogue with China, withdrawal from Afghanistan, and steps towards disarmament—on Soviet foreign policy.[4] India responded by opening up a dialogue with China, Pakistan, and also the United States. The disintegration of the Soviet Union in 1991 did not create an abrupt end to the flow of relations between the two countries. The two countries extended the 1971 agreement during the visit of the former President Yeltsin to India in 1993 and subsequently in 1994 several agreements including those that dealt with military and technical cooperation were signed during Russian Prime Minister Victor Chernomyrdin's visit in 1994. In October 2000 President Putin visited India and both countries signed the Declaration of Strategic Partnership.[5] This visit was reciprocated by Prime Minister Vajpayee who during his visit signed a Declaration on Further Consolidation of Strategic partnership between the two countries. The provision of regular summit-level meetings between the two countries made in the first agreement has helped to continue the mutual dialogue. There was a significant forward movement in the area of defence cooperation during the Putin regime. Over the past years major weapon systems were acquired or contracted for[6] and joint development of weapon systems like the BrahMos supersonic cruise missile was initiated.[7]

Whether out of compulsions of reliability or difficulties faced due to dependence, India has now sought to diversify its defence procurements. The earlier compulsions of being tied to the Soviet Union have almost ended and India now avoids the 'exclusivity' that existed in those bilateral ties. The Indo-US security dialogue began sometime in the late 1980s. In 1995, the two countries signed the Agreed Minute on Defence Cooperation[8] covering service-to-service and civilian-to-civilian cooperation, as well as cooperation in defence production and research. The Indian nuclear tests of 1998 broke the early momentum of the bilateral relationship. The tests were followed by a prolonged dialogue between the Indian Foreign Minister Jaswant Singh and the American Under Secretary of State Strobe Talbott. This dialogue sought to re-establish the broken links between the two countries. It was only after September 2001 that Indo-US security ties gained real momentum. Both countries came to acknowledge a desire for greater bilateral interaction on security issues. In

July 2005 President Bush and Prime Minister Manmohan Singh vowed to work on achieving 'full civilian nuclear energy cooperation with India.'[9] The finalization of the agreement in 2010 ended the nuclear 'apartheid' for India and it became eligible to gain access to nuclear material and technology from the suppliers. The Modi government has set its agenda with a focus on Southern Asian neighbours as priority. It has sought to extend the 'Look East' policy further and build itself in the Indo-Pacific region as also further strengthen its ties with the United States. One of the key initiatives being taken is in the area of self-reliance in defence production under the 'Buy (Indian)' and 'Buy and Make (Indian)' policy. There appears to be a realist perspective being brought in, ending the ideological overtones in India's world view.

Issues of defence industry and production bring in debates about self-reliance and research and development capabilities, they also raise the prospect of private sector participation in defence production. In India, the context of these developments would be dependent upon the availability of infrastructural facilities or the lack of it; or the ability or otherwise to indigenize, and innovate and produce in the face of trade and other restrictions.[10] Speaking at the Defence-expo the then Indian Defence Minister argued that Indian defence expenditure would increase 'in proportion' to India's economic growth rate. He linked Indian defence spending to the Indian industrial growth and also emphasized the need for achieving a higher degree of indigenization. This according to him would be possible with a greater cooperation between the private and the public sector and would enable India to achieve its goal of defence modernization.[11] However, defence spending in India has not increased Indian military capability. Cohen and Dasgupta[12] argue that the modernization effort has been visible mainly in the Navy and the Air Force while the Army continues to face problems. There remains an imbalance within the services with no integration of strategic planning. India has emphasized on technology as the key to modernization and not on organizational change. The problem, according to Susant Singh and Mukul Asher[13] is not of allocation of finance that the Defence Minister routinely states would continue to be available, but with the fact that the defence budget is only an allocation of funds and does not have any relation to strategic planning. The problem is not of availability of funds, but of the long-term strategy of their effective utilization.

Issues

It is in this context that the Nehru Centre decided to hold a series of seminar discussions on India's Defence Preparedness inviting experts and practitioners from the field of armed forces, intelligence agencies, scientific community, academia and diplomacy. Independence, internal security, and territorial integrity have always been over-riding priorities in India's strategic perspectives. These, along with the approach to peace, constituted the 'governing image' of India's policies during the early years of Indian Independence. One may argue that India's geopolitical location; its history and culture; its political and socio-economic system have contributed in different ways to evolve its strategic perspectives. But does India have a 'National Security Strategy'? How does one understand India's defence preparedness?

The volume begins with a survey of India's defence preparedness in the context of the three services in the first section and then moves on to understand the discourse on the making of a national security policy, its political implications, linkages with foreign policy and the issues of civil-military relations. The third section has a specific focus on the issue of defence research and development and the role of the State and participation of the private sector in defence production. Finally, the volume takes a look at two specific applied cases where the issue of defence preparedness is likely to impinge, that of Pakistan and China.

Defence Preparedness, **Maj Gen Shashikant Pitre (Retd.)** argues, is the synthesis of tangible factors like strength of the armed and paramilitary forces, quantity and quality of the weapons and equipment, stocking of ammunition, supplies and other war-like materials and intangible factors like morale, motivation and dedication of soldiers, state of their training, efficacy of force structure, soundness of tactics and strategy, quality of military leadership, higher defence management, will power of the policy-makers and the national will and awareness. The comments made by General VP Malik, the then Chief of the Army Staff (COAS) at the onset of the Kargil War, that the Indian Army will fight with whatever they have or the letter written by the former COAS, General VK Singh to the Prime Minister expressing great concern about defence preparedness sets the tone of Maj Gen Pitre's paper. He goes on to examine the challenges that India faces, the threat scenarios; acknowledges that the debate on defence preparedness is now conducted in the public domain; laments the discrepancies in the equipment profile of the Indian Army and calls for a process wherein the Government initiates processes for the Services to have a say in the national policymaking.

Air power has two important features which according to **Air Marshal BN Gokhale (Retd)** remained somewhat obscured during India's post-Independence period. First is that the air power is inherently offensive in nature, best used pre-emptively, forcing the enemy on the backfoot and the second important feature is the strategic effect, often achieved by timely use of air power. In the years ensuing after Independence, due to the baggage from the Colonial days, many military experts continued to consider the Indian Air Force (IAF) as a Tactical Air Force, a thought process that almost shackled the IAF as an extension of field artillery, playing a 'limited' role on the battlefield. Air Marshal Gokhale takes a survey of the role played by the IAF since independence and stresses on the need for jointness in operations on the battlefield.

In case one views the map of the world in an inverted manner one can see India jutting out in the Indian Ocean area. Pointing out this reality, **Vice Admiral Vinod Pasricha (Retd.)** maintains that in comparison to the other navies of the world the Indian Navy has had an excellent performance. There are areas of concern like planning for defence in India that is usually of five years, whereas there is a need for a long-term perspective planning. This is especially so in case of shipbuilding activity in India. Some concerns about ammunition are, according to him, resolvable. He believes that the Indian Navy can handle the presence in the Indian Ocean area of Pakistan navy and the Chinese navy or any other navy in the world.

George Tanham's essay on Indian strategic thinking led to a debate in Indian academic circles on Tanham's argument that India lacks strategic thinking. Two other works that **Mr Nitin Gokhale** cites are those of Manjari Chatterjee Miller and Ashley J Tellis, the former follows the

Tanham line while the latter talks of Indian strategic autonomy. The questions raised by Gokhale are based on these perceptions about India. While there is no documented policy on Indian's 'National Security Strategy,' not at least is public domain, one finds that the terms 'grand strategy' and 'national interest' are used for almost anything. Grand strategy, Gokhale argues, is not a product or a document that can be manufactured by a group of experts and policy wonks. It is, in many ways, a by-product of history that needs further nurturing by way of political direction. So while India may not articulate a 'grand strategy,' it will do well to pursue one—in a pragmatic, understated and commonsensical manner. Gokhale makes a specific mention of the Naresh Chandra Committee (2011) and calls for a public debate on the report so as to overcome systemic weaknesses and structural shortcomings in its national security decision-making apparatus.

Ambassador Rakesh Sood's presentation seeks to spell out the understanding of national interest in terms of the structuring and implementation of India's foreign policy. He traces the historical roots of Indian foreign policy during the British times and the freedom movement and argues that in 1947, the Indian government inherited two competing schools of thought that were to have a bearing on foreign policy—realpolitik from the colonial practice and moralpolitik from the Congress national movement. He traces the changes that Indian foreign policy has witnessed since Indian independence and its close linkage with concerns of Indian security and concludes that the role of foreign policy today in safeguarding India's national interest and contributing to defence preparedness is more vital than ever before. India needs to go beyond the 'labels' which often get wrapped up in ideology and seek a healthy mix of pragmatism, a willingness to learn from past experiences, a readiness to accept change and convert challenges into opportunities, an ability to synergize efforts and policies and a wise leadership that can keep the focus on bringing about the transformation of India into a secure and prosperous nation.

This 'pragmatism' would be a product of the manner in which political guidance is used to shape India's 'hard power' meant for external threats. The hard power of a nation represents the coercive power of a State and in combination with soft power determines its ability to exert influence in the international system. **Lt Gen (Dr) Prakash Menon (Retd)** focuses on the scope, content and form of India's politico-military interaction required to shape India's military forces during peace so as to understand this continuing interaction between hard and soft power and its role in the defence of the land. Menon laments that currently, India's hard power is being shaped by bureaucratic inertia instead of a military strategy that ought to bridge the space between envisaged political objectives and national resources available. He recommends that there is a need for creating a group of national security professionals in government; that strategic studies be introduced in the university system, so as to provide an adequate supply of national security professionals and the appointment of a Chief of Defence Staff or any other equivalent entity who can provide military advice in contrast to service-specific advice, evolve a joint military strategy, harmonize inter-service differences and, at the same time, mitigate the problem of prioritization of acquisition.

The politico-military interaction constitutes the core of the debate on civil-military relations, an issue that has been widely debated in India. The political and military leadership would naturally carry different perspectives from which each approaches the issue of national security. The military leadership would place greater stress on the ways and means of overcoming security threats while the political leadership would have to operate on a wider canvas as they would be responsible for both the security issues and other equally important economic and social objectives as well as preserving the legitimate political order and the constitutional foundations on which it rests. This is the debate that **Dr S Kalyanaraman** focuses on in his presentation on the civil-military relations. It is the interaction between the security and social imperatives and, by extension, the interaction between civilian and military leaders charged with addressing these imperatives that according to him is 'the nub of the problem of civil-military relations.' Kalyanaraman argues that India's practice of civil-military relations is the product of three major concerns that have dominated the thinking of the political leadership: the need to ensure that defence and development go hand in hand; the imperative of subordinating the military leadership to civilian authority; and three, not empowering the military leadership in any manner that might contribute to their assertiveness.

Lt Gen VR Raghavan (Retd.) carries this argument further when he argues that the interplay of responsibilities between the political and military establishments of any nation is a principal component of its military security policy. This policy should aim at developing a system of civil-military relations that will maximize military security at the least sacrifice of other social values. Raghavan refers to the flawed civil-military relations during the 1962 conflict and contrasts it with the excellent manner in which the two were able to work together in 1965, a lesson that was helpful in the 1971 conflict. He traces the recommendations by various committees like the Kargil Review Committee Report and the Group of Ministers' Report of the Naresh Chandra Group and points out that the causes of political and civil service unwillingness to modernize the Ministry of Defence and introduce the recommendations of Expert Committees and Groups are rooted in historical, cultural and organizational beliefs of political and bureaucratic privilege or gains. This has led to actions that are self-evidently needed in national security interests being opposed or sidelined due to unfounded fears and unstated prejudices.

Intelligence is an important instrument for anticipating, assessing, planning, and operationalizing national security situations like waging wars for expanding territorial boundaries, resisting foreign aggressions and quelling internal rebellions. This is an area where the civil and the military expertise are likely to work together for national security. **Mr V Balachandran** traces the evolution of intelligence organizations in India and some other countries like the United States and Russia. He points out that Intelligence is not mere collection of information, it is a long and often tedious process of bare facts becoming policy inputs and ground action through an alchemic process—collection of facts, analysis, evaluation, assessment and dissemination to the consumers by the agencies, then arbitration by a higher body like the National Security Council to plug gaps in intelligence, report to the policy-makers (Cabinet), policy adjudication by the Cabinet, policy implementation by different ministries, review and accountability at the end. This is called the 'Intelligence Cycle'. If any one of these steps is missed an impression arises about 'Intelligence Failure'. Commenting on the Indian scene he argues that there is a high-powered coordinator and that despite setting up a high-profile National Security Council with a big secretariat, India has not been able to do satisfactory intelligence integration to anticipate security threats.

The last decade or more has seen momentous changes take place in the approach to war, changes that have been a product of technological innovations that were first witnessed in the Gulf War of 1990. If technology is likely to dominate the discourse on defence preparedness one needs to understand the capabilities of a nation in this regard. The volume takes a look at the Indian scenario in this regard with two articles, one by Dr Amitav Mallik dealing with the status of Indian defence technology, especially with reference to the objective of self-reliance and the other by Dr Deb Mohanty focusing on the role of the private sector in defence.

Dr Amitav Mallik focuses on India's policy of 'self-reliance' that has led India to make impressive progress since 1962 to be recognized as an emerging world-class democratic power with its own techno-military capacities. He identifies some of the technologies that are critical to the existing requirements for Defence, including Fly-By-Wire Flight Control technology, Advanced Gas Turbine Engines, Ram Rocket & Hyper velocity missiles, Atmospheric Re-entry technology, Infra-Red Search & Track technology, etc. Some of the technologies that would be vital for new capabilities for defence and security may include Smart Weapon sub-systems, Sensors and Active Arrays, Intelligent Terminal Guidance, Supersonic and Hypersonic Propulsion, Satellite-based Communication and Intelligence, Advanced Radars and Stealth detection, etc. Self-reliance, according to Dr Mallik, in these technologies can be achieved only when indigenous knowhow and competence is backed with in-country availability of all critical materials and components as well as the necessary integration and test facilities for some of these highly complex advanced systems. He argues that the perception of India being a potential regional power could now attract adverse attention of other powerful competing nations and also the weak neighbours who may be apprehensive of India's influence.

The Indian position on the participation of the private sector in defence production is peculiar. It recognizes the need to involve the private sector, calls for a private-public participation, seeks to give preference to 'Buy

(Indian)' and 'Buy and Make (Indian)' but at the same time seeks to retain the dominant/controlling position of the public sector. **Dr Deb Mohanty** does not appear to share the confidence of Dr Mallik about India's defence science and technology and industrial base and argues that India has already missed the defence industrial base (DSTI) for a variety of reasons, and that it needs double the effort to nurture its domestic DSTI base in order to be counted as a formidable power on the global stage and Technology and Industry base in India. He traces the history of private sector participation in the defence industry in India to identify the problems and opportunities. The Indian government, in May 2001, decided to open up the defence production sector for private participation. The private sector was allowed to produce any defence item, with foreign direct investment (FDI) up to 26 per cent. However, its participation was subject to obtaining industrial license and security clearance which became a major bottleneck for the industry. The new government has now increased the FDI Component to 49 per cent. Dr Mohanty feels that the state would have to take a firm decision as to how to engage the private sector for maximization of overall DSTI capability. However, India's weaknesses, most of which are self-created, outnumber its strengths, leading the entire sector to excel in some pockets only. Corrective measures in the form of a defence industrial and technology vision document as a guiding force, a pragmatic politico-bureaucratic direction, flexibility in structural arrangements with horizontal inter-disciplinary interactions and diffusion on the other, periodic reviews and accountability within the institution and at the higher governance levels need to be undertaken for India to forge ahead in this area.

In the final part of this volume an effort is made to see the application of India's defence policy to two critical countries: China and Pakistan. China's foreign policy according to **Ambassador Jayadeva Ranade** has begun to acquire a sharper and more muscular edge that will impact India, Japan, Vietnam and other countries with which it has territorial disputes. In the intense debate underway in China for the past couple of years on China's international security environment, arguments advocating an uncompromising approach appear to be gaining ground. China has assertively sought to expand its footprint in South Asia, in the process encroaching on India's strategic space and encircling it. The challenge for

India is essentially to manage relations with China, as their interests overlap to an extent and any undue tension or conflagration could derail the aspirations and economies of both countries. The greatest impediment to the India-China relations, however, remains the boundary issue. The ability of both sides to contain incidents on the border will be a prominent feature of the region's geo-politics in this decade.

India and Pakistan, though emerging from a common colonial past, have followed radically different paths of political evolution. Pakistan has been plagued by persisting insecurity about its very identity. In terms of military analysis, **Mr R Banerji** identifies six general characteristics of Pakistan's strategic culture that have been commonly enumerated: (i) Opposition to Indian hegemony; (ii) Primacy of Defence requirements; (iii) Nuclear Deterrence; (iv) Acceptance, but not over-reliance on outside assistance; (v) Stability on Western border—quest for 'strategic depth' for conventional and nuclear assets and (vi) Identification with conservative Islamic causes. There is a miniscule opinion among fringe Pakistani liberals or intelligentsia that suggests beginnings of introspection to change this national narrative, but prospects for internally or externally driven shifts in the Army's strategic culture, according to Banerji, have not manifested sufficiently.

The post-cold-war era saw three transformative events in India's national life that had far-reaching implications for its world view: one, the economic watershed when India started the irrevocable economic liberalization and reform process under the compulsion of an economically perilous condition; two, the foreign and defence policy watershed when India declared itself a nuclear weapons power; and three, the Indo–US Civilian Nuclear Cooperation agreement that ended the Indian isolation in the world of dual-use technology transfer and sought to end the ideological blinkers on foreign policy. The efforts at modernization of the Indian armed forces in terms of equipment and training; the building up of nuclear and missile capabilities; the opening up of a strategic dialogue with the United States; the opening up of arms purchases from the Western sources, including Israel; etc., are some of the indicators of the acceptance of a more open realist posture in international relations. The technological dimensions of this debate came to be demonstrated in the context of India's success in the fields of nuclear, space and electronics. The nineties saw the opening up of East Asia as an area of interest under what came to be termed as a 'Look East' policy. Today, with economic concerns of energy security taking over the debates on external affairs, India has embarked on a more global reach for itself. Yet concerns about India's neighbours continue to dominate Indian thinking. This volume seeks to place issues of India's defence preparedness in the context of this changing environment.

NOTES

1. Estimates Committee, 1992-3, 10th Lok Sabha, 19th Report, Ministry of Defence: Defence Force Levels, Manpower Management and Policy (New Delhi, 1992).
2. There is a lot of literature on India-China relations, especially border conflict and its management. The central thrust of this argument is what K Subrahmanyam has pointed out. See: K Subramanyam, '50 Years of Security,' *The Times of India*, 15 July 1997, p. 14. See also the Special Issue on *Chinese Aggression*, International Studies (New Delhi), Vol. V, July-Oct. 1963.
3. Government of India, Ministry of Defence, Annual Report 1963-4, p. 2.
4. Sestanovich, Stephen, 'Gorbachev's Foreign Policy: A Diplomacy of Decline,' *Problems of Communism*, Vol. XXXVII (1), Jan-Feb, 1988, pp. 4-5.
5. See Text: *Declaration on Strategic Partnership between the Republic of India and the Russian Federation*, 3 October 2000.
6. *India News Online*, 5 March 2001.
7. Bakshi, Jyotsna, India-Russia Defence Cooperation,' *Strategic Analysis*, Vol. 30 (2), April-June 2006, pp. 458-61.
8. Steven, Sboto, 'Indo-US Military Cooperation—Taking Stock,' in *Foreign Area* http://www.faoa.org/journal/sboto1203.html
9. Paranjpe Shrikant, 'Beyond the Defence and Development Debate : A Framework for Analysis of Indian Defence Expenditure,'*Mondes en Development*, Vol. 21, no. 83, 1993, p. 148.
10. *DNA* (*Daily News and Analysis*) Mumbai, 15 February 2010.
11. Cohen, Stephen and Sunil Dasgupta, *Arming without Aiming: India's Military Modernization*, New Delhi: Penguin Publications, 2010, pp. 143-5.
12. Quoted in Ibid., p. 144.

I. THE SETTING

CHAPTER I

DEFENCE PREPAREDNESS OF THE INDIAN ARMY

Shashikant Pitre

Introduction

The Indian psyche from time immemorial firmly believed that the land was protected from the north by the impregnable Himalayas and from the south by the vast Indian Ocean. The residents could rest assured of their security provided by these natural barriers. To their peril, the first invader came in the tenth century surmounting the same Himalayas. He gained a foothold and then by crafty application of Chanakya's philosophy of '*Sam, Dam, Dand and Bhed*,' consolidated his empire. A series of invasions followed at regular intervals, one aggressor replaced by another kin from his land till Babur laid the foundation of the legendary Mughal Empire in AD 1526, which ruled for over two centuries. The final invasion came from the sea by a medley of European powers. The second citadel had also failed the Indians. The Englishmen succeeded in establishing the largest colony of the British Empire and guided India's destiny for over 150 years.

The ancient Indian security thought enshrined in Kautilya's *Arthashastra* was replaced by the Panchsheel philosophy of Emperor Ashoka, deeply influenced by the 'Live and let live' preaching of Buddhism.

Forgiveness and 'Vasudhaiva Kutumbakam' were the guiding principles. Chakra and Lion were the symbols. There was no place for a sword or gun in this idealism. Peace, diversity and an all-inclusive culture were the primal nuances. It is but natural that this evolution would have a profound influence on the Indian strategic culture. It subdued the national strategic temper.

This strategic inadequacy has been the bane of Indian polity. Despite five wars and a crawling proxy war launched by our adversaries, the fact that we do not have a comprehensive National Security Doctrinal Document is undoubtedly a matter of great regret. There existed no exclusive organization to deal with the vital subject of National Security till the late 1990s, when it was overseen by the Principal Secretary to the Prime Minister. It was only on 19 November 1998 that the National Security Council (NSC) was instituted. However, even their parleys were few and far between. These are a few pointers to the neglect of strategic thought in the initial years of the Republic. This aspect of defence preparedness fails to receive the attention of policy-makers even today.

Defence Preparedness

Defence Preparedness is the synthesis of tangible factors like strength of the armed and paramilitary forces, quantity and quality of the weapons and equipment, stocking of ammunition, supplies and other war-like materials and intangible factors like morale, motivation and dedication of soldiers, state of their training, efficacy of force structure, soundness of tactics and strategy, quality of military leadership, higher defence management, will power of the policy-makers and the national will and awareness.

Walter Lippman in 1943 postulated that 'a nation has security when it does not have to sacrifice its legitimate interests to avoid war and is able, if challenged, to maintain them by war.' Thus the defence preparedness of a country on the one hand should be a deterrent against any challenge by its adversaries to the country's sovereignty and on the other, enable it to wage a successful war against any inimical interests, when the situation so demands.

Lately, India's defence preparedness has been under public gaze apropos the statements of two recent Army Chiefs. At the onset of the Kargil War, General VP Malik, the then Chief of the Army Staff (COAS) had said, 'We will fight with whatever we have.' A letter to the Prime Minister written by the former COAS, General VK Singh in 2012 revealed that 'the state of defence preparedness of the country is a matter of great concern.' He reportedly wrote, 'The state of the major (fighting) arms, i.e., Mechanised forces, Artillery, Air Defence, Infantry and special forces, as well as the Engineers and Signals, is indeed alarming.' A few major issues raised by him include:[1]

- The army's entire tank fleet is 'devoid of critical ammunition to defeat the enemy tanks.'
- The air defence is '97 per cent obsolete and does not give the deemed confidence.'
- The infantry is crippled with 'deficiencies of crew-served weapons' and lacks night-fighting capabilities.
- Elite Special Forces are woefully short of essential weapons.
- There are large-scale voids in critical surveillance.

General VK Singh has revealed only part of the malady. It is not that the previous Army Chiefs had not brought to the notice of the policy-makers concerns about lack of adequate attention to the vital subject of the defence preparedness of the Indian Army (IA), but the leakage, ostensibly a blessing in disguise, has brought this into India's public domain. This narrative endeavours to delve into various aspects of the defence preparedness of the IA.

Challenge

India is a huge country covering an area of 30 lakh square km, spanning 3200 km from Kashmir to Kanyakumari and 2700 km from Kolkata to Kutch. It has land borders measuring 16500 km with seven neighbours and it has a maritime boundary of 5600 km. It has a complex border dispute with China on the eastern border and an obdurate and unreasonable adversary, Pakistan, on the western border. India is a major littoral nation on the Indian Ocean, the world's energy interstate, the link for megaships carrying hydrocarbons from the Middle East to oil-guzzling countries like Indonesia and Japan.

In size, it is the seventh largest country in the world and second largest in Asia. With a population of 1.3 billion, it is an attractive market for the developed countries. It is the largest democracy in the world, with deep democratic roots evolved in a short period of six and a half decades. India is the third largest economy with a GDP of more than USD 4 trillion. India's growth rate had touched 8 per cent, which of late has waned.

Due to its size, eminent geo-political position, economic credentials and political maturity, it has the potential to be a regional power in Asia and a natural responsibility to lead the South Asian countries. It follows that India should possess a formidable armed clout to preserve and enhance its national interests. India has the third largest armed force in the world, amply battle-tested having fought five wars with its neighbours. The challenges, both to its borders as well as to its internal security, are humongous.

The principal role of the IA is the protection of India's territorial integrity against both internal and external threats. Guarding India's borders with Pakistan and China is an unenviable task, particularly when of its 16500 km shared borders, 7000 km are disputed. These are hot borders where artillery duels and other confrontations are routine. There is a raging insurgency both in Kashmir and on the North-eastern borders.

C Christine Fair, a noted US Defence Analyst, has this to say about the IA:

> India has the largest army of any democratic country, a highly regarded, well-trained and professional army that has operational flexibility and niche warfare capabilities. It has conducted operations successfully in desert and jungle terrains, tackled rural and urban insurgencies and operated at home and abroad including on UN peace-keeping missions. Notably, the IA has well-honed and exceptional high-altitude warfare capabilities, which few countries can boast.

Clearly, the IA has the potential, but is it backed by equipment wherewithal?

General Bikram Singh, COAS, outlined the following security challenges to the IA, in an interview to SP's Military Year Book 2013:

- The geo-political environment in Asia and South Asia is dynamic, which poses challenges to the IA across the entire spectrum of conflict in conventional and unconventional domains. Challenges range from traditional land-centric threats along borders to asymmetric threats including proxy war and insurgency. Rapid and exponential growth in the information and communication technologies and cyberspace has created fresh technological challenges. Threats emanating from the cyber domain have become an everyday reality.

- Threats have hybridized. There is a conventional threat concurrent to the ongoing proxy war in Jammu and Kashmir (J&K) and in the Northeast. IA needs to prepare for both.
- Requisite modernization and capability enhancement is planned and is being undertaken.

While the security challenges have been well spelt out, it is difficult to share the optimism of the Chief regarding materialization of the enhancement of capabilities.

Threats

Battlefield Environment

There has been a paradigm shift in the nature of conflict. Developments in Pakistan and Afghanistan have brought South Asia to the centre stage of sub-conventional conflict and instability. In addition, terrorism, low-intensity conflict (LIC) motivated by economic disparity, religious fundamentalism, narcotic trade and the threat of nuclear weapons falling into wrong hands remain issues of concern in the region. The entry of non-state actors has added a new dimension to LICs.

The continuum of warfare has expanded with the proxy war at one extremity, the nuclear war at the other and the conventional war in the middle. There is an increased avoidance of conventional warfare and preference for extremities. The enormous destructive power of conventional and nuclear capabilities of strong adversaries has resulted in weaker states and non-state groups adopting sub-conventional and irregular means to achieve their political objectives. The conventional conflict is increasingly becoming intertwined with sub-conventional conflict, with irregular forces using unconventional means and tactics. The lethality of irregular forces is on the increase with their access to technology.

The characteristics of future conflict will be as under:

- The spectrum of conflict will range from conflict between states to conflict with non-state actors and proxies. The weaker states will utilize non-state actors to achieve their political objectives against their stronger adversaries.
- Distinction between conventional operations, proxy war and unconventional means is increasingly blurring due to the hybrid nature of warfare. Conventional conflict could be either preceded or succeeded by a period of irregular conflict.
- The future wars will be technology-driven. Increased use of precision munitions at ever-increasing ranges, loss of distinction between day and night operations, increased fatigue due to non-linearity and incessant pace of operations and ever-increasing technological threshold to operate sophisticated weapon systems will add to the complexity of war.
- Space and cyberspace will be active battlegrounds. Cyber-warfare may emerge even more dangerous than the nuclear threat due to ambiguity in the source of attack and potential to cripple critical infrastructure. The conflict will become five-dimensional to include aerospace, land, sea, electromagnetic and cyberspace. Laser-based Direct Energy Weapon (DEW) system and Anti-satellite (ASAT) weapons will be the technical demonstrators.
- Thus the battlefield will be hybridized blending conventional, irregular and cyber-warfare.

The major impact of technology on warfare is in the following areas:

- Increase in range and lethality.
- Reduced collateral damage, sophisticated target systems and stealth techniques.
- Less boots on the ground. This is not applicable in the Counter-insurgency Operations (CI Ops).
- Battlefield transparency turning night into day and real-time surveillance.
- Digitalized battlefield, which demands accelerated decision cycle.

Network-centric Warfare (NCW) capability is perhaps the most salient component of the future battlefield.

Nuclearization of China, Pakistan and India has had a major impact on the war-waging concepts of the three adversaries. The effect is more pronounced in case of Pakistan, which is the weakest of the three. The nuclear collusion between Pakistan and China is particularly significant, since Pakistan's nuclearization has been empowered by China with a view to giving Pakistan strategic parity with India and isolating India. While China is a world nuclear power and India has declared 'no first use policy,' it is Pakistan which wears its nuclear status on its sleeves and has utilized it to the hilt juxtaposing it with irregular warfare. This has turned the South Asian subcontinent into a dangerous flashpoint.

China Factor

India has fought a full-fledged war with China in 1962 in which it suffered a humiliating defeat. There were two subsequent encounters between the People's Liberation Army, Army component (PLAA) and IA, one at Nathu La in Sikkim in 1967 and the other at Sumdorong Chu in the Kameng Division of Arunachal Pradesh in 1987, when the PLAA tried its coercion tactics. In both cases the IA took a firm stand and the PLAA units/ formations chose not to escalate the situation. Other than these two major events, the India-China border has remained placid except for minor patrol incidents.

The territorial dispute between the two countries took a concrete shape after the 1962 conflict. China is in occupation of 38000 sq km of Indian territory in Ladakh (Western sector), while it lays claim on 96000 sq km of the entire Arunachal Pradesh (Eastern sector) which is part of the Indian Union. There is also a minor dispute over about 2000 sq km on the Uttar Pradesh (UP)-Tibet border (Central sector). Pakistan ceded 5180 sq km of Pakistan-occupied Kashmir (POK), which is part of J&K in Shasgam Valley of Northern Area, to China. India does not recognize this unauthorized and illegal transfer.

There have been two major agreements between the two countries; Border Peace and Tranquillity Agreement (BPTA) in 1993 and Agreement on CBMs in Military Field in 1996. Both are to India's military disadvantage. By the first Agreement the entire border was named as Line of Actual Control (LAC), its name implying that it can be altered by military force. The second stipulates that no exercise can be held close to the LAC unless the other side is informed. The Chinese Border Guards man their border, while the PLAA units are located deep inside, where they can easily carry out any movements. The IA units guard the border and hence are unable to carry out even brigade-size exercise movements.

After his 'successful' China trip in 1988 Rajiv Gandhi as a goodwill gesture, ordered the suspension of Operation Falcon, which had commenced in 1980 with a view to carrying out a phased build-up of forces on the Indian border and undertaking compatible infrastructure development of the border area. The Chinese counterpart, Mr Deng Xio Ping laid no such restrictions and permitted unhindered development of the Tibet Autonomous Region (TAR). As a result, all-weather roads totalling 58,000 km have been constructed so far. A rail line has been constructed between Gormo and Lhasa, which is to be extended to Shingatse and then on to Kathmandu. Five fully operational bases have been built at Gongar, Pangta, Linchi, Hoping and Gar Gansa. New missile bases, helipads, storage sites for ammunition and fuel are under construction. These have resulted in substantial reduction in the time required for deployment of forces in the TAR for an offensive against India.

In the 1980s and early 1990s, the assessment of the IA was that the PLAA will require three campaigning seasons, after taking a decision, for launching a sizeable offensive across the TAR; two seasons for move and deployment of troops and dumping of ammunition, specially the artillery ammunition, and the third for launching the offensive. This provided adequate warning time to IA. However, with the phenomenal infrastructural development of the TAR, the PLAA can now launch an offensive in a single campaigning season. It is capable of mobilizing a force of up to thirty-two divisions on the LAC against the IA in one season. However, due to terrain restriction, it is assessed that this force will be limited to a maximum of twenty divisions.

IA assesses four levels of military threat from the PLAA: non-contact war (coercion and intimidation), low, medium and high-level threats, with force levels the PLAA likely to bring against the IA in the latter three cases being five to six, eight to twelve and eighteen to twenty divisions respectively. The Chinese border is being manned by the Border Guards (Militia). Even that is located well inside. For instance, the Chinese Militia brigade (two Border Guards regiments) opposite Tawang is stationed at Tsona Dzong, 40 km deep inside. While IA units are on the LAC, the PLAA is nowhere to be seen. Further, unlike on the Indian side, the Chinese Border Guards are not physically present 24x7, they rely instead on technology. The LAC has a network of tactically networked surveillance devices. The Border Militia is placed under the command of the PLAA. There is a good network of gravel (not black-topped), well-drained roads which are serviceable even in the monsoons.

The strategic advantages of the PLAA are efficient border management, close politico-military interaction and possession of tactical nuclear weapons. The IA is weak in the first two and deficient in the third.

The PLAA's advantages at the operational level are unity of command (including Aerospace) at TRA theatre level, its special forces with potent vertical envelopment capability, operational logistics with adequate stocks of ammunition, missiles and supplies in the theatre to support an offensive and build-up of force multipliers like electronic support measures (ESMs), battlefield command and control systems (BCCS), increased surveillance capabilities and PGMs. India's four Army Commands and two Air Force Commands deal with the TAR theatre. The IA is inferior with respect to all the operational capabilities outlined above.

The Chinese have adopted a new concept called unrestricted warfare, a war conducted in non-war spheres. Joseph S Nye in his book titled *The Future of Power* writes, 'Chinese strategists have developed a strategy of unrestricted warfare that combines electronic, diplomatic, cyber, terrorist proxy, economic and propaganda tools. The first rule of unrestricted warfare is that there are no rules.' The IA is far behind in these departments.

Pakistan Factor

Pakistan is in illegal occupation of one-third area of the Indian State of J&K, where the Line of Control (LC) is 740 km long. In addition to Kashmir, other problems between India and Pakistan are Siachen Glaciers and Kutch. India and Pakistan have fought four wars, in 1947, 1965, 1971 and 1999. Pakistan is waging a prolonged proxy war against India since 1989 with the help of extremist terrorist organizations which its national intelligence organization, Inter-Services Intelligence (ISI), with extra-constitutional authority, has helped to raise, finance and guide.

After its ignominious defeat in the 1971 war and subsequent dismemberment, Pakistan realized that it cannot risk another conventional war against India to capture Kashmir. It then evolved an ingenuous policy against India. On the one hand, it engineered a successful proxy war with the help of religious fundamentalists and Kashmiri separatists 'to bleed it through a thousand cuts' and on the other, it sought to combine that with 'nuclear blackmail' by developing nuclear capability to deter India from responding militarily. After 1989, the Pakistan Government decided to employ cross-border terrorism as an instrument of state policy. The irregular (terrorist) forces under the ISI could act independently, as well as become a vanguard for conventional forces, the Kargil misadventure in 1999 being a case in point.

The Pakistan Army (PA) is 6,17,000 strong and is divided under nine corps headquarters. It has twenty infantry divisions (including two mechanized divisions), two armoured divisions and fifteen independent mechanized/armoured brigades. It has two Army Reserves for offensive operations: Army Reserve North located at Mangla and Army Reserve South located at Multan. It has about 2565 battle tanks of various makes and about 4000 Armoured Personnel Carriers (APCs). Pakistan has craftily diverted millions of dollars the US gave it during the 'war against terror' to modernize its Armed Forces. Consequently, the PA has gained a certain edge in the level of modernization over its Indian counterpart.

Though a small part of this force is committed to fighting insurgency in Federally Administered Tribal Areas (FATA) and Baluchistan, the PA can marshal most of this force on its Eastern border against the IA. With the IA's commitment on its Eastern Border, the PA can hope to create a situation of near parity of force levels on the Indo-Pak border, though the IA will maintain superiority with its ability to switch forces between its borders.

China has helped Pakistan in its nuclear quest. It gave Warhead technology, fissile materials and transferred M9/M11 missiles. Pakistan also received Nodong and Taepodong missiles from North Korea and is now trying to develop TNWs Hatf 9 (Nasr) of 60 km range to checkmate India's Cold Start Doctrine.

Threat Analysis

The threat of an adversary is the synthesis of his capability and intention. There is no doubt that the Chinese have created a quantum gap between the capabilities of the PLAA and IA. The Chinese are focused on establishing their claim on the territory they have captured in Ladakh in the Aksai Chin area through which their lifeline of Karakoram Highway runs and will go to any extent if challenged, including another border war. However, they are aware that it will not be a cakewalk like in 1962. Since the status quo facilitated by the 1993 Agreement meets their requirement, they may not like to rock the boat unless some extraordinary situation or extraneous domestic reasons compel them, though repeat of Somdorong Chu type of incidents cannot be ruled out.

The Chinese will, however, continue to keep the pot boiling on the LAC by their tactics of intimidation and coercion. They have prudently avoided exchanging the maps of the LAC alignment so as to maintain the ambiguity and to endeavour to claim areas as in the recent Depsang Valley incident.

Pakistan is unlikely to give up cross-border terrorism as an instrument of the state policy as well as support to proxy war by irregular forces aided and abetted by the ISI. In case of a war between India and China, Pakistan is more likely to open its front with India to assist China by presenting a 'two-front war' scenario to India. However, in case of a war between Pakistan and India, China is unlikely to participate militarily and will offer only moral and diplomatic support to Pakistan. It may even go to the extent of mildly censuring Pakistan, as it did during the Kargil conflict, if it finds Pakistan on the wrong foot.

Perspectives: Strategy

Capability

In December 2009, the then COAS, General Deepak Kapoor while replying to a media question, stated that the IA was 'preparing for a two-front war.' This initiated an intense discussion on whether the Indian Armed Forces were in the process of upgrading their capability to deal with China and Pakistan simultaneously. India since its independence had planned for a 'one and a half front war,' which meant incidence of war either with Pakistan or with China, one at a time, leaving the remaining 'half front capability' for holding the 'non-active front' and for internal security.

In any case, such a core change had to apply to all three services across the board, at least to the IA and IAF, and being a major policy change would always be in the political domain. Obviously, the statement of the Chief was misconstrued. All that he may have meant is that the IA should build capability to face a conflict covering both fronts, a likely situation which has been brought out in the threat analysis above, and not that India should fight a two-front war. So the policy 'per se' has not changed.

There has, of late, also been talk of changing from 'threat-based' planning to 'capability-based' planning. The army hierarchy ostensibly holds differing perceptions on this, as revealed by the views of two previous chiefs. In a recent interview to *SP's Military Year Book 2013*, General Bikram Singh while replying to a question, 'to what extent can the IA meet a dual challenge and talking of two-front capability, what is it in terms of capability building?,' replied thus: 'IA's primary mission is to secure the territorial integrity of the nation. In the ongoing force structuring and modernization process, our focus is on development of various essential capabilities towards achieving the primary mission, without being "country"-specific.'

The IA is transforming from a threat-based to capability-based force to meet the challenges of the entire spectrum of war below the nuclear threshold: conventional to sub-conventional war, capabilities to secure island territories, out of area (intervention) capability, assistance to friendly countries and 'soft' tasks such as disaster relief, humanitarian help and participation in United Nations (UN) peace-keeping missions.

China

In respect of China, the IA's strategy is 'strategic defence and tactical offence.' This envisages a strong defensive component as not to permit any aggression beyond the Tawang-Lohit line and a small but credible offensive component. While the IA has near adequate defensive force to dissuade China and blunt its offensive, it lacks an offensive component which would act as deterrence. With this in view, a proposal to raise a mountain strike corps has been mooted. Two mountain divisions have already been raised in 2010.

The roads and tracks in the Eastern Sector are narrow, single-way, fair-weather, in poor state of maintenance and highly susceptible to the 'friction of terrain' like landslides. In 1980, a strategic military plan, codenamed Operation Falcon, was approved. It envisaged forward build-up of forces along with development of the infrastructure over a fifteen-year time span. This was abandoned in 1987 apropos Prime Minister Rajiv Gandhi's visit. Having realized the folly, the Government allotted funds and cleared construction of 73 strategic roads in March 2001 to be completed in a decade, out of which only 13 were built by December 2011. Massive funds have now been allotted for infrastructure including advanced landing grounds (ALGs), bunker and storage facilities. Additional plans for 277 roads of 13000 km length are also afoot. This is an important aspect of defence preparedness in the Eastern Sector.

China considers India's quest for infrastructure development as a violation of CBMs contained in the 1996 Agreement. India needs to ignore any such protestations by China and continue the effort to neutralize the existing asymmetry in infrastructure, at least to some extent. The IA should be extremely vigilant to identify any border violations by the PLAA, specifically when done by large detachments, and checkmate them firmly to defeat the PLAA's coercive and intimidation tactics.

Pakistan

The IA's strategy against the PA is 'strategic defence and operational offence.' India failed to respond militarily to the terrorist attack on Parliament in December 2001 and to the Mumbai attack in November 2008 (26/11), both stage-managed by the ISI. During Operation Parakram, the two armies remained face to face on the border in battle readiness from 18 December 2001 to 16 October 2002 without firing a shot. This highlights that the luxury of launching an offensive as retribution to PA's misdemeanours has been lost due to the nuclear risk, thereby closing the option of 'strategic offence.' The major reason for failure of 'Parakram' was that the IA took twenty-two days for build-up of the strike forces, which provided adequate time for preparation to the PA to block any ingress.

The IA believes that there is still a space between the proxy war terrorist attacks and the nuclear threshold which can be explored for launching limited offensives, taking due care that the nuclear redline is not crossed. It proposes to adopt a new concept titled 'Cold War Doctrine' to undertake this limited offensive. The Doctrine has the following major elements:

- Carry out adjustments to enhance the offensive capability of defensive ground-holding forces (pivot corps) so as to enable them to launch offensive operations virtually from a cold start to deny the PA the advantage of early mobilization.
- Formation of a number of 'integrated battle groups' (IBGs) of division-size forces for launching a series of limited offensives across a shallow depth to capture sizeable enemy territory across the border.
- Success achieved by one or two IBGs to be enlarged by the Strike Corps without violating the 'red lines.'
- IAF's assurance of 'area air superiority' taken as a prerequisite.
- The Strike Corps cantonments to be brought closer to the border, if possible, to save deployment time (more easily said than done!)

The assessment of the IA is that this Doctrine will act as a deterrent for waging a proxy war and Pakistan will be forced to dismantle it, an optimism not shared by everybody. Be that as it may, the IA will have to find ways and means to launch limited offensives. The only other options to retaliate against terrorist strike are either 'Hot Pursuit' to destroy militant camps, which is fraught with a possibility of failure or heavy bombardment, which has only limited effect.

Instant retaliation against minor terrorist strikes on the LC, like the beheading of a Jawan in February 2013, is an important aspect of counter-infiltration operations. General Bikram Singh had openly declared that local commanders down to battalion level have been authorized to take instant retaliatory action, without waiting for approval; rather 'he expects them to react expeditiously.' This is a welcome measure and its implementation will be a deterrent to the extremists.

Nuclear

India published its Draft Nuclear Doctrine on 17 August 1999 and the Official Doctrine on 4 January 2003. It envisages credible minimum deterrence, no first use, punitive retaliation, a threat of use against chemical and biological strikes and no threat of use against non-weapon states. Estimates of warheads (WHs) with India range from few dozens to 400. Its missile structure is based on SSMs (Prithvi, Agni I to V) with the IA, under slung bombs on Mirage 2000 and SU 30 FB with the IAF and SLBMs with the Indian Navy (IN).

The policy of 'second strike capability' devolves on India the responsibility to ensure survivability of its nuclear arsenal after the first strike. Measures to ensure this in the form of underground silos and a protected command and control apparatus are essential. It can be said that India's defence preparedness in the nuclear zone is adequate and backed by a logical policy.

Perspectives: Force Structuring

The primacy of 'man behind the gun' has been an age-old maxim. Strength, capability, organization, tasking and 'head to tail' ratio are a few important factors of force structuring. Future wars will require troops who are technically adept and capable of exploiting high-end equipment. The IA's focus is on minimum enhancement in force levels, upgrading of technologies and induction of force multipliers. Effective cyber defence capability is needed to dissuade and deter any cyber threats. The Naresh Chandra Committee has pointed out that India needs to enhance its unconventional and special warfare capabilities.

The 1.3 million strong IA is the second largest standing army in the world. It has eleven corps headquarters, thirty-seven infantry divisions including three armoured divisions, five force headquarters (each equivalent of a division) specially designed for CI operations and ten independent infantry brigades. Approval has been accorded to raise a strike mountain corps, of which two mountain divisions are already raised. A corps headquarters, two more infantry divisions and one artillery division will be raised in the 12th Five-Year Plan. The 54 Infantry Division will be reorganized as Air Assault Division in the 14th Plan (2022–7).

Out of this force, twelve divisions and three independent brigades are located against China, five to six are deployed along the LC against Pakistan and two to three divisions are committed to fighting the insurgency in the Northeast. In modern armies, the stress is on reduction of manpower and increase in modernization of equipment. However, in case of the IA, the requirement of 'boots on ground' to meet the man-intensive nature of the task justifies the high strength and negates any possibility of reduction in manpower in the foreseeable future.

Perspectives: Equipment Profile

Of various components of the defence preparedness, the dismal equipment profile of the IA is the biggest cause of concern. General VK Singh's letter to the PM has laid this bare. Today's IA ails due to ill-equipped infantry, outdated artillery, obsolete air defence, aging helicopters and shortage of special ammunition. The maladies of indecisive policy-making, slipshod modernization, lethargic procurement and paltry indigenization are taking a toll on the defence preparedness.

The story of the Rifle is a case in point of the lack daisy of the Indian system. In 1962, the men were pushed into battle with World War vintage .303 Lee-Enfield rifles. In the midst of the China War, 7.62-mm Self-loading Rifles (SLRs) were hurriedly imported from the US and supplied to the soldiers on the frontline. Its production started in the Ordnance Factories and mercifully, the 1965 war was fought with 7.62-mm SLRs. Faced with Punjab and Liberation Tigers of Tamil Eelam (LTTE) militants armed with Kalashnikovs, a few AK47s were imported. The realization that 7.62 is an 'overkill' calibre led the NATO countries to adopt the 5.56 calibre for the future. In the late '80s the Indian Small Arms System (INSAS) project to develop a 5.56-mm carbine, rifle and LMG for the IA was undertaken by the DRDO's ARDE. The project was delayed. Use of INSAS during the Kargil conflict revealed faulty design, poor metallurgy and shoddy craftsmanship leading to stoppages, breakages, overheating and barrel bulge. INSAS could not fire a rifle grenade, hence 7.62 SLR had to be retained. The INSAS LMG took a long time to come and the INSAS carbine never made its appearance.

In 2011, the IA declared its intention to import new-generation assault rifles from the world market and opted for a multi-barrel assault rifle which can fire both 5.56 and 7.62-mm ammunitions. Beretta, Ceska, Colt, IWI and Sig are in the field out of which, only Beretta has a multi-calibre. The IA plans to import 65,000 pieces to equip 120 infantry battalions in the first phase and then extend it to about 360 infantry and Rashtriya Rifle (RR) battalions which, hopefully, will be completed by 2020. Forty-four thousand pieces of carbines will also be imported to replace 9-mm carbines. Decision on the INSAS LMG is yet to be taken. The process may begin in 2014 and will cost a whopping US $ 2 billion. Thus the Indian nation, sixty seven years after independence, does not have a standard indigenous rifle!

The major areas of anxiety in the equipment profile of the IA are as under.

Infantry

Personal weapons of the infantry battalion include pistols, carbines, rifles and light machine guns (LMGs). All are struggling with enduring obsolescence. The Defence Acquisition Council (DAC) has approved a new assault rifle with interchangeable barrel, a new-generation carbine, LMG and a sniper rifle. The procurement of new bullet-proof jackets, ballistic helmets, boots anti-mine has not materialized. The IA is in search of man-portable mortars, thermal images night sight for assault rifles.

F-INSAS, 'Future Infantry Soldier as a System,' is aimed at making the infantryman a weapon platform with situational awareness, increased lethality and sustainability in a digitalized battlefield. This is to be implemented in three stages: first, weapons, body armour and equipment; second, target acquisition systems and third, computer and radio sub-systems. This will form part of the Battlefield Management System (BMS) of the IA.

Special Forces (SFs)

These are force multipliers for trans-border tasks such as asymmetric warfare, special operations and psychological operations. Their present state of equipping is sub-normal. The seven battalions need to be fully equipped before any accretion.

Mechanised Forces

The Armoured Corps has an assortment of tanks which, it must be granted, total to a viable number. Two regiments have been equipped with 124 Arjun MBTs. Another 124 Arjun Mark II tanks for two more regiments have been ordered. Six hundred and fifty-seven T 90S assembled at HVF, Avadi have been inducted into the IA. The effects in their Fire Control Systems are being remedied. BMP2 Infantry Combat Vehicle (ICV) Sarath is the mechanised infantry's main vehicle. 1000 ICVs have been manufactured in India since 1987. The IA has planned Futuristic ICV (FICV) and, for the first time, has invited private participation, a welcome step indeed! The state of the mechanized forces is satisfactory.

Fire Power

The last major acquisition of artillery guns was in 1986, when 410 pieces of 155m FH 77 Howitzers from Bofors of Sweden were imported. During this period of abject neglect, old 100-mm and 122-mm Russian field guns as well as indigenously developed 75/24 Howitzers have become obsolete, leaving a yawning gap. The proposal under the Artillery Rationalization Plan to acquire a mix of around 3000 155-mm/52-calibre Howitzers through imports and local licensed manufacture has not made any progress. Likely induction of 145 M777 ultra-light Howitzers from the US is the only ray of hope. An early lead in producing a prototype of 155 mm/39 calibre, even exploring the private partnership route, is the need of the hour. Induction of two missile groups Prithvi SS SRBM, the raising of one Agni Group and successful firing of BrahMos Cruise Missile's army version provide a silver lining to an otherwise dark cloud.

Air Defence

The IA holds four-decade-old L70 guns, ZU 23-mm Twin, Schilka, Kwadrat, OSA AK and Igla systems which are to be replaced by Akash and Trishul SAMs, the project for the latter being foreclosed. Only Tanguska is moderately recent. It is proposed to acquire medium-range missiles or develop them jointly with Israel. As successor to Igla SAAB RPS 70, MBDA and Mistral have been short and are to go for trials. The state of Air Defence is dismal.

Army Aviation

Army Aviation Corps (AAC) has four squadrons of Dhruv, which will increase to eight. Cheetahs and Chetaks have been in service for long. Armed version of Rudra, which in addition to guns and rockets has Air to Air Missiles, is an army project. Rudra units will form part of holding corps. Out of 197 recce and surveillance helicopters, for which RFP was floated a few years earlier, 131 are meant for the AAC.

Perspectives: Procurement and Indigenization

Inefficiency in procurement and absence of indigenization are two evils which have plagued the Indian defence machinery and have been the main cause of obsolescent, expensive, dependent and ill-modernized Indian Armed Forces. Modernization is a continuous process driven by the 'one-third rule,' i.e., technology of one-third of the inventory should be of 'cutting edge,' of one-third current and of the rest obsolescent.

Acquisition is a complex and intricate process. Over 70 per cent of Indian hardware is imported, and 20 per cent is produced by forty-one Ordnance Factories (OFs) and nine Defence Public Sector Undertakings (DPSUs). In the current profile, the state-of-the-art equipment is only 15 per cent against the desired 33 per cent, while 85 per cent is matured and obsolescent.

The Defence Procurement Procedure (DPP) came into effect in December 2002, was modified in 2003, in 2008 and finally in April 2013, but 'the more it changed, the more it remained the same.' It incorporates 'buy' and 'buy and make' through transfer of technology (TOT).

The Defence Acquisition Council (DAC) was set up in 2002 to meet emergent demands and establish a single control and monitoring organisation under the RM with RRM, Service Chiefs, Secretaries of defence, DP, R&D, finance and CIDS as members. The DAC's main functions are:

- Accord in-principle approvals to Capital acquisitions in long-term perspective plan (LTPP) covering a fifteen-year time span.
- Identify projects as 'Buy' (outright purchase), 'Buy and Make' (purchase followed by licensed production/indigenous development) and 'Make' (indigenous production and R&D).
- Monitor progress of major projects on feedback from DPB.

The new order of precedence for acquisition categories is: first, buy Indian; second, buy and make Indian through joint ventures with overseas vendors; third, make Indian in which domestic companies are asked to design, develop and build a full-fledged system; fourth, buy and make Indian through TOT which would come from overseas firms, and fifth, buy global. 'Buy Indian' entails only 30 per cent indigenous content, while 'Buy and make Indian' entails only 50 per cent. The DAC has approved release of fifteen-year Long-Term Integrated Perspective Plan (LTIPP 2012–27). The maintenance of TOT (MTOT) is no longer through only nomination, earlier reserved only for OFs and PSUs.

The major problem areas are:

- Slow procurement procedures in replacement of guns, other weapon platforms and ammunition hit road blocks and heavy capital budget amounts remain unspent. The approach breeds indecision, fear, suspicion, scams and scandals leading to blacklisting of firms, which is the path of least resistance. The IA's 600-odd modernization schemes amounting to Rs 70,000 crore in the 11th Five-Year Plan (2007–12) are enmeshed in bureaucratic procedures. The government has now sanctioned the 12th Five-Year Plan. These two plans together will create Rs 1,25,000 to Rs 1,75,000 crore (US $ 25 to 35 billion). The procurement mechanism must bridle to meet this challenge.
- OFs and PSUs have monopolized the process pushing private players to the periphery. They must give way to the private sector as committed partners in defence for full integration of India's technological prowess.
- Defence R&D in the private sector must be funded by the Government as in the US.

- Non-nomination of TOT should be meticulously implemented to encourage the private sector to enter the fray.

India is the biggest importer of arms in the world. This demonstrates that India has not been able to throw away the vestige of foreign dependence of the colonial era. India has developed a humongous technological base during the past six and a half decades. The following measures need to be instituted for boosting private participation in defence production:

- The Defence Ministry should initiate proactive motivators like tax holidays for production of major weapon platforms and war-like equipment.
- Business without exports may not be cost-effective. Hence export of the manufactured defence equipment should be liberalized.
- The Indian Industry should be encouraged to enter into an understanding with foreign OEM to develop together the required systems and undertake manufacture under a technology-sharing arrangement.

Higher Defence Management

There is a glaring absence of institutional coordination between the Indian political leadership and the Indian Armed Forces. Whether it is a vestige of the colonial psyche or a subconscious response to dictatorial regimes in the vicinity or plain lack of strategic temper is another matter, but the defence hierarchy has always been kept on the periphery and 'remembered' only in the time of crisis. This was succinctly articulated by the Kargil Review Committee (KRC) constituted under K Subrahmanyam: 'India is perhaps the only major democracy where the armed forces headquarters are outside the apex government structure.' As a matter of fact, most of the fault lines in India's defence preparedness are primarily due to this enigma.

The slide can be traced to 25 March 1955, when Prime Minister Jawaharlal Nehru discarded the designation of Commander-in-Chief and in 1961, persuaded by the wily bureaucracy, designated the three service headquarters as 'attached offices of the Department of Defence under the Government of India Allocation of Business Rules.' Distancing the Services from participating in the policymaking, the bureaucracy succeeded in interposing itself between the soldier and the politician, thus pushing the armed forces to the periphery of the policymaking apparatus. It took five wars for the realization to dawn that the Services need to be 'counted.'

A taskforce led by Mr Arun Singh on 'Defence Management' recommended the creation of Chief of the Defence Staff (CDS) and integration of defence services headquarters with the defence ministry. The CDS was to form a single-point military advice, enhance tri-service planning process, formulate joint service doctrine, exercise control over the Defence Intelligence Agency (DIA), ensure 'jointness' and also discharge functions in respect of the tri-service commands of Andaman and Nicobar Islands (ANC) and Strategic Forces Command (SFC). Before the ink dried, the proposal was watered down by sanctioning only staff-level Chief of Integrated Defence Staff (CIDS), assuring a step-by-step approach and re-designating the three services headquarters as 'Integrated Headquarters of Ministry of Defence,' a mere cosmetic gimmick. That ended the 'exercise.' Strangely, objection to the creation of CDS came from an insider, the IAF! It is nobody's case that the creation of CDS is the panacea of higher defence management, but surely it is the beginning. The least that the Government could do is to accept the recommendation of the Naresh Chandra Committee and appoint a four-star General or equivalent to be the permanent head of the Chief of Staff's Committee (COSC) as a stopgap measure.

The following two suggestions have been made in the Institute for Defence Studies and Analyses (IDSA) Monograph titled 'A call for change—Higher Defence Management in India,' (6 July, 2012) which is germane to the subject:

- Greater Parliamentary involvement in defence reforms and the urgent need to re-examine the rubric of higher defence management. For this an Act of Parliament along the lines of the Goldwater-Nicholas Act of the US should be enacted.
- The MOD needs to be restructured and the GOI Rules of Business, 1961 suitably amended so that the role of the military in national defence is recognized and the military hierarchy accorded recognition as an integral component of the Government structure.

Verdict

Three decades back, discussion of critical deficiencies of the IA outside its four walls was a taboo for a variety of reasons like national interest, secrecy of information vital to the enemy, adverse effect on the morale and motivation of the force and a host of others. Today, there is a paradigm shift in the ideas about 'security' due to the accessibility to information on the internet. That the defence preparedness is now discussed threadbare in the public domain is an acknowledgement of the awareness of the common man about the national security, the pragmatism of the Armed Forces and the maturity of the system.

The battlefield environment of today is hybridized and is becoming increasingly technology-driven. The electromagnetic spectrum and cyberspace will dictate the pace. This technologically surcharged future battlefield calls for an aptitude change. There is a visible asymmetry in the capability of the IA vis-à-vis the adversaries. On this background, the discrepancies in the equipment profile of the IA—ill-equipped infantry, outdated artillery, obsolete air defence, aging helicopters and shortage of special ammunition—become more glaring and pronounced. India is the biggest importer of arms and yet there is inadequate push to indigenize despite availability of a huge technological base. The modernization is way behind schedule.

The IA is unlikely to be required to fight on two fronts, except for an odd chance that Pakistan activates its front to assist its benefactor, China in an India-China conflict, chances in itself of which are remote. That is no reason for the IA to loosen its guard. It has rightly decided to develop a 'two-front' capability. No army is ever 'fully prepared' for war. The IA has fought four wars 'with whatever they had' and has won them when it was in similar situation. The Government must initiate processes for the Services to have a say in the national policymaking. Inauguration of the CDS would be an appropriate beginning and a step in the right direction.

NOTES

1. DNA (Pune) 28 March 2012

CHAPTER II

The State of the Indian Air Force: Challenges and Opportunities

BN Gokhale

'Unfortunately, you can change friends but not neighbours.'

Atal Bihari Vajpayee,
Former Prime Minister of India[1]

Introduction

The medium of air and its contiguous medium of space have not only added a third dimension but have, in turn, compressed the dimensions of distance and time. It is no wonder then that in just over a decade of the first flight in 1903, use of aircraft for carrying out offensive support in the First World War, ushered a Revolution in Military Affairs (RMA). Rapid technological advances have enabled this medium to grow into a potent power, complementing its inherent characteristics of speed and flexibility.

The nascent IAF made a decisive contribution in October 1947, when, with Spitfires and Tempests giving fire cover, the Dakotas flew in troops and supplies to Srinagar to save the valley from Pakistani attack. Presently the IAF has embarked on modernization of its ageing inventory; however, budgetary constraints along with slow pace of indigenization are hampering this effort. With aerospace power becoming the most preferred option being exercised at the beginning of most conflicts, this fourth largest air force[2] in the world needs to infuse quality as well as quantity. The urgent need for modernization is necessary not only for the IAF but also for the nation to maintain a decisive deterrence and cutting-edge potential to exercise this option, if and when needed.

Threat Perception

In a hostile neighbourhood with two adversarial countries armed with nuclear weapons and in many areas collaborating with each other, the challenges faced by India are far greater today than ever before. Added to this external threat is the dimension of internal strife and terrorism including the spread of Naxalism. Non-traditional security threats emanating from issues such as space and cyber security, increasing demands on food, water and energy also need to be factored into the gamut of overall security preparedness. In this complex security scenario, the Armed Forces need to be prepared for conflicts across the spectrum, from Low Intensity (LICO) on the one hand to an all-out war on both fronts,[3] including the undesirable nuclear exchange. This makes equipping and training that much more complex and expensive especially for an equipment-intensive service such as the IAF.

The Indo-Pak scenario has witnessed three wars of 1947, 1965 and 1971. In addition there have been two major conflicts, Siachin in 1984 and Kargil in 1999. However, in keeping with ZA Bhutto's strategy of a 'thousand-year war,' and Gen Zia's doctrine of 'bleeding India through thousand cuts,'[4] Pakistan has been waging a proxy war with India by supporting acts of terrorism. The policy of sponsoring terrorism suits her best as a prolonged war is not in the interest of Pakistan due to her limited geographical depth, which results in most of the civil or military installations within reach of Indian strike aircraft. However, with the US and International Security Assistance Force (ISAF) troops slated for withdrawal from Afghanistan by end 2014 and likely resurgence of Taliban, India will need to factor in a possible realignment in the Af-Pak scenario.

Considering the nuclear overhang, including Pakistan's recently tested

Tactical Nuclear Weapons (TNW) it is felt that her ill-defined nuclear threshold will need to be factored in by India while selecting the overall aim of an all-out overt war against Pakistan. Ideally for India a full-scale overt war will be won by swift and accurate strikes at Pakistan's military and industrial complex by delivering maximum punch at the very start of a conflict. However, due to the low threshold for use of nuclear weapons and the international pressure for de-escalation, in all likelihood the future scenarios will be limited in geography and duration akin to the Kargil conflict.

Against China, the reverse is true for India in terms of waging a protracted war. Till adequate modernization is achieved India will not be able to sustain a long-duration war with China. The statistics indicate that 'China's "comprehensive national power" exceeds India's by a wide margin with China's economy over four times the size of India's in 2012, and over eight times the size when adjusting for purchasing power parity (PPP). China's official military budget of $119 billion in 2013 was over three times larger than India's $38 billion defence budget.'[5] In addition, with the geographical advantage China enjoys, India will need long-range weapon systems to hit where it will actually hurt. As such the conflict scenario presently seems to be that of local confrontation like the one in the Daulat Beg Oldie (DBO) sector in April 2013, with both China and India avoiding escalation.

There are some other aspects of the Chinese strength which also need serious consideration. The Chinese have invested heavily in Cyber Warfare terming it as the modern-day RMA. They have raised special battalions to neutralize the adversary in the classical Sun Tzu maxim of 'the supreme art of war is to subdue the enemy without fighting.'[6] Added to this is her increasing strength in the arena of Space with Anti-Satellite Weapon (ASAT) capability. Her rapid modernization and that too based on indigenous capability, allows the Chinese to exploit weapon systems independent of external pressures. This is one of the many important advantages China enjoys vis-à-vis India.

These challenges therefore, need to be weighed against both, current preparedness of the Armed Forces and possible opportunities. This paper attempts to look into the various challenges and opportunities from the perspective of Aerospace power and its main practitioner, the IAF.

Important Features of Air Power

Apart from swift action and compressing the dimensions of distance and time, there are two very important features of Air Power, which remained somewhat obscured during India's post-Independence period, leading to unnecessary debates. First is that the air power is inherently offensive in nature, best used pre-emptively, forcing the enemy onto the back foot. Here offensive need not necessarily mean the use of weapons alone but also air-landing or dropping combat-ready troops, as was the case in October 1947. While Air Defence is intrinsic in any offensive action, it would be befitting to call the three Services as Armed Forces instead of Defence Forces. It not only does well to the psyche, but also to the type of equipment being inducted and to the Doctrine.

The second important feature is the strategic effect, often achieved by timely use of air power. During the Second World War, RAF and USAF used to fly the bomber aircraft based in India; whereas the IAF was equipped with Hurricanes and Spitfires typically designed for Air Defence and Army support operations. In the years after Independence, due to this baggage from the Colonial days, many military experts continued to refer to the IAF as a Tactical Air Force.[7] This thought process almost shackled the IAF as an extension of field artillery, to be allotted in penny pockets to the Army field formations. There were endless debates on the roles and tasking, as also on the type of aircraft and weapons best suited for such a 'limited' role. It is worth quoting USAF Gen Hoyt S Vandenberg who in 1951 said, 'Air power is indivisible. We don't speak of a "strategic" or a "tactical" Army or Navy, yet those terms are constantly applied to the Air Force.'[8]

Historical Perspective and Strength of the IAF Combat Squadrons

When comparing the preparedness of the Armed Forces it is best to compare the combat force potential. Such potential of course is not solely dependent on combat units but also on support capability, logistics, maintenance, human resource and infrastructure, et al. However, an analysis of the strength of IAF's combat squadrons will effectively illustrate various policies, plans and offensive potential. As such the historical perspective illustrates the build-up of IAF's squadrons since independence.

Formative Years

The Indian Air Force was formed on 8 October 1932. Coincidentally the late JRD Tata himself piloted the first commercial flight from Karachi to Mumbai in a Puss Moth aircraft on 15 October 1932 to start Tata Airlines[9] to be known as Air India later, when it was nationalized in 1951. The formative years of the IAF were spent basically in support of the British action in the Northwest Frontier region and later in the Eastern front against the Japanese during World War II. However, the operational experience gained by the IAF pioneers was of great value, laying a strong foundation of the IAF. It was this experience which came in handy to rescue the grave situation in the Kashmir valley during October 1947. At the time of independence, out of the original ten squadrons, the IAF had only six combat and ½ transport squadrons manned by about 1700 personnel.[10]

In 1941, at the start of the British India campaign against the Japanese, it was planned by the Chatfield Committee[11] to establish an air force with strength of twenty-one combat squadrons and six coastal defence squadrons. These were to comprise eleven RAF and ten IAF squadrons with about 325 aircraft. It is important to compare these figures in the context of the post-1947 expansion of the IAF. Despite the belligerent attitude of Pakistan from its very inception and the threat of another war in 1951, the IAF force level was not raised by the Central leadership beyond fifteen squadrons. It was only after Pakistan had joined the Southeast Asia Treaty Organization (SEATO) in 1954 and the Central Treaty Organization (CENTO) a year later[12] that the Indian authorities gave directions for increasing the squadron level to twenty-three of which eighteen would be for combat and five for transportation. However, the deployment remained Pakistan-centric with no squadrons being deployed in the east despite steadily worsening ties with China.

Absence of Air Power in the 1962 Indo-China War

Even fifty-two years after the debacle with China in 1962, the policy of not using IAF offensively against the Chinese continues to baffle the historians. With bilateral relations worsening with China and coinciding with the exile of Dalai Lama to India, it was only in 1959 that one British-made Vampire Photo Reconnaissance squadron was moved to Tezpur followed by one more French-built Toofani fighter squadron. However, these combat aircraft were neither used offensively against the Chinese troops nor employed for interdicting their advances through the narrow defiles of the mountains of Ladakh and Arunachal Pradesh. The second option though benign in nature would have made the Chinese advances and later their withdrawal difficult, as they would have taken a heavy toll on their logistics chain. White House Intelligence summary of December 1962 states 'Use of combat air power would have made a material difference to the war on ground.'[13] Although not yet declassified, some portions of the Henderson Brooks-Bhagat report are now available in the media. According to these it seems that inadequate preparation, incorrect assessment of intelligence inputs and lack of synergy in decision-making were some of the many reasons for not using air power offensively. The misplaced notion that use of air power was escalatory stymied the use of this option, which on the other hand had been used so very favourably in 1947.

The 1965 War with Pakistan

In the aftermath of this debacle, in March 1963 the government decided to increase the strength of the IAF and set up a committee under the late JRD Tata to recommend the numbers of squadrons the IAF should possess. The Tata Committee[14] recommended a sixty-four-squadron air force to cater to the requirements of both the Eastern and Western fronts. While this figure had been accepted by the Emergency Committee of the Cabinet, it remained only on paper. At the time of the 1965 war with Pakistan the IAF was in the process of expanding to a newly approved strength of thirty-five combat squadrons and was stretched to its limit in terms of resources, infrastructure and shortfall in manning. The Pakistan Air Force on the other hand was equipped with American F-86 and supersonic F-104 combat aircraft and better radar cover.

Pakistan also had the advantage of surprise aided with the initiative of clandestine infiltration of troops into the Kashmir Valley under code name Operation Gibraltar. Intelligence failure has been the bane of Indian preparedness, forcing a reaction than a pre-emptive action, which can be decisive in war. The Pakistan Air Force (PAF) had also started the war preparation well before with war plan No 6/65 issued on 29 June 1965, almost two months before the actual war, codenamed Operation Grand Slam. In the initial days of the war the IAF suffered a number of losses in the East. This is because the IAF was constrained by the initial Indian policy of not retaliating to the PAF attacks from East Pakistan due to misplaced apprehension of alienating the predominantly Bengali population.

On the day of Chinese withdrawal from India on 20 November 1962, the late YB Chavan took over as the Defence Minister in place of his much criticized predecessor the late Krishna Menon. Within a short period of time he made a very important contribution to the Indian Armed Forces by initiating reequipping and modernization, rebuilding trust and morale, and more importantly bringing about synergy between the politicians, bureaucrats and military personnel.[15] This paid dividends in the 1965 war and India could foil the initial Pakistani advances. Regarding the use of air power, Chavan took a calculated and prompt decision of using the IAF in the nick of time when the Indian Army was on the verge of losing control in the Chamb Jaurian sector. The urgency of the situation was such that Chavan, unable to contact the Prime Minister on phone, took this important decision himself.[16]

1971 Bangladesh Liberation War

It was to the credit of leadership and synergy that India emerged victorious in the 1971 Bangladesh war. In the interim years the IAF strength had been increased to forty-five squadrons including thirty-five for combat role. Pakistan, on the other hand, possessed thirteen combat squadrons. This higher strength of the IAF was adequate if China did not interfere. The IAF was well-equipped and trained; it was motivated and was used in unison with the overall joint plan. Not only did the IAF ensure air superiority over the PAF in the East but it also ensured that the PAF was almost ineffective in the Western theatre of war.

The IAF had established Heli-bridging over the Padma and Meghana rivers by helicopters to rapidly advance towards Dacca and had successfully carried out one of the biggest airdrops over Tangail in Bangladesh on 11 December 1971. The subsequent bombing of the Governor's Palace in Dacca on 14 December 1971 hastened the surrender by Lt Gen AAK Niazi on 16 December 1971. The IAF had thus ensured that the overall war aim of the early fall of Dacca was achieved by an effective air campaign. Although MiG-21 aircraft were used for the bombing raid, they had achieved strategic effect in this war.

Dwindling Strength of the IAF

The Defence Plan of 1966–71 had reiterated the need for a sixty-four-squadron air force. However, the IAF was able to achieve the sanctioned level of forty-five squadrons only by 1971. After the war, the strength of the IAF was allowed to dwindle possibly because of the perception that Pakistan had been cut to size and that the Chinese People's Liberation Army Air Force (PLAAF) was yet to be modernized. However, an important aspect was missed out, that of human resource. The pilots and technicians need to be kept abreast of technology and also need adequate flying experience to ensure operational capability.

Later when the Siachen conflict took place in 1984, the IAF realized the need for multi-role platforms capable of also operating at high altitudes. The MiG-23 and MiG-27 were used in this conflict but their numbers had started dwindling rapidly. The lack of new induction resulted in the IAF getting caught on the wrong foot during the Kargil War of 1999. Constrained with the Government directive of not crossing the Line of Actual Control (LAC), it lacked aircraft which could carry out accurate and effective attacks on the infiltrators using the higher reaches of the mountains. It is only when the IAF used Mirage-2000 aircraft with Laser-Guided stand-off weapons[17] that the enemy logistics build-up was destroyed, in turn shortening the war in India's favour.

The lessons of Kargil once again brought into focus the issue of adequacy of strength and also that of quality of platforms. Since the First Gulf war of 1991 and later Kosovo, it was evident that newer generation of aircraft and weapons would be needed. While the IAF possessed a number of MiG-21, MiG-23 and MiG-27 squadrons, it lacked adequate numbers of 4th and 5th-generation aircraft such as the Mirage-2000 and

Su-30. Delay in induction of the Light Combat Aircraft (LCA) was also affecting the IAF strength. Meanwhile, the PAF was armed with F-16 and Chinese J-10 aircraft and the Chinese PLAAF was also modernizing rapidly with aircraft like Su-27 and indigenous J-10 and FC-20, 5th-generation fighter aircraft. Apart from combat aircraft the Chinese have been rapidly building infrastructure in terms of airfields, logistics depots, supply routes and radar cover in the Tibet Autonomous Region (TAR).

Since the 1980s the IAF had been demanding an increase in the strength of the fighter fleet including additional Mirage-2000 aircraft, which could have been operationalized very quickly since the IAF had enough experience and trained manpower. However, this case was not sanctioned and the IAF had to upgrade the older aircraft like MiG-21, MiG-27 and Jaguar. During the year-long stand-off known as Operation Parakram, after the attack on the Indian Parliament on 13 December 2001, the IAF had to move the combat squadrons from Central and Eastern sectors to the West. This once again brought into focus the inadequacy of strength to cater to both the Pakistan and China fronts.

The IAF currently has only thirty-three combat squadrons, which is hopefully the lowest it can get. Amongst these only about fifteen squadrons consisting of Sukhoi-30 and Mirage-2000 can be considered as modern 4th and 5th-generation aircraft. This is woefully short of the desired strength of forty-five squadrons. There is need therefore to induct 126 MMRCA Rafale aircraft along with FGFA being developed with Russia. If adequate budgetary support is made available, it is expected that by 2027 the IAF would once again build up to strength of forty-two squadrons.[18] In comparison 'China can throw at least twenty-one fighter squadrons against India, from its eight airbases in Tibet and other airfields to their north. More Chinese fighters can join forces if they are allowed to overfly Myanmar. Similarly, Pakistan can deploy twenty-one to twenty-five fighter squadrons against India.'[19] With limited strength presently, the IAF will need to use squadrons from either fronts with air-to-air refuelling in a 'swing role' as was practised in a major exercise 'Live Wire' in March-April 2013.

Gaps in Combat Support Systems

While the strength of combat squadrons has been discussed above it is equally important to comment on other requirements such as Radar Cover, Air Defence Missiles, Combat Support Systems and infrastructure. Efforts are being made to enhance all these but will need continued budgetary support especially in the area of Air Defence. To cater for gaps in radar cover the IAF has inducted Aerostats, Airborne Warning And Control System (AWACS) aircraft and is in the process of accepting indigenous Airborne Early Warning and Control (AEW&C) configured by Defence Research and Development Organisation (DRDO) on Embraer[20] platform. Similarly, to cater to the shortfall in Air Defence missiles the DRDO-made Akash system caters to intermediate threats, and longer range interceptor missile systems are also being developed by DRDO.

Joint Operations

In all the recent wars such as the Gulf War of 1991 and 2003 as well as in Kosovo 1998 and Libya 2011, it was air power which was not only used first but with its immense reach and firepower it made it easier for the land forces to achieve their objectives rapidly and with far less causalities. No wonder then it is said that 'Air Forces may not win the war by themselves but no war can be won without them.' The protagonists of Air Power on the hand, must equally appreciate the need for Joint Operations, wherein the combined effect would not be just linear but exponential.

After the 1962 debacle with China, the newly appointed Defence Minister, the late Shri YB Chavan needs to be credited with re-establishing the practice of periodic review meetings between the Service Chiefs and officials of the Ministry of Defence as well Cabinet Secretariat. Frank dialogue and discussion is the key to such meetings and he certainly brought about synergy in decision-making.[21] Frank advice on the timing of the war by the late Field Marshal Manekshaw ensured that there was no interference by the Chinese in the 1971 war with the Sino-Indian border being snowbound during the months of November-December.

After the Kargil War, jointmanship once again came in for a lot of criticism. The reasons were many. While lack of intelligence was the root cause, the Indian Army having realized the gravity of the situation wanted the IAF to use Mi-25 and Mi-35 Gunships to attack the intruders. However, these helicopters did not have the capability to reach such higher heights with the other irritant being the necessity of Cabinet clearance for using air power in the Pakistan-occupied Kashmir (POK) sector.

The Kargil Review Committee constituted under the late K Subrahmanyam recommended new structures for joint working of the Services and the Ministry of Defence. Lack of coordination in gathering Intelligence and quick dissemination of analysed information also came under scrutiny and led to formation of another entity, National Technical Research Organisation (NTRO). While some recommendations have been implemented there is a lot more to be put into place. HQ Integrated Defence Staff does plan on joint areas of operation and acquisition, but the true integration with the Ministry of Defence and Service HQs has not taken place. In the US, a model often talked about regarding jointmanship, it is only a decade after implementation of Goldwater-Nichols Act of 1986[22] that the Services integration has taken place. However, it must be understood that there is a vast difference between the limited scope of roles and operations of the Indian military as compared to the US engagements globally. We therefore need to develop a model best suited for India's vision. With considerable delay in the implementation of the Subrahmanyam committee recommendations, the Government had set up the Naresh Chandra Committee in July 2011 to once again review the higher defence management and make suggestions to enhance National Security. While this report has also been submitted, it is yet to be acted upon.

Undoubtedly, joint planning is the key to success and the joint operational plan should dictate whether a particular Service should lead or carry out parallel warfare. However, it needs to be understood that new structures may help but essentially it is the understanding of the core competencies of each other, which is far more important. After all, in 1971, the Indian Armed Forces achieved unparalleled success without any formal joint structures. Absence of joint planning can lead to losing initiative as emphasized by Air Cmde Kaiser Tufail of the PAF. He has blamed the Pakistani Army for not keeping the PAF informed of the planned infiltrations in Kargil, which resulted in the PAF not being able to retaliate against the IAF.[23]

Synergy in intelligence sharing, logistics management, use of space assets, and cyber warfare are areas in which the three Services can cooperate without worrying about 'transgressing the turf.' Apart from the existing joint commands of Strategic Forces and Andaman Nicobar, there is an urgent need to set up joint commands in the areas of Space, Cyber Warfare and Special Operations.

Modernization Drive

In the last decade or so, the IAF has witnessed a comprehensive drive towards modernization of its aircraft and equipment. It is comprehensive because it has truly added to the reach and capability including a wide spectrum of platforms, sensors, upgrades of older platforms and training assets such as the Hawk Advanced Jet Trainer (AJT). Some of the unfilled gaps are on the anvil for induction, both qualitatively and quantitatively. This of course is a continuous process, but what is important is that the IAF is moving in the right direction. The years 2009–11 were important, during which the IAF operationalized the AWACS and also achieved network centricity to a large extent. With Flight Air Refuelling (FAR) capability on aircraft such as Su-30, Mirage-2000 and Jaguar, IAF is now capable of long-range missions in India's extended neighbourhood. Added to this is the space-enabled extended footprint with Rohini multi-sensor satellite series and Global Positioning System (GPS)-Aided Geo-Augmented Navigation (GAGAN) programme for better navigation. With the induction of C-17 Globe Master and C-130 Hercules aircraft the IAF has also acquired strategic airlift capability for inter and intra-theatre movements.

However, all is not well regarding replacing the obsolescent inventory as mentioned earlier. Ideally, the inventory should consist of 33 per cent or less leading to obsolescence with 33 per cent new inductions and the remaining matured systems. However, presently the IAF is grappling to maintain an edge with more aircraft and equipment becoming obsolescent. This is because of many challenges such as budgetary support, policy directives as well as lack of indigenous equipment.

The budget provision for 2013–14 has been the lowest since the 1962 War.[24] It was only 1.74 per cent of the Gross Domestic Product (GDP) as compared to 2.5 to 3 per cent in earlier years. What is more important is the marginal increase for new induction or capital acquisition. At Rs. 31817 crores, it is much lower than needed for inducting 126 MMRCA and other equipment. This is because not only the inflation and adverse exchange rates have eroded the allotment but bulk of this amount is for earlier inducted (rollover) schemes, for which payments have to be made. Meanwhile, the US and Russia spend around 4 per cent of GDP on their militaries, the UK and France spend 2.3 to 2.5 per cent, Pakistan spends close to 3 per cent, and China declares an expenditure of slightly over 2 per cent, but is believed to actually spend 3 per cent if hidden funding is included.

With almost US $35 billion expected to be spent in the next ten years to boost its air combat power, the IAF needs urgent infusion of funds. However, with the Army and Navy also in similar need of funds it will be difficult to manage adequate budget allocation for capital acquisitions. The IAF is inducting more Sukhoi-30 aircraft from Russia for US $10 billion[25] with another $20 billion required for MMRCA Rafael aircraft. There is also a plan to induct more combat support aircraft and ground systems. As such it will be quite some time before the IAF can truly acquire capability to fight on both Eastern and Western fronts.

Indigenization and Self-reliance

India having gained independence through the non-violence movement, the initial policy abhorred production and export of weapons. Added to this was the policy of non-alignment which further affected development and export of weapons. It is a well-known fact that to avail advantage from the 'scale of economy,' export of defence systems is a must. India, however, never ventured into this lucrative market, in turn denying herself an opportunity to build a comprehensive military-industrial complex. On the other hand, efforts in fits and jerks affected the indigenous development as massive financial outlays had to be set aside later for projects such as Tejas Light Combat Aircraft (LCA) and Arjun Main Battle Tank (MBT) with no satisfying results. To illustrate, after successful design of HF-24 fighter aircraft, India did not follow up with other designs, leading to loss of expertise and the art of manufacturing complex systems.

After the success of Kiran Jet Trainer had India pursued with advanced models of trainer alone, by now India could have been a leader in manufacturing and exporting trainer aircraft. Instead India imported Swiss-made Pilatus basic trainers and the British Hawk AJT. While India has produced many weapon systems under license, India continues to be hampered in many critical core areas such as engines, metallurgy, sensors and seekers to name a few. The challenge therefore is of ensuring self-reliance and to minimize dependence on foreign suppliers. The indigenous product support will also ensure very high states of serviceability of aircraft and equipment.

There are new opportunities for the Indian industry, both in the public and private sectors to take advantages of the prioritized clauses such as 'Buy (Indian),' 'Buy and Make (Indian)'[26] promulgated in DPP 2013 and the 'off-set' clause. However, there are many issues including deft handling of contracts, which would be very important. While provisions have been made, unless the 'know-why' is acquired, India will once again be confined to 'transfer of manufacturing process' and not the essence of 'transfer of technology.' With a sizeable revamp of inventory in the near future, the IAF could be instrumental in energizing this process and therefore a major stakeholder in realizing the indigenous, self-reliant capability.

There is a need to encourage larger participation in private industry and let them collaborate with foreign partners than to allow Foreign Direct Investment of 50 per cent as being mentioned recently. Such collaborations should also have a clause for export. Another important aspect is of accepting indigenous equipment with scope for incremental improvement in next versions. A similar approach termed as 'Mark-I to Mark-II philosophy' has been adopted by the Chinese to encourage use of indigenous equipment and to learn lessons, which are then incorporated for improvement in the next version. India started a similar approach and the Akash surface to air missile is one such example. Induction of LCA by the IAF is another such incremental project. Brahmos[27] is a classic case of a collaborative project, which has benefited not only DRDO but also the private industry. DRDO has now got expertise in early-warning radars, surface to surface and air to air missiles, AEW&C aircraft and need encouragement by the Services. However, more indigenous efforts are needed to acquire latest technology and 'know why' in areas of engines, metallurgy and sensors. Unmanned Aerial Vehicle (UAV) is another area in which India is fast acquiring indigenous capability. Netra,[28] UAV made by R&D (Engrs) Pune along with IIT, Mumbai is a classic case of using expertise in such academic institutions.

Strategic Vision

With her growing economic potential, need for increased energy resources as well as buoyant trade and commerce, India now looks way beyond her traditional borders. Apart from trade, the Indian cultural ties with littorals of Indian Ocean and beyond makes the country envision her strategic boundaries all the way from the Malacca straits in the East to the African coast in the West and from Central Asian Republics in the North to Antarctica in the South. Engaging in a globalized economy is another reason for such a strategic vision. The Indian Armed Forces have to be prepared therefore to protect the interests arising from such strategic vision.

Space: the New Frontier

With such a large area of interest, there is now a need for a bigger footprint in satellite-aided communication, navigation, remote sensing and many other space-based applications. Inherent to the globalization of the economy is competition amongst nations, which leads to implications of space security. Space as a continuum of air above us will then be a dominant medium, which needs to be safeguarded. The Chinese Space Doctrine[29] refers to space as the 'ultimate high ground' during a conflict situation and use of 'space territory' for creating military imbalance. Recently, the Chinese President Xi Jinping urged further integration of air and space defence capabilities, in response to militarization of space by rivals.[30]

The IAF with its extended reach and capability to respond quickly in any scenario is acquiring network centricity. It therefore needs to use space-based assets along with a terrestrial backbone. For many years now, the IAF has been advocating creation of an Aerospace Command, jointly with other Services. While discussing this one must clearly understand the difference between militarization and weaponization of outer space. While the first one relates to using space-based assets for enhancing military capabilities, the latter refers to using offensive weapons such as the ASAT capability demonstrated recently by China and USA. Unfortunately, there is no international treaty obligation against use of space for operating offensive platforms except for the conduct of nuclear tests. The proposed Tri-Service Space Command will be focusing on the area of enhancing military capabilities. It is heartening to note that such a need has been accepted by the higher echelons in the government. However, it must get off the ground urgently.

Air Vector for Nuclear Option

Developing Air Vector for carriage of nuclear weapons was undoubtedly a technological challenge. Due credit must be given to those who configured a bomb load constrained by size and weight. Today India maintains a credible deterrence to retaliate while exercising the 'No First Use' doctrinal approach. While the surface to surface missile capability has grown exponentially with consecutive successful flights of Agni-5 IRBM capable of 5000+ km ranges, the submarine-launched missile capability is also improving steadily. India is also developing her own Ballistic Missile Defence system and has had successes in both 'exo and endo' atmospheric interceptions.

China has launched a massive programme of developing and deploying newer versions of SSM, Dongfeng 31 and 41, and long-range cruise missiles like YJ-62 and DH-10. The Chinese have also developed a GPS-enabled anti-shipping missile DF-21D. It is a very capable programme and hence India will have to ensure that on the one hand the nuclear threshold is not reached against China and on the other to develop our capability for a viable deterrence like Agni-5, as well as improving BMD capability. After all for the Chinese the Himalayas offer some sort of insulation against fallout if a low-yield nuclear weapon is used by them against India.

'In Pakistan's nuclear strategy, the primary task of its nuclear weapons is not to deter India's nuclear weapons, but to avoid an engagement with a superior military capability.'[31] The Pakistani response is therefore a complex situation both in terms of indiscretion of threshold on the one hand, including deployment of Tactical Nuclear Weapon Nasr as well as Cruise Missile, Babur and the insider conniving into nuclear terrorism, on the other. The second aspect has raised concerns the world over with possible extremist ideological inroads into the Pakistani establishment leading to 'lose nukes.' Peter Topychkanov sums up the Pakistani programme, 'Pakistan's missile programme is based on cruise missiles and tactical nuclear weapons, because no Indian antimissile system will be able to protect its territory, especially the areas in the vicinity of the Indian-Pakistani border, from strikes by cruise missiles and tactical nuclear weapons. Given that Pakistan has limited resources, it is prepared to respond asymmetrically.'[32]

The National Security Advisor Shivshankar Menon had signalled a significant shift from 'No First Use' to 'NFU against non-nuclear weapon states' in a speech on the occasion of Golden Jubilee celebrations of the National Defence College in New Delhi on 21 October 2010, a doctrine that Menon said reflected India's 'strategic culture, with its emphasis on minimal deterrence.'[33] In April 2013 Shyam Saran, convener of the National Security Advisory Board, affirmed that regardless of the size of a nuclear attack against India, be it a miniaturized version or a 'big' missile, India will retaliate massively to inflict unacceptable damage.[34]

Incidentally, on occasions there is debate as to whether a Triad is needed and that the Air Vector should be done away with. Instead of debating such issues, it is important is to develop all the three vectors for better and robust designs and keep options open for newer technologies to be configured in later years. India is too early in stage to deny her an option later on, for having succumbed blindly into following some models in the Western world.

Cyber Security

While addressing the Staff College in March 2000, Former Chief of Army Staff Gen VP Malik rightly said 'The Armed Forces must be fully joint: doctrinally, institutionally, organizationally, intellectually and technically because Cyber War will be to the twenty-first century what the blitzkrieg was to the twentieth century.'[35] The importance of Cyber Warfare cannot be understated in today's digitally connected communication and command systems. While the net-centricity has helped in shortening the Observe Orient Decide Act (OODA) loop, Cyber security is also the biggest challenge. In the recent Russo-Georgia war of 2008 the reported large-scale hacking of Georgia's essential networks, resulted in degradation of her military response. Similar cyber assaults had earlier taken place against Estonia in April 2007 and by the Israeli Air Force in their attack over a Syrian nuclear reactor under construction at Al Kibar on 6 September 2007 in what is known as 'Operation Orchard.'

Presently with increasing dependence on computers and networking, clogging or disabling civil utility networks of communications, power grids and many others including banking and finance; equally affect nation's war preparedness. It would be even more catastrophic then, if a hacker can disable exclusive intra-nets using embedded software bugs and Trojans. 'One of the great technical blockbuster in malware history'[36] is that of Stuxnet, a computer worm, which was embedded in the Siemens' industrial control units and in turn affected the Iranian enrichment plant at Natanz in 2010. Incidentally it is reported that almost 60 per cent of Iranian nuclear installations were affected by such malware and the US computer security company Symantec had reported that 8 per cent of Indian nuclear installations using Siemens' equipment could also be susceptible to this bug.[37]

Owing to this force-enhancing capability the US has set up United States Cyber Command in 2009, which is a joint command with a mandate to execute both, offensive and defensive operations. The Chinese are also known to give a lot of importance to cyber warfare and refer to cyber warfare as the latest RMA. Chinese view cyber pre-emptive attack as 'The supreme art of war to subdue the enemy without fighting.'[38]

On many occasions in the past few years, important Indian Government sites and intra-nets have been affected, with investigations pointing towards foreign involvement. Unfortunately, India has invested a lot in creating software but almost all of the susceptible hardware is imported, leaving a room for embedded malware. Many terrorist groups are also known to be active in this field. Therefore the IAF along with the other two Services have been creating their own expertise in this field. However, there is a need for better synergy with other civilian national agencies working in this specialized field. Therefore, another long-pending demand for a tri-service Cyber Command needs to be formed urgently to give a concrete shape to both defensive and offensive capabilities.

Aerospace Commission for Comprehensive Eco-System

Today when we see a great surge in civil aviation, one cannot help but recount the contribution made by the IAF in every facet of this growth. The IAF's involvement has been varied such as seconding trained pilots and maintenance personnel to Air India and Pawan Hans, ensuring maintenance of requisite medical standards for the aircrew, synergy in aviation meteorology observation and setting up airspace management across the country. Initially the majority of Air India pilots were from the IAF and continue to be seconded even today. The helicopter pilots, seconded from IAF, formed Helicopter Corporation of India in 1985, which was later renamed as Pawan Hans. These pilots carried out pioneering work of flying to distant offshore oil-rigs of Bombay High.

Vested with the responsibility of air defence, the IAF has a major stake in air space management of both civil and military aircraft. For a number of years after independence, Director Generals of Civil Aviation and of Airport Authority of India (AAI) were senior IAF officers, who helped in ensuring synergy of operations and also streamlining procedures. In those formative years, far-flung airfields across India were networked and many of the Air Force airfields were either completely handed over to the AAI or civil enclaves were established at IAF bases to allow use by civil aircraft. Now that the civil aviation in India is witnessing an impressive growth, there are over twenty-two IAF airfields from which civil aircraft operate. A network of Advance Landing Grounds (ALGs) and helipads operated by the IAF for air-logistics delivery will also come handy for air connectivity to inaccessible areas. In the recent past, concepts such as flexible air space have been introduced by the Air Force jointly with AAI, to facilitate efficient flow of air traffic. This would result in avoiding circuitous route flying; in turn saving time and fuel as also avoiding air-traffic congestion.

There is a need therefore to ensure coordinated growth in aviation, not looking at only the Western models, but also those from countries which have overriding requirements of air defence as in the case of India.

In 2007 as part of IAF's Platinum Jubilee celebrations, when two young pilots from the IAF flew a micro light around the world in eighty days, while over-flying the eastern coast of China, this benign aircraft had to zigzag many times,[39] possibly to avoid naval installations en route.

Apart from the opportunities for indigenous development and manufacture in military aviation, there are similar opportunities in civil aviation. While about 30 per cent of the indigenous content is being developed for the Armed Forces, there is practically 'nil' production for civil aviation.[40] Indigenous content will not only save sizeable foreign exchange but will also lead to establishment of a manufacturing base. In turn the sector will also help in creating more job opportunities within India. The resultant scale of products and the spin-off into other sectors such as auto, medical equipment using laser, fibre optics, nano and micro technology will attract sound investment by the private sector in a PPP or other models.

Already some of the private companies like Mahindra, Reliance, L&T and Tata are manufacturing smaller aircraft, UAVs, high-fidelity simulators and parts of aircraft and helicopters to name a few. More companies, namely Godrej, Kirloskars and Bharat Forge have set up subsidiaries in these fields. In order to encourage these and for nurturing many Small and Medium Enterprises (SMEs) we will need a sound policy mechanism with adequate safeguards for security and redundancy.

With mediums of air and space becoming pivotal in various fields of transportation, navigation, surveillance, imaging, and communication backed by high-technology aerospace industries, there is a need for establishing an enabling eco-system for synergy in all aspects of R&D, manufacturing, human resource training, etc. Undoubtedly, the Indian Air Force, Indian Space Research Organisation (ISRO), Civil Aviation and Public and Private enterprises will be the major stakeholders to ensure a concerted end result. As the IAF celebrates its 82nd anniversary this year, it would be befitting to form the much-needed Aerospace Commission to deal with the challenges and opportunities in this vital sector.

Conclusion

In the past few years due to various constraints the combat potential of the IAF has been eroding. To overcome this shortfall the IAF has been struggling to maintain deterrence on both fronts with innovative use of various platforms and inter-theatre deployments. However, further reduction in the IAF's potential will be detrimental to national security. Therefore, adequate budgetary support and timely decision-making is urgently needed. Emphasis also needs to be laid on indigenous manufacturing capability of defence systems to reduce dependence on foreign suppliers. An enabling eco-system will help in achieving this synergistically. With resurgent policy-making and budgetary support, the IAF will overcome various challenges and grow from strength to strength in the years ahead. I am also confident that the Air Warriors with their innovative approach will turn every challenge into an opportunity, so as to reach greater heights in future to 'Touch the Sky and Space with Glory.'

NOTES

1. Interview of Shri Atal Bihari Vajpayee with the *Financial Times*, New Delhi, 7 October 2002.
2. *The Military Balance 2014*, London: International Institute for Strategic Studies.
3. Standing Committee of Indian Parliament, April 2012. See also: *Asia Pacific Defence Forum*, 10 May 2013.
4. Vijaya Dar, 'India's Destiny—Thousand Cuts on a Thousand Branched Tree' *India Opines*, 26 July 2013.
5. Jeff M Smith, 'China and India: end of cold peace,' *The National Interest*, 10 February 2014.
6. Sun Tzu, *The Art of War.*
7. Jasjit Singh, *Defence from the Skies*, p. XV.
8. Myers *Aerospace Power, The Case for Indivisible Application* (September 1986).
9. *Remembering JRD Tata, 1904–93.*
10. *Official Website of Indian Air Force.*
11. Jasjit Singh, *Defence from the Skies*, p. 11.
12. Mohammad Ayub Khan, 'The Pak American Alliance' *Foreign Affairs*, January 1964.
13. Jasjit Singh, *Defence from the Skies*, p. 70.
14. Vivek Kapur, 'IAF Equipment and Force Structure Requirements to Meet External Threats 2032 ' *IDSA*, January–March 2014.
15. RD Pradhan, *Debacle to Resurgence, YB Chavan, Defence Minister (1962-6).*
16. This event is also depicted in the recently released Marathi film on him by Jabbar Patel. 'Yashwantrao Chavan—Bakhar Eka Vadalachi' (2014)
17. VK Bhatia, 'Laser-Guided Bombs—Building LGB Capability,' *SP's Aviation*, 30 June 1999.
18. IAF Transformation Maturing with New Aircraft, More Squadrons, *India Strategic*, October 2012.
19. Sushil Singh, 'India will use fighter jets to defend two borders,' *Asia Pacific Defence Forum*, 10 May 2013.

20. India receives first EMB 145 AEW&C aircraft from Embraer, *Air Force Technology.com* 17 August 2012.
21. RD Pradhan, *Debacle to Resurgence, YB Chavan, Defence Minister (1962-6)* p. 23.
22. 'Beyond Goldwater-Nichols,' *Centre for Strategic & International Studies* (CSIS), 13 May 2014.
23. Kaiser Tufail, 'Himalayan Showdown,' *Air Forces Monthly*, June 2009.
24. Ajai Shukla, 'Budget Analysis,' *Business Standard*, 21 February 2014.
25. Rajat Pandit, 'Dwindling number of fighters biggest challenge for new IAF Chief,' *Times of India,* 1 January 2014.
26. Salient Features of Defence Procurement Procedure-2013, *Press Information Bureau*, 1 June 2013.
27. 'Army test-fires BrahMos in Pokhran,' *Times of India*, 8 April 2014.
28. 'DRDO develops UAV 'Netra' to aid anti-terrorist operations,' *The Hindu*, 3 July 2010.
29. Ashley J Tellis 'Can China Threaten the United States in Space?,' *Carnegie Endowment for International Peace.*
30. *Channel News Asia,* 15 April 2014.
31. Manpreet Sethi, 'Responding to Pakistan's TNW,' *Eurasia Review*, 19 January 2014.
32. Peter Topychkanov, 'Indian Agni-4 launch stirs fears of local nuclear war in South Asia' *Voice of Russia*, 23 January 2014.
33. Speech by NSA Shri Shivshankar Menon at NDC on 'The Role of Force in Strategic Affairs,' *Media Centre*, 21 October 2010.
34. Indrani Bagchi, 'Even a midget nuke strike will lead to massive retaliation,' *The Economic Times*, 30 April 2013.
35. Address at Defence Services Staff College, Wellington, *The Tribune*, 31 March 2000.
36. Michael Joseph, 'A declaration of Cyber-War,' *Vanity Fair*, April 2011.
37. W32.Stuxnet, Symantec, 17 September 2010.
38. Sun Tzu, *The Art of War*, Chapter 3, Attack by Stratagem.
39. 'IAF duo holed up in Haikou,' *Times of India*, 9 June 2007.
40. 'CEOs call for indigenization, single certifying agency,' *Times of India*, 14 March 2014.

CHAPTER III

THE STATE OF INDIA'S NAVY

Vinod Pasricha

The Indian Ocean appears to be a relatively neglected area in Indian history during the medieval era. Most of Indian's medieval rulers regularly chose to neglect the seas. The era before them had considerable maritime activity, accompanied by economic prosperity and political stability. Till the twelfth century, maritime trade was at its best and the Indian share of world GDP was higher than most nations. However, in the thirteenth century, Indian rulers from Central Asia had a totally continental outlook, which led to a total decline of Indian maritime activity. By the time the Europeans came to India, Indians neither contested nor had the inclination to challenge their control of their ocean. This led to two centuries of foreign domination, with no maritime orientation in Indian strategy.

Background

The India maritime outlook was again articulated by Sardar KM Panikkar, when in 1945 he stated:

> 'While to other countries the Indian Ocean is only one of the important oceanic areas, to India it is a vital sea. Her lifelines are concentrated in this area and her freedom is dependent on the freedom of this water surface. No industrial development, no commercial growth, no stable political structure is possible for India unless her shores are protected.'

When India gained independence, there were hardly any warships or merchant ships. Fortunately, the Indian continental mindset started dissipating and it began thinking of new ships, other than the hand-me-downs from the Royal Navy. India started improving its ports and shipbuilding capabilities. At that time, Mazdocks and Scindia were India's only shipyards, with its shipbuilding and repair facilities being very weak. There was a need for urgent action, as nearly 93 per cent of Indian trade requirements came by sea, its merchant ship industry was weak and the number of merchant ships that India had built was small in number, even for its own requirements.

Earl Mountbatten and Pandit Nehru had together planned the growth of the Indian Navy, with Admiral Parry preparing the perspective plan as early as December 1947. However, financial constraints, the first Indo-Pakistan conflict over Jammu and Kashmir and the Korean War delayed Indian plans. Notwithstanding this, Indian naval personnel left for England in 1949 and India bought its first aircraft carrier, INS Vikrant and a variety of aircraft. Soon the Long Range Maritime Patrol role shifted to India and the IAF transferred their Super Constellations to the Navy. Recently, India also acquired the P81s from the United States. Today, India is one of the very few countries that have used this changeover to great advantage ensuring that its naval strength is adequate.

Navies are generally classified either as *Blue Water* or as *Brown Water*, depending on their ability to remain, operate and fight either in the *open seas* or in *coastal waters*. Because India had very few ships in the sixties and most had inadequate endurance, it was considered a *Brown Water* navy. However, since nearly all Indian import and export requirements were by sea, it had little option but to concentrate on sea-trade. Today, because indigenous warship-building capability and its naval mettle have been proved during the 1971 War, the world now recognizes that India has a *Blue Water* Navy.

Geopolitics

An important component of Indian foreign policy has been that it would never be the aggressor. Instead, it uses defence forces primarily to defend its territorial integrity and sovereignty. It has been possible for India to convey this through a display of its Navy's size and capabilities. Whilst it needs to grow much more, so that its long coastline, Island territories, Exclusive Economic Zone (EEZ), oil platforms and Sea Lanes of Communication remain safe, a closer look at its maritime boundaries and EEZ would be opportune.

Two laws that govern the oceans are of vital importance. The first relates to the concept of EEZ and the territorial waters. Most countries have declared territorial waters to extend up to 12 nautical miles from their coastline. This allows foreign warships to reach close to the coastline to this limit and yet remain within the purview of international law. They can thus exert pressure on an adversary, before hostilities actually break out. This law remains India's trump card, which was exercised successfully during the Kargil Conflict. India is also fortunate to have the Andaman and Nicobar and the Lakshadweep Islands as an integral part of India. This has enhanced its EEZ, as well as the control of all ships that transit across these islands. The second relates to the *Right of Innocent Passage* through restricted waters. The advantages of this are indeed manifold for the Indian Navy, as it allows it to maintain its presence at all Choke Points of the India Ocean. These being the following: in the west are the Strait of Hormuz, Suez Canal and the Red Sea, Strait of Bab-el-Mandeb and the Horn of Africa; in the East are Malacca Strait, Lombok Strait, Sunda Strait; and along the Indian coast line are the Six Degree Channel and the Nine Degree Channel.

It would be interesting to look at an inverted map of India (see map). Over centuries, India has only been watching its Northern frontier and had not paid attention to the vast number of countries that actually form India's maritime neighbourhood. This view has great significance and would help India in meeting the challenges that emanate from the sea. Whilst conventional wars remain possibilities, conflicts are now taking amorphous forms with the emergence of terrorism epicentres. The effect of non-state actors has also been highlighted recently by maritime pirates, who are indulging in widespread hijacking and the commandeering of merchant vessels. The Indian Navy has made a determined effort to cope with these requirements and is amongst only a handful of countries that build and operate diverse platforms on the surface of the ocean, below the surface and in the air. India now has a multitude of indigenously built ships and submarines that can perform all roles at short notice, both during war, as well as for search and rescue missions in peacetime.

Capability

India has sought to become a *Builders' Navy* and not a *Buyers'* one. By enhancing its shipbuilding capacity India is producing warships, which compare with those of all advanced nations. Even when India purchases a ship from abroad, it has a large amount of Indian-made equipment and sensors. This multi-dimensional capability which is so necessary in modern warfare has become the Indian Navy's major strength. However, one area in which India still needs to enhance its capability is to build indigenous naval aircraft.

The Indian Submarine Arm, which started in the mid-sixties, has now matured into an extremely potent force, with India embarking on a thirty-year-plan to build submarines, including nuclear ones. In all this, the Indian strengths remain the ability to conjoin the technologies that exist on foreign acquisitions into indigenous ships. India is one of the very few countries that have managed to combine the Western and Eastern bloc technologies, as well as improve on these systems with totally Indian characteristics. This is specifically so in all Indian software and communication activities, where deep understanding of the different protocols has ensured excellent mergers. It has also enabled it to achieve very high standards in all its Command, Control and Communication Channels and in Data Linking.

The mainstay of the Indian Navy remains its ships. It now has a second aircraft carrier, INS Vikramaditya. The MiG-29K that have been purchased have folding wings, a tail hook, fly-by-wire electronics and a rear cockpit, that can become a fuel tank with extra endurance. All new Indian ships are capable of carrying a variety of missiles, both the surface-to-surface, as well as the surface-to-air variety, which is capable of shooting down low-flying aircraft. Similarly, torpedoes and anti-submarine rockets remain India's main ammunition against enemy submarines. However, because of hydrology, whenever submarines dive deep their sound-beam echoes cannot be heard on the ship's sonar. This gives a submarine an inherent advantage, particularly so in the tropical waters of the Indian Ocean. Because the sea surface is so much warmer here, the substantial temperature differential makes detection problems very acute. For this, the Naval Physical and Oceanographic Laboratory has designed excellent HUMSA (Hull-Mounted Sonar Advanced) and APSOH (Advanced Panoramic Sonar Hull-mounted) sonars, along with a variety of airborne sensors. These help to detect submarines and thereafter attack them. Also, Passive Towed Array Systems (PTAS) are becoming the main stay on our anti-submarine ships. These permit ships to employ gambit tactics, which make it difficult for enemy submarines to attack them.

Some of the achievements that the navy has besides the ships are in the area of tankers. The gas turbines consume a lot of fuel and the ships need to be refuelled. To resolve this problem the Indian Navy converted a lot of ships, particularly the LSTs which have a lot of fuel for long distance into tankers so that wherever the tankers are not there with three to four ships going on a task, one of these ships could go along and fuel them just about 200 miles away from the enemy coast. The communications network is also totally computerized. The navy lays stress on systems not on platforms therefore an effort is being put into developing systems—radars and communications.

An important feature of a Blue Water Navy is *Staying Power* and the capability to operate in rough seas. Here again, the Indian Navy has progressed tremendously and the new-construction ships are specifically designed for this. India has also built its own fleet tankers, which are capable of fuelling all ships at sea, so that there is no requirement for them to frequently return to harbour for replenishment. Stealth has become an essential requirement to successfully avoid detection and wage a battle at sea. Thus, aspects gaining ascendancy are the ability to ensure that radar signatures, infra-red emissions and self-noise levels of all new ships remain low. The Indian Navy has introduced design features to ensure low self-noise levels, radar signatures and infra-red emissions. India is also the only Indian Ocean country with Amphibious Warfare capability. The acquisition of INS Jalashwa with her huge helicopter-deck, from which up to six medium helicopters can operate simultaneously, have given India a tremendous capability. Jalashwa can also launch four mechanized landing craft. The helicopter deck can also be used to operate vertical takeoff and landing (VTOL) aircraft, like the Sea Harriers. The ship can embark over a thousand troops and is fully equipped with extensive medical facilities, including four operation theatres, a twelve-bed ward and a dental centre—both in war and during peacetime relief operations.

As the three defence forces work in total unison in these operations, they have been classified as truly 'joint-service' and also include the Coast Guard as an integral component. Many civilian organizations also take active part and have now understood the nuances and intricacies that are involved in these operations. Regular training and interaction along with the Indian Army and the Air Force, have added tremendously to jointmanship capability.

The Indian Navy also conducts Commando Operations, whenever the need arises, both at the regional and global levels. It has now worked upon Marine Commandos (MARCOS), with one thrust area being the build-up of their professional acumen. This elite force, that demands a tremendous amount from each individual, continues to be a front-runner in special war conditions and during disaster management in peace time. Further, in *Amphex* exercises the Navy has regularly also taken merchant ships from trade to add to the carrying capacity of troops, tanks/weapons and equipment. These ships are referred to as STUFTs, which is short for '*Ships Taken up from Trade.*'

The Indian role of building bridges with its neighbours in the Indian Ocean, as well as with the major Navies of the world has brought about some changes in Indian thought-processes, as well as highlighted its capabilities to these countries. Whilst enhancing India's indigenous shipbuilding capacity, one factor that must remain paramount is its ability to drastically reduce the eight to ten years now being taken for a new ship to become fully operational. India must cater for all roles that may be required in the future, including internationally, as was displayed in Lebanon and in all the multi-navy exercises. Despite all this, there is need to improve the weapon-manufacturing capability, as also an early decision to manufacture indigenous carrier-borne naval aircraft. These require a totally co-ordinated approach between the Government, Research and Development (R&D) and shipbuilding organizations. There is also a need to enhance the ability to protect Indian merchant ships against piracy at sea.

Though the Indian Navy's indigenization plans have remained well ahead of the other two services, co-ordinated work ethics between the Government, R&D organizations and defence manufacturers lacks the desired initiative. This interaction must be at a much faster pace.

Areas of Concern

India has not been able to produce good indigenous weapons, the research and development in this aspect remains problematic. The other area of concern has been the defence budget, especially where it relates to equipment. There is a need to ensure that the process of integrating the three services would benefit the procurement of equipment that is common for the services. The other aspect about integration relates to the Andaman and Nicobar command which is a tri-service command, commanded headed for 2 years each by the army, air force and the navy. This is a purely island command which has about 1100 or 1200 islands. Such a command may be placed permanently with the navy and some other command of the north like the air command and the air tactical command be given permanently to the Air force. This logic is extended to the CIGS who changes from service to service with a two-year tenure thus not providing enough time to know the issues relating to the other services.

Indian defence planning is based on a five-year plan system. A ship takes fifteen years to build and the fear is of uncertainties that may come in due to changes in government policies. Fortunately, the navy has three to four plans and the nuclear submarine is one of them where it was given a thirty-year tenure. But the budget allocation is still on the short term with the result some of the armaments take six years to come through.

Economies of scale constitute another area which needs to be worked on. India was able to procure seven ships from Korea within a span of two years while the production time in India can run up to twenty-five years. This is where the shipyards need to change totally. The issue is the procedure for import of spares. Today if a system is not working, by the time one can import the spare that is needed for the system it can take as much as eight to ten months. While certain powers have been given to the Chiefs in this regard the insistence on indigenous procurement needs to be kept on hold until the Indian R&D is able to produce the necessary material.

Recommendations

i. There is a need to lay down and ensure time-bound programmes for the construction of ships and their major components.

ii. Till India masters new technologies for indigenous weapons, systems and aircraft, India will continue to pay huge costs to import these. By directly purchasing such technologies and by hiring foreign experts/scientists, India would be able to obtain these services on a contract basis.

iii. The concept of budget allocations only during each *Five-Year Plan* needs a relook. Whilst the Navy has been fortunate in a few projects, since most naval projects extend over long periods, there is a need to convert all major programmes into long-term strategies.

iv. The Defence industry needs to work on the concept of *Economy-of-scale*. Each yard should not be working independently to produce each item. They all must link up to one common manufacturer, who must be given suitable concessions by the Government, to produce specific items.

v. The question of import of spares and equipment that are urgently required needs to be addressed. Whilst indigenization is a good thing and must definitely happen, to hold back a full system/equipment either by not permitting import or by charging colossal duty for certain items needs a review.

vi. Remotely Operated Underwater Vehicles (ROVs) have a tremendous future and these need urgent action to develop indigenous ones.

vii. There is a need for a long-term policy by the Government for merchant ship construction.

viii. There is a need for a totally co-ordinated approach between R&D, the Government, the Navy, shipbuilding yards and all other organizations involved.

Map 1: Inverted Map of the Indian Ocean

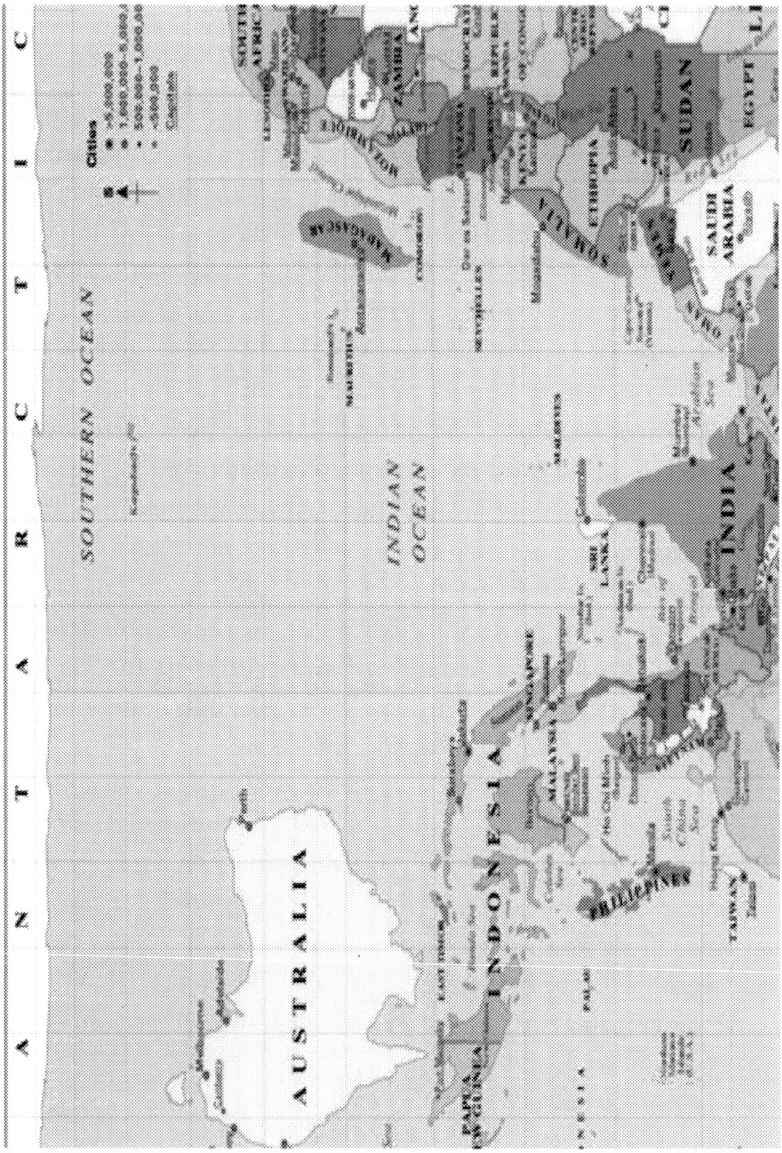

Map 2: Choke Points in the Indian Ocean

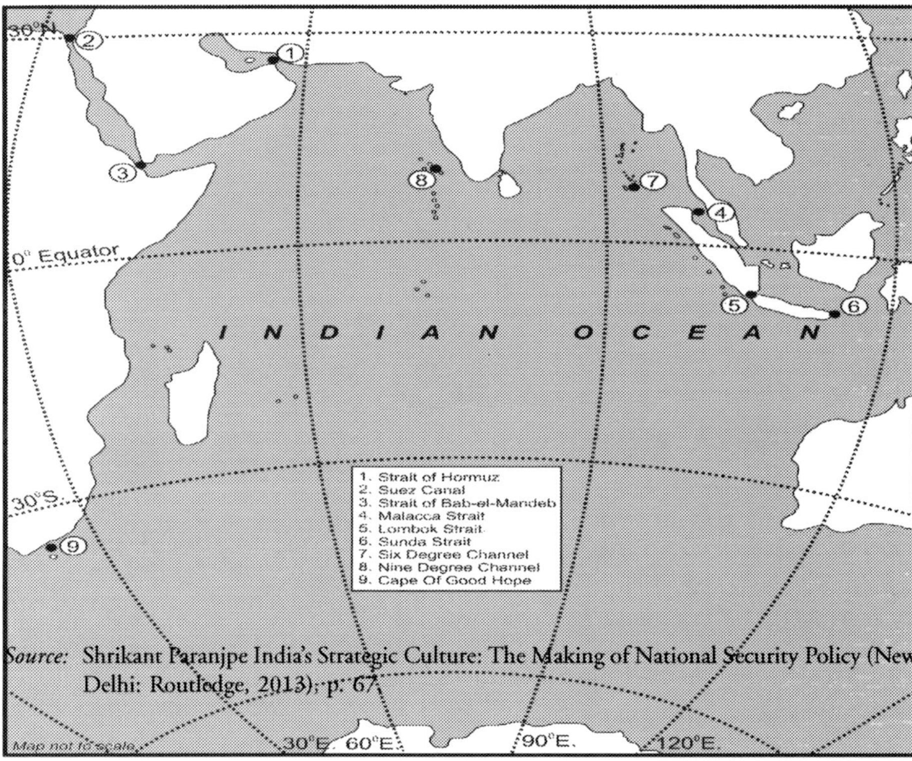

Source: Shrikant Paranjpe India's Strategic Culture: The Making of National Security Policy (New Delhi: Routledge, 2013), p. 67.

II. THE CONTEXT

CHAPTER IV

THE NEED FOR A NATIONAL SECURITY POLICY

Nitin Gokhale

In the early 1990s an American scholar, George Tanham, published a monograph in which he argued that India was bereft of coherent strategic thinking. Entitled *Indian Strategic Thought: An Interpretive Essay*,[1] the monograph provoked many Indian thinkers to take Tanham apart. Most of them pointed out that Tanham did not understand India's core values of pacifism and that he had tried to analyse India's policy through Western eyes. Others like Professor Manjari Chatterjee Miller[2] (writing in *Foreign Affairs*) found an Indian government without a strategic objective. She writes of policy being made by individual foreign-service officers without a strategic umbrella. Ashley J Tellis, an avid and expert India watcher, has been more nuanced. He lauds India for having successfully navigated the international system since 1947. In doing so, he outlines the contours of India's 'grand strategy' and recalls her success in surviving as a unified entity despite great poverty and diversity; he also praises India for the courageous feat of preserving its strategic autonomy in the face of substantial material weakness.[3]

Almost two decades after the Tanham report, the *Economist* had a cover story, '*Can India become a Great Power*?'[4] raising the question again by commenting: 'Despite a rapidly rising defence budget, forecast to be the world's fourth-largest by 2020, India's politicians and bureaucrats show little interest in grand strategy... That India can become a great power is not in doubt. The real question is whether it wants to.' The article was written strictly from a militarist point of view. It ended with the observation that 'India's strategic shortcomings are a liability and an obstacle to India's dreams of becoming a twenty-first-century world power.' This raises a reaction: Is there an agenda set by the world's biggest arms companies eager to sell more arms to India?

National Security Strategy

These articles and essays have helped revive an old debate about 'grand strategy.' So what exactly is National Security Strategy?

In India there is no documented policy, not at least in the public domain. Indeed, the terms 'grand strategy' and 'national interest' are used for almost anything. That India needs a grand strategy is a matter of consensus amongst academics and practitioners alike. However, what this really means is a matter of conjecture. For instance, in 2010 Prime Minister Manmohan Singh's pledge to send a spacecraft to Mars was called a 'grand strategy' in the 'national interest.' India's aspiration for a permanent seat in the United Nations Security Council is said to be India's 'grand strategic objective' too. Yet, what serves as one group's definition of 'national interest' can well be another's nemesis. Signing on the dotted line to enter nuclear commerce with a range of nations was considered central to India's 'national interest' by the Congress party. For the Left, it was a matter of humiliation. So who defines and produces a nation's grand strategy?

Grand strategy is not a product or a document that can be manufactured by a group of experts and policy wonks. It is, in many ways, a by-product of history that needs further nurturing by way of political direction. To put it simply, the idea is to bring together a nation's mind and resources with the view to get to a certain destination, a sort of man-made guiding star. What we call comprehensive national power in today's parlance. So while India may not articulate a 'grand strategy,' it will do well to pursue one—in a pragmatic, understated and commonsensical manner.

Interestingly, Deng Xiaoping told the Chinese to adopt the 'hide your strengths, bide your time' policy which has acquired the status of national strategy in China over the past four decades. Ever since then China only talks of 'a peaceful rise' but packs it with the punch of an annual defence budget of 180 billion dollars and a prescient military modernization programme which some analysts describe as the most massive in the history of mankind; one that is set in precise timelines and choreographed with deft politico-military signalling of intent and capability through a series of Defence White Papers and periodic military manoeuvres. In May 2014, China published its first national security blue book. The book listed problems Beijing sees itself facing in internal security—including Western nations' cultural hegemony threatening China's socialist values, terrorism, and the 'export' of Western democracy threatening Chinese ideology, among others. More importantly, it outlines the role of China's National Security Commission.

India

Each country will have to have its own unique set of principles and practices that frames National Security Strategy or Grand Strategy. Whatever course India adopts, here are a few random thoughts, which may help to flag some criticalities in our emerging worldview/strategic outlook/grand strategy.

Among the strategic challenges facing India are those relating to defence policy, nuclear strategy, and governance. At present, defence policymaking is ad hoc, short-term, and service-specific. The political executive has ceded space to the professional bureaucrat in deciding policy matters. Sixty-seven years after Independence, it is no secret that the political-military interface is all but absent in India's institutional set-up. The armed forces are completely under the day-to-day as well as policy control of the Ministry of Defence (MoD). The desirable politico-military interface is now reduced to weekly, sometimes fortnightly meetings chaired by the Defence Minister. According to several former chiefs this author has spoken to, these meetings are informal, without any agendas or note-taking and have no official status although in theory, the Defence Minister is deemed to have given policy directions in these meetings.

Former Army Chief Gen S Padmanabhan, who was leading the Army in the crucial period when India mobilized its entire Army under Operation Parakram in 2002, has rarely written or spoken about matters of national security since his retirement in 2003. However in his book,[5] published in 2005, Padmanabhan had this to say about the meeting of Service Chiefs with the Defence Minister:

> Even at the level of the Defence Minister and Service Chiefs, exchanges on major matters of defence policy were few and far between, the Defence Minister's weekly meetings with the Service Chiefs being used to update the minister and equip him to negotiate questions in Parliament. Often, these meetings were deferred, as 'more important' activities claimed the time of the minister...The result was...the greater role and authority assumed by the Defence bureaucracy. The Defence Secretary, with his nearness to the Defence Minister, often began to exercise power on the minister's behalf and was, quite often, regarded as de facto defence minister. The 'supremacy of the civil over the military' was thus effectively changed from supremacy of the political authority to that of the civilian bureaucracy.

Through the seventies, eighties and the nineties, the bureaucracy continued to acquire disproportionate powers vis-à-vis the Service Chiefs and now it is a given that the Defence Secretary and not the Service Chiefs, is the single-point adviser to the Cabinet on matters military. For he and the Cabinet Secretary have a consistent interface with the political leadership, with the Service Chiefs attending the meetings of the Cabinet Committee on Security (CCS) only if invited.

On the other hand, the National Security Council, which had been expected to address policy incoherence and inadequate strategic planning, burdened itself with executive responsibilities. The services intelligence directorates are ill-equipped for long-term intelligence assessments, and area specialists are few, suggesting a greater need for think tanks. The armed forces have also not fully thought through important aspects of nuclear policy and strategy. In a nuclear era, the role of the military becomes, essentially, preventing wars from breaking out through appropriate weapons' acquisitions, force deployment patterns, the development of infrastructure, military exercises, and defence diplomacy. This is a far more demanding task than peacetime operations in a pre-nuclear age.

So how does one formulate grand strategy? And is there a need for one in India? Some experts have raised the question: Does India need a grand strategy that will inform and influence policymakers across ministries, across political party lines and over time? The answer to this would be in the affirmative. Should this be publicly articulated? While there may be a disagreement of this, doing so offers a way to assess whether or not policymakers are sticking to the given script. A government-funded think tank, the Institute for Defence Studies and Analyses (IDSA) had in 2007 launched the National Strategy Project (INSP) that aimed to bring together a wide range of scholars, analysts and experts and jointly shape a grand strategy.

Indian leaders always pursued a grand strategy with just one objective: preserve the unity of this country. The survival and security of the state, the most economical definition of the national interest, has been and remains India's grand strategy. However, the extent that India's grand strategy caused India's leaders to be inward-looking, both the opportunities and threats emanating from outside have been neglected. In the highly competitive times of the twenty-first century, India cannot afford to miss either. So there is a case to rethink grand strategy. There is a need to shake up the foreign policy and security establishment from one that was defending a weak India from an anarchic world order, to promoting the interests of a stronger India in a world where there are opportunities as there are threats.

Since India does not have a spelt out grand strategy or a national security strategy or even a white paper, perhaps it is desirable to consider whether there is a need to have one and what would an exercise to formulate such a strategy entail. It is not unusual sometimes to hear even some knowledgeable people say that a grand strategy is relevant only for countries indulging in great power politics. And therefore, India—a non-aligned country which won its freedom through a non-violent struggle—did not need one. To dispel such notions it needs to be clarified that grand strategy is simply an academic term, referring to plans and policies undertaken to balance national ends and means at the highest possible level. Grand strategy includes strategies dealing with the military, economic and diplomatic resources of a country, as well as trade-offs across those domains. It thus encompasses all elements of national power—military, economic, technological, diplomatic, social, cultural and even psychological.

Influential elements within government, political parties and the strategic elite believe, justifiably, that India's non-alignment, crafted by Jawaharlal Nehru, was itself a grand strategy. But six decades later, India and the world have transformed in fundamental ways. India's economy has opened up and has seen an unprecedented dynamism; the world economy has been rapidly globalizing; Asia is becoming the new theatre of geopolitical and economic action; new powers are rising in a multipolar world; and power is increasingly being diffused among non-state actors. Can a strategy designed for a different era be effective today? Or does the ongoing transformation at least call for a fresh look at the old assumptions? At the very least, a vigorous debate is needed to revalidate the relevance of the non-alignment strategy in a changed world order.

What can one expect from such an exercise to review India's grand strategy? First, it will help to reassess how the global and regional security environment has changed; which emerging strategic trends are shaping the future; and what the principal challenges are to our national interests and objectives. It will also help to determine priorities among competing objectives. As resources are finite, not all goals can be attained simultaneously. Without inter se priority among competing objectives, all interest and threats would be treated as equal. That would be a fundamental flaw in the strategy. As Frederick the Great had aptly observed: 'He who attempts to defend too much defends nothing.' Once core interests and objectives are determined, a strategy can be formulated to apply to all elements of national resources to secure those interests and achieve those objectives in the most effective manner. The exercise will involve trade-offs between competing ends and available resources.

The process of strategy formulation, especially in a democracy, is not easy but is essential. A strategy developed through an open debate will impart legitimacy to the process and its outcomes. It will promote greater awareness of the rationale behind policies and key decisions. The process will help develop a strategic vision, a long-term view on core issues and minimize knee-jerk reactions and ad hoc decisions.

Finally, is a grand strategy valid for all times to come? It must be emphasized, especially in the present context, that grand strategy is not a mechanical exercise but a dynamic process, which requires constant adaptation to shifting conditions and circumstances. Strategists should examine assumptions when necessary and modify them, if warranted. Grand strategy debates thus never end, they resurface in different forms and different shapes. In making their strategic decisions leaders may not follow a master document on grand strategy, but their decisions will be made in the backdrop of informed debates.

The then Indian Government appointed a high-level committee under former Cabinet Secretary Naresh Chandra in 2011 to look into various aspects of National Security. While the report has not been made public it apparently recommended the following:[6]

- Appointment of a Permanent Chairman, Chiefs of Staff Committee (CoSC)
- Integration of Service HQ and Ministry of Defence by allowing more cross-postings
- Shifting focus of India's national security strategy from Pakistan to China
- Better Intelligence Coordination between all agencies
- Creation of a dedicated financial Institution for access to energy, rare earths and raw materials from across the world

From some of the occasional interaction that this author has had with a few members of the Task Force, before and after the submission of the report, one aspect is very clear: There was no consensus on the creation of the post of the Chief of Defence Staff (CDS), leading to, what one believes, a half-hearted recommendation to appoint another four-star officer as permanent chairman of the Chiefs of Staff Committee (CoSC). According to the Task Force, this officer will be in charge of the two existing tri-services commands—the Strategic Command Force (SFC) and the Andaman Nicobar Command (ANC)—while the three service Chiefs will continue to command and lead their respective services, the Task Force said. The Permanent Chairman CoSC, according to the recommendation of the Naresh Chandra Task Force, will have a fixed tenure of two years and will be rotated among the three services. This officer will be assisted by the existing Integrated Defence Staff (IDS), headed by a three-star officer from any of the three services.

Given what is known publicly, it appears that another opportunity to reform the national security mechanism has been lost. The National Security System does not have to depend on seeking Least Common Multiple (LCM) solutions. It does not have to seek to appease lobbies and turfs. The government is duty-bound to take urgent steps to reform the higher defence management in the interest of the nation. As a first step, the government owes it to the people of India to make the Naresh Chandra Task Force report public and let a healthy debate ensue if India has to overcome systemic weaknesses and structural shortcomings in its national security decision-making apparatus.

NOTES

1. George Tanham, *Indian Strategic Thought: An Interpretative Essay*, New York, 1992.
2. Manjari Chatterjee Miller, 'India's Feeble Foreign Policy: A Would-Be Great Power Resists Its Own Rise, *Foreign Affairs*, Vol. 92 (3), May-June 2013.
3. Ashley Tellis, 'Between the Times: India's Predicaments and its Grand Strategy' *India in Transition (IiT)*, Center for the Advanced Study of India, 3 December 2012. Source: https://casi.sas.upenn.edu/print/271
4. *The Economist*, 30 March 2013.
5. S Padmanabhan, *A General Speaks*, New Delhi: Manas Publications, 2005.
6. Naresh Chandra Task Force's Report on National Security: An Appraisal. See more at: http://www.vifindia.org/article/2012/july/16/naresh-chandra-task-force-s-report-on-national-security-an-appraisal#sthash.CUpJ6uaG.dpuf

CHAPTER V

National Interest and Role of Foreign Policy

Rakesh Sood

India's national interest can be defined in three general terms—ensuring security against both internal and external threats, pursuing economic development to raise the economic standards of the Indian population, and seeking to create and benefit from a regional and global environment that is conducive to these objectives. In each of these three dimensions, foreign policy has a role, though its importance could vary over time.

Salience of Foreign Policy

In 1947, India's first challenge was the consolidation of the Indian state. While the integration of over 550 princely states that constituted 40 per cent of undivided India was primarily an internal exercise, in three cases—Junagadh, Hyderabad and Jammu and Kashmir—foreign policy became relevant because of Pakistan's involvement. While the disputes over the accession of Junagadh and Hyderabad died fairly quickly, the dispute over Jammu and Kashmir has not been resolved to this date. For addressing external security threats, the normal approaches include negotiating treaty arrangements, pursuing alliances, or non-alignment, as we chose, all of which fall naturally in the domain of foreign policy.

Self-reliance remained the chosen policy for pursuing economic development. During the early decades, our trade relations may have been modest, but India was a major recipient of foreign aid, both from bilateral sources as well as from multilateral agencies like the World Bank and the ADB. India's energy dependency created the need to secure resources and therefore, another kind of diplomacy, particularly with the oil-rich Arab world. Today, the Indian economy is far more open and globally integrated, with greater trade and foreign direct investment (FDI) inflows and outflows demanding greater engagement and attention to developments across continents and oceans as it manages multiple inter-dependencies.

The regional and global environment changed dramatically after World War II. The shift of power was away from the erstwhile imperial powers. The emergence of newly created multilateral institutions like the United Nations, the growing ideological rivalry between the US and the USSR leading to the Cold War, and the coming into being of new states following decolonization were developments that needed to be carefully assessed. The chosen policy of non-alignment was seen to offer the greatest freedom of action while providing a certain ideological mooring. It should be added though, that closer examination would reveal that Nehru's foreign policy was not driven purely by idealism; it also reflected a strong strand of realpolitik. Moulding and exploiting the regional and global environment required a combination of policies in which foreign policy too had an integral role.

The Foreign Policy Legacy of the Raj

Having established the salience of foreign policy in promoting and safeguarding national interest, it is relevant to examine historical sources to trace the role that foreign policy has played since 1947. While Pandit Nehru had his own world view, which was earlier described as 'liberal idealism,' subsequent writing indicates that whatever his other qualities, he was also a 'realist.' He understood the compulsions of geography and developed an appreciation of the role of the British Indian Empire (or the Raj) in the region, even though its imperial underpinnings were often at variance with his and the Congress's ideology, shaped by the freedom struggle. The territorial sweep of the Raj was undoubtedly larger than independent India, including Pakistan, Bangladesh, and Myanmar at one time, and this shaped the Raj's interests. The changed boundaries after 1947 greatly impacted India's challenges, but interestingly, certain continuities remained because even after Partition, India remained the pre-eminent power in the Indian Ocean region.

The external threats to the Raj originated from other empires—Czarist Russia, Persia, France, China and Siam—at different times in history. To address these challenges, the Raj engaged in a purposeful foreign policy, developing a system of protectorates and buffer states and special treaty arrangements from Zanzibar in East Africa to Singapore in the South East. At the same time, the Raj also developed its own military strength, which became known as the British Indian Army and the Bombay Marines.

Lord Curzon described and refined the Raj's approach in the 'triple frontier' or 'the two-ring' concept. The first frontier defined the limits of the territory that was directly administered by the British, excluding the princely states, which were under indirect rule; the second frontier (or the first ring) included the territory administered by a Political Agent with the cooperation of the local tribal leaders, who were given subsidies and allowed self-governance in internal matters (NWFP in the West and NEFA in the East); the third frontier (or the second ring) included states with strong alliances where the foreign and defence policies of these 'sovereign' states were subjected to 'advice' by the British Resident (Afghanistan, Nepal, Tibet). In addition were agreements negotiated with Oman, British Somaliland and Zanzibar on the Western seaboard and Penang and Singapore on the Eastern seaboard, which allowed the Raj to set up listening posts to monitor the activities of rival empires and station personnel and military and naval assets as and when needed.

The policies of the Raj enjoyed a fair degree of autonomy and responded to the then regional, political, and geographical challenges and constraints, as did its economic and trade policies. At crucial moments of wars where London was involved, the Raj responded with its own resources, but the 'diplomacy of dependence' that it pursued in its extended neighbourhood made it a net security provider from Suez to Malacca. Gradually, as its resources grew and responsibilities expanded, it developed its military assets.

The Bombay Marines came into being in 1686, when the East India Company moved its trading hub from Surat to Bombay. The port of Aden was captured in 1830 and the Marines were increasingly deployed in patrolling and mapping coastlines along both seaboards, and protecting the trade routes. Renamed the Royal Indian Marines in 1892, they saw action during World Wars I and II, in Iraq, Egypt, East Africa, and Sicily.

The Madras Regiment, raised by the British in the 1750s to fight the French in South India, is the oldest regiment, after it incorporated the Nair Brigade which had been raised by the Maharaja of Travancore in 1704. The British Indian Army helped expand the Raj's colonial frontiers and participated in operations to quell local uprisings and restore stability, from Southern Africa and Egypt to China and the Philippines. It was also used to deal with internal threats to the Raj posed by the growing freedom movement. During World War I, the over 1 million strong Indian Expeditionary Force saw action in France and Belgium as also in Egypt and Mesopotamia. Seventy-four thousand Indian soldiers died, five times the total number martyred in all the wars since 1947, and 80,000 were taken POWs. In addition, India provided 10,000 nurses and £146 million in revenue. During World War II, the Indian Army was deployed in Western theatres including Italy, the Middle East, and North Africa. In the East, it was a 750,000 strong Indian force that liberated Indo-China, Malaya, and Burma from the Japanese. By the end of World War II, the Indian Army was the largest standing army, with a strength of 2.5 million. Incidentally, the reason Britain never raised a Marine Corps was because the armies and navies of the Raj acted as its expeditionary forces.

The Foreign Policy Legacy of the Freedom Movement

Together with the British legacy, the second input in independent India's foreign policy was the anti-imperialist strand of the Congress ideology. After World War I, the nationalist movement gained momentum and the Congress began to oppose the deployment of the Indian Army for imperialist purposes, without seeking the consent of the people. Part of the reason was the apprehension that such expeditions would lead to increased taxation in India. Gradually, a divergence in the world view of the imperial power and the nationalist leaders of the Congress began emerging. During the 1920s, the Congress leadership began to express solidarity with other people under colonial rule and in 1927 the Congress demanded that the (British) Indian Government withdraw all Indian troops from all British colonies and foreign countries.

During World War II, these growing differences came into the open when a group led by Netaji Subhash Chandra Bose refused to join in the anti-fascist war, proposing instead that India exploit the opportunity to advance towards early independence. Gandhi and Nehru took the line that this would be opportunism and that an independent India would stand together with other democratic forces against fascist forces, as long as this was an alliance between 'equals' by mutual consent. Eventually, the Gandhi-Nehru view prevailed, though a British assurance on 'independence' never came. While Netaji created the Azad Hind Fauj to join the Axis powers, the Congress, in 1942, disappointed with the British vacillation, raised the banner of the Quit India movement.

Defining India's National interest and Shaping its Foreign Policy

In 1947, the Indian government, therefore, inherited two competing schools of thought that were to have a bearing on foreign policy—realpolitik from the colonial practice and a moralpolitik from the Congress national movement. Even after Partition, India was still the predominant power in the region, though the leadership was preoccupied with the challenge of integrating the princely states, drafting a new Constitution, dealing with externally sponsored aggression in Jammu and Kashmir, and coping with the refugee crisis following the creation of Pakistan. Under Nehru's leadership, the government sought to secure India's frontiers by signing treaties with neighbours, by objecting to major foreign powers' presence in the region, and by adopting a policy of non-alignment, which would provide it room for manoeuvre on the international stage. Having witnessed the consequences of war among major imperial powers, India wisely chose to steer its own course, which was critical of imperialism and imperial dominance and supportive of liberation movements and decolonization, and sought engagement with a new world order symbolized by the United Nations, whose Charter was based on respect for territorial integrity, non-interference in internal affairs, peaceful resolution of disputes, opposition to use of forces, and solidarity among newly independent states to work together for economic development.

There were some suggestions that the Himalayan states of Bhutan, Sikkim and Nepal should be integrated into India, but Nehru adopted a more nuanced approach. India chose to respect the sovereignty of the Himalayan kingdoms, while also drawing them into treaty arrangements that retained the substance of the linkages that these states had enjoyed with the Raj. In fact, the early need for consolidating ties with the new Indian republic was equally reciprocated by these kingdoms, unsettled as their rulers were by the Communist takeover in China, followed by the takeover of Tibet.

In 1947, a tripartite agreement with the UK and Nepal was signed to continue the practice of recruiting Nepali Gurkha nationals into the Indian Army, a practice that continues to this day. New treaties of 'peace and everlasting friendship,' with clauses pertaining to 'defence cooperation and close consultation,' were signed, which also contained references to respect for each others' sovereignty, to replace the earlier (more unequal) treaties with the Raj. The 1949 Treaty with Bhutan replaced the previous treaties of 1865 and 1910 just as the 1950 Treaty with Nepal replaced the 1816 and 1923 treaties. Sikkim became a Protectorate in 1950, continuing the relationship established in 1890. The centrality of the Himalayan frontiers for India's security, which Nehru was sensitive to, clearly continued the same thinking that had guided the Raj, and was also reflected in Nehru's writings and speeches in the Indian Parliament at the time.

In 1949, Myanmar leader U Nu sought military assistance to tackle the growing Communist insurgency, a request to which Nehru responded with alacrity. Indian support was acknowledged and the Treaty signed with Myanmar in 1951 provided for cooperation in security and defence matters. A few months earlier, a similar treaty had been signed with Indonesia, which was followed by separate agreements for cooperation between the Services. Sukarno, Nu, and Nehru also shared the vision of a re-emerging Asian identity and, facing similar challenges of national consolidation, sought to deepen security cooperation among themselves.

Looking Westwards, the first significant treaty was with Afghanistan (which had a strained relationship with the newly created state of Pakistan, having opposed its membership into the UN) in 1950, followed by Iran in the same year. Unlike the Raj, though India no longer shared borders with these countries, Nehru's reaching out to them was based on his assessment of their importance for India's security. By this time, he had already become disillusioned with the political machinations in the UN Security Council over the Kashmir issue. In the following years, links with Arab and Islamic states were built, with agreements signed with Turkey (1951), Syria (1952), Oman (1953), and Egypt (1955). In fact, there was active and significant defence cooperation with Egypt for over a decade, particularly in the aerospace sector.

Along both the eastern and western seaboards, India's regional diplomacy was clearly guided by security interests and reflected a continuity of the geographical compulsions that had shaped the Raj's policies. That many of these agreements gradually faded away was due to other developments, both domestic and external. However, it clearly shows the realpolitik strain in Nehru's foreign policy in the early years after independence. These arrangements came under strain because independent India was not as paramount a power in the region as the British Indian empire had been. The situation was further aggravated by growing tensions with China, even after India's acceptance of Chinese suzerainty over Tibet in 1954. The 1962 debacle with China altered the scenario with both Myanmar and Indonesia, whose leaders adopted a pro-Chinese tilt. Meanwhile, Nepal discovered the usefulness of playing the 'China card'. The Cold War dynamic led to the creation of South East Asian Treaty Organization (SEATO) in South-east Asia and Central Treaty Organization (CENTO) in West Asia. Pakistan readily joined both alliances. The non-aligned policy, an instrument of strategic autonomy, became the Non Aligned Movement, often long on rhetoric but lacking both economic resources and strategic technologies which developing countries needed.

India lost its role as a net security provider in the region and correspondingly, its foreign policy grew more inward-looking. However, the India-Soviet Friendship Treaty, the intervention in East Pakistan leading to the creation of Bangladesh, the integration of Sikkim in 1975, and the reorganization of the North-east into separate states in the 1980s reflected a security calculus and a re-assertion of foreign policy in securing the frontiers. More, recently, we saw the induction of the Indian Peace Keeping Force (IPKF) into Sri Lanka, which became controversial, though assistance to the Maldives to put down an attempted coup in 1988 was appreciated.

Despite India's loss of power in the region, Nehru's 'liberal internationalism' carved out a role for the country as the leading contributor to UN-mandated peace-keeping operations. This was also consistent with the notion of 'collective security' and Nehru's desire to see India on the international stage. From the Korean peninsula in 1953-54 to South Sudan in 2011, Indian soldiers, policemen, doctors, and civilians have participated in more than sixty operations worldwide, under the UN flag. These have included Indo-China, the Congo, Lebanon, Yemen, Cyprus, Costa Rica, Namibia, Angola, Cambodia, El Salvador, Iran-Iraq, Iraq-Kuwait, Mozambique, Somalia, Liberia, the former Yugoslavia, Rwanda, Haiti, Sierra Leone, Sudan Burundi, the Ivory Coast, East Timor, Eritrea and the Golan Heights.

From the 1960s onwards, the former USSR emerged as the principal supplier of defence equipment. This seemed a natural foreign policy choice, with Pakistan a member of the US-led SEATO and CENTO and later, an 'all-weather friend' of China. This situation began to change with the end of the Cold War, first with respect to Israel in the early 1990s, after India established diplomatic relations with it, and then during the last decade with the US, as both countries tried to develop new partnerships and foreign policy convergences.

To reiterate, foreign policy played an important role in helping us with our defence preparedness, in addressing security threats and developing linkages with other countries in the region and beyond as we pursued the policies of 'non-alignment' and 'self-reliance' in a Cold War environment. These policies combined both, realpolitik and moral politik, the two legacies of our colonial past and the freedom movement, under a distinct Nehruvian stamp. Prime Ministers Indira Gandhi and Rajiv Gandhi followed the same policies as has been briefly mentioned.

Post Cold War—Opportunities for Readjustment

The world today is different. The Cold War is over and the centre of gravity is shifting, slowly but surely, from the Atlantic to the Asia-Pacific or as some would like to suggest, Indo-Pacific. The flattening of the world by the forces of globalization, India's growing economic integration, our far-flung diaspora, our growing energy dependency and stronger military capability will involve us more and more in regional and global affairs that will unfold now at our doorstep. Indian national interests have not changed—there are still security threats, both internal and external (some new ones have emerged and some old ones have persisted) and economic development remains a priority, but it is clear that this requires more trade and FDI inflows as well. A growing trend towards greater regionalism and globalization has led to a change in the nature of state power and a diffusion of power away from centralized authority.

New security threats have also appeared on the horizon. Left-wing extremism is now increasingly perceived as an internal security threat, though it also has an external dimension that has diminished as we have helped bring Nepal's Maoists into the political mainstream and improved relations with both Bangladesh and Myanmar, thus choking the supply of illegal weapons. International terrorism and its possible link to the proliferation of weapons of mass destruction are globally accepted as a principal threat requiring concerted action. In addition, food security, energy security, cyber security, and climate change are challenges that require collective responses and foreign policy engagements. Regions around India are troubled by uncertainties—Afghanistan, West Asia, and large parts of the Arab world, and a rising and more assertive China in East Asia. New technologies are threatening the global commons of outer space and cyber space.

Indians are adapting to these changes. 'Self-reliance' in the economic sphere has given way to a more open Indian economy. At \$ 800 billion today, India's foreign trade stands at 40 per cent of our GDP, compared to \$20 billion in 1980. Inward FDI is more than \$ 350 billion and the target for infrastructure investment during the current five-year plan is a trillion dollars, of which half is to be raised by the private sector, both domestic and foreign. FDI limits in insurance, railways, and defence are being reviewed and liberalized. The assistance programmes of the World Bank and ADB are now dwarfed by the much larger asset bases of private equity funds and global foundations. All this is creating new equations of engagement between private and public institutions, outside the state-centric frameworks that were the dominant factor in the decades after 1947.

After the Cold War, there was a brief period of a decade and a half that could be described as a unipolar moment, of a world where the US was often described as the sole super power. It was a period during which the practitioners of Indian diplomacy created new openings following the nuclear tests of 1998, when India declared itself a nuclear weapon state. They realized that strategic autonomy was only meaningful if it enabled the development of multiple options. Strategic analysts are still seeking labels for India's new policy, but it is clear today that policies have to be adaptable or they become 'constraints' rather than 'enablers'. This pragmatic approach guided Indian foreign policy even as our economic crisis in 1990-1 forced us to liberalize our economy, and the disintegration of the USSR, pushing it into internal disarray, deprived us of a steadfast partner.

Diplomatic recognition of Israel, the 'look-east policy' to re-engage with Association of Southeast Asian Nations (ASEAN), and following up on Rajiv Gandhi's historic visit to China were initiatives taken by the Narasimha Rao government. The Vajpayee government took charge when India's 'nuclear option' was shrinking in the face of new export controls on dual-use technologies, a growing norm against nuclear testing reflected in the Comprehensive Nuclear-Test-Ban Treaty (CTBT), and continuing assistance from China to develop Pakistan's nuclear and missile capability. While the decision to test was an internal one, managing the regional and international fallout was the first foreign policy challenge for the Vajpayee government. In tackling it, Indian foreign policy successfully developed new partnerships even as the world became more aware of the threat posed by Islamic extremism, especially after 9/11.

Foreign Policy Challenges Beyond 2014

The unipolar moment appears to be ending and with the global economic crisis of 2008, a fundamental shift in economic and military terms seems to be underway. Moreover, in maritime terminology, the reordering will take place in the Indian and Pacific oceans and not in the faraway Atlantic Ocean or the Baltic Sea. With India's size and growing economic and military strength, our policies will impact this change and India cannot insulate itself from this reordering of economic and military rebalancing, which will create new demands on our foreign policy. The key factor in this change is the rise of China. Even though the US remains the largest economy and the biggest military power, the gap with China is narrowing. Further, there is a sense of US foreign policy turning inwards after the unproductive engagements in Iraq and Afghanistan, compared to the emergence of a more assertive Chinese foreign policy. The US has announced its 'Asia pivot' but its contours have yet to take shape. How far the US will go in safeguarding the global commons or in upholding its security guarantees to its allies in the Asia-Pacific who may feel concerned about Chinese muscle flexing—this remains the key question.

India needs a peaceful environment and has to manage its relations with China by building convergences where possible (on World Trade Organization (WTO) and climate change), while working towards a permanent boundary settlement, which continues to remain a work in progress, often affected by reports of incursions by Chinese troops and aircraft. Economically, China has emerged as our largest trading partner, though the relationship is skewed in China's favour. To address this imbalance, the idea of setting up an SEZ to attract Chinese investments is being explored. India's growing relationship with the US, particularly in the defence and strategic sectors, often attracts adverse comment in China, while hardliners in the US establishment question India's reliability as a partner in managing security in the region. For India, China's all-weather friendship with Pakistan and its continuing cooperation to build up Pakistan's nuclear, missile, and defence capabilities (despite its concerns about Islamic extremism in western China) pose questions that do not yield clear answers today.

The renewed focus on India's immediate neighbourhood announced by the Modi government has been received well. Most of these countries would like to benefit from the economic opportunities offered by a growing Indian economy. India can afford to be generous while setting out clear red lines so that ambiguities that have often led to misperceptions in the past can be avoided. Political transitions in Nepal need to be monitored carefully, particularly as we share an 1850-km-long open border. The exit of the International Security Assistance Force (ISAF) from Afghanistan by the end of 2014 opens up questions about the continuation of our role, which has been carefully built with an impressive cooperation programme of $2 billion since 2002. In opinion polls in Afghanistan, India is always described as 'the most friendly nation,' a position that will need to be maintained in the post-Karzai era. With the geopolitical shift to our part of the world, India will need to be more active in the neighbourhood to consolidate our periphery, even as we sought to do immediately after 1947.

Pakistan is in a different category because it is still struggling to redevelop its sense of nationhood other than in anti-Indian terms, an exercise that has been periodically derailed by the dominant role of the military in domestic politics, which resorts to inflating the Indian threat to serve its vested interests. Nawaz Sharif has traditionally had a difficult relationship with the Army in each of his tenures as Prime Minister, and this time is no exception. Reports of differences between him and his appointee General Raheel Sharif have already surfaced in the media. Yet Pakistan is a nuclear weapon state and India has no choice but to manage its relations with Pakistan in a manner that can help strengthen its democratic and civil society institutions. Finding a lasting solution to the issue of Jammu and Kashmir is certainly a desirable goal, but only feasible after Pakistani polity has undergone a transformation that enables it to develop an identity that does not deny its geographical roots.

Eastwards, relationships with ASEAN have been growing steadily, following the look-east policy announced by Prime Minister Narasimha Rao in 1992 and reiterated by successive governments since. High-level interactions have become regular, with intensified Indian participation in the Summit processes and the ASEAN Regional Forum. Under Prime Minister Abe, Japan is seeking to intensify its relations with India, a process that will gain momentum with Prime Minster Modi's forthcoming visit.

On the Western side, there is growing turmoil and uncertainty, set into motion by the US intervention in Iraq in 2003, which is now assuming grave proportions, with multiple conflict lines emerging with the Iran-Saudi Arabian rivalry, Arab spring movements and their backlash, and the emergence of the ISIS in parts of Iraq and Syria. It is a region of vital importance as two-thirds of India's oil is sourced from this region that also hosts more than 6 million Indians who repatriate more than $ 70 billion a year. While India has steered clear of these internal conflicts, ensuring the security of the Indians there and organizing their evacuations from conflict zones will require across-the-board diplomatic engagement with different groups and close coordination with intelligence agencies that will need to expand their networks in the region.

Europe will remain more concerned with internal developments, particularly its changing demographic, and managing the integration of East European states. Further, as the geopolitical focus shifts towards Asia-Pacific, only those European countries with significant capabilities and interests will emerge as players—possibly the UK and France. Nevertheless, for India, the European Union (EU) as a group is a significant trading partner and a source of investment and high technology. Today, Russia still accounts for more than 70 per cent of our defence imports even as we diversify our sources and build our own defence industry, making it a vital relationship in forthcoming years.

Since the turn of the century, a new revolution in military affairs has been underway, driven by Information and Communication Technology (ICT) and its increasingly diverse applications. The use of space-based assets for real-time information and surveillance, cyber capabilities for communications and intelligence gathering, and exploiting social media for public mobilization as witnessed during the Arab spring and in Karnataka (India) in 2012, which led to an exodus of north-easterners from the region, are only some of the domains emerging on the security horizon. Securing these new spaces as the global commons assumes greater importance. Fortunately, our capabilities in some of these areas are well established and this time around, we will need to ensure the new rules of the game do not impede our access to technology, as happened in the nuclear domain during the 1960s and 1970s.

Additionally, the growing importance of the Indian Ocean and our growing dependence on sea lanes for our foreign trade and energy supplies require us to devote greater attention to maritime security. Once again, as in the period after independence, we have begun to develop exchanges with our maritime neighbours, beginning with the Maldives, Sri Lanka, and Mauritius, but we need to expand our outreach further. Oman and

Chabahar on the Iranian coast and Myanmar, Singapore, Vietnam, and Indonesia in the South-east are countries with which maritime links need to be strengthened.

The importance of food security is evident from the stand just taken by the Modi government on the Trade Facilitation Agreement under negotiation at the WTO. Despite being among the largest producers of food grains and building up a security stockpile, our agricultural sector as a whole needs modernization and the infusion of modern technology and management practices, for more green, white, and blue revolutions. Similarly critical is securing energy supplies and sourcing critical rare earths and raw materials for sustained industrial growth as we develop our manufacturing sector.

The absence of an overarching security architecture in the Indo-Pacific is a lacuna that needs to be addressed. During the Cold War, the bipolar structure imposed its own order and rules, with competing military alliances led by two super powers that were also circumscribed in their behaviour by nuclear deterrence. In today's world, with super powers having receded into history and newly emerging major powers jostling for space in the Asia-Pacific, nuclear deterrence equations are being rewritten, the old rules of the game no longer apply, and new rules are yet to emerge.

In sum, the role of foreign policy today in safeguarding India's national interest and contributing to defence preparedness is more vital than ever before. What we need for an effective foreign policy are not labels, which often get wrapped up in ideology, but a healthy mix of pragmatism, a willingness to learn from past experiences, a readiness to accept change and convert challenges into opportunities, an ability to synergize efforts and policies and a wise leadership that can keep the focus on bringing about the transformation of India into a secure and prosperous nation.

CHAPTER VI

POLITICAL GUIDANCE IN SHAPING INDIA'S HARD POWER

Prakash Menon

Introduction

The hard power of a nation represents the coercive power of a State and in combination with soft power determines its ability to exert influence in the international system. The hard power of India resides in institutions that are under the Centre and the states. At the Central level, it mostly rests with the Ministry of Defence (MoD) and Ministry of Home Affairs (MHA). The Armed Forces of India comprising the Army, Navy and Air Force represent the sharp end of India's hard power and is primarily shaped to counter external threats. The Central Armed Police Forces (CAPF) under the MHA represent the hard power available for internal threats.

At the state level, the armed police forces and the local police form the first responder component against any threat that is internally manifested. Taken as a whole, India has nearly 30 lakh armed forces personnel to deal with external and internal threats. It is a considerable number. The armed forces alone comprise 12.25 lakh personnel and due to its equipment and other requirements, needs a substantial portion of the Union budget. The MoD has on an average been allotted nearly 17 per cent of the Annual Budget and consumes nearly 1.7 per cent of the

GDP. In terms of GDP, India's Defence Budget has remained modest considering the nature and scope of threats against it. But Defence expenditure in absolute terms is substantial and its planned equipment procurement programme involves an expenditure of nearly $100 billion in the five-year defence plan 2012–17.

This paper seeks to examine the issue of political guidance that is shaping India's 'hard power' meant for external threats. Hence it focuses on the scope, content and form of India's politico-military interaction required to shape India's military forces during peace. Admittedly, wartime politico-military interaction would be more complex since it involves two opposing wills and so outside the ambit of the paper.

The Politico-Military Problematic

The fundamental difficulty in providing political guidance to shape the nation's hard power is derived from the politico-military problematic. The politico-military problematic acquires its character from the divergent outlook that animates their preferences. As the politician operates in the vicious world of politics wherein compromise for political survival and harmonization of differences is an imperative, he is primarily focused on the short term, prefers to deal with contingencies and because he is extremely susceptible to populism, calculates the impact of his actions on vote bank politics. In contrast, because the role of military leadership mandates a contribution to the evolution of policy and strategy, he is also expected to play the role of the strategist.

The strategist outlook, shaped by complex international and domestic political dynamics, has to be based on the long term. For the military leader the evolution of military strategy is his main domain and it requires being frame-worked within the Ends-Ways-Means paradigm. The Ends represent policy from which political objectives, through use of force are derived. But policy itself cannot be formulated without consultation with the military, because policy might otherwise, either under-utilize the military potential or ask the military instrument to do what is simply beyond its capacity. Therefore, political objectives for the military require to be evolved through a process of continuous dialogue between the political and military leadership. Such a dialogue requires mutual understanding of each other's perspective, which, by the nature of their worldview, is difficult to reconcile. This makes policy evolution a challenging proposition.

Evolution of Policy and Strategy

India's policy and strategy evolution process is better understood through the organizational structures that have been put in place especially after the Kargil Committee Report in 2001.After the acceptance of the Group of Ministers (GOM) Report, the Cabinet Committee on Security (CCS) constituted the National Security Council (NSC) through an executive order. The Prime Minister heads the NSC, which has the same composition as the CCS, and its members include the ministers of Home, Defence, External Affairs and Finance. The Cabinet Secretariat, services the CCS and the National Security Council Secretariat (NSCS), the NSC. The National Security Advisory Board (NSAB) and the Strategic Policy Group (SPG) also support the functioning of the NSC and the National Security Adviser (NSA) coordinates the functions of the NSC and its constituent bodies.

The NSC has an advisory function and no financial powers. It is expected to formulate policy and strategy with the support of the NSCS, NSAB and SPG, with all its decisions being finally approved by the CCS. The NSC can initiate the policy/strategy formulation process by identifying issues; as well also approve policy/strategy that has been formulated through the NSCS, NSAB or SPG. However, the point to be noted is that these are not the only routes for policy/strategy formulation.

It can also take place through the ministries in the form of a CCS note. The Allocation of Business Rules specifies the allocation of business that shall be transacted in the ministries, departments, secretariats and offices of the government of India, with a distribution of subjects amongst the departments being specified. Therefore, any ministry in charge of a subject can act as a nodal ministry to initiate the CCS note. Elaborate instructions exist regarding the preparations of the CCS note wherein all stakeholders are to be consulted in finalizing the policy and if the note has any national security implications, the NSCS has to be consulted. The system therefore caters for widespread consultations and facilitates a holistic appraisal of issues.

The NSAB, a body of eminent persons who are outside government, is tasked to provide advice on national security issues to the NSC. While it is authorized thirty members, it normally consists of fifteen, drawn from all domains pertinent to national security and has a two-year tenure. The NSC can either task it to examine issues or the NSAB could identify pertinent ones on its own. In the recent past, the major task given to the NSAB has been the evolution of a National Security Strategy (NSS). While two previous NSABs had finalized the document, which did not find political acceptability, the present NSAB has prepared an NSS, which is under consideration. A major hindrance of the NSAB functioning is that although in principle they have access to classified documents, in practice, they are frequently denied the requisite access.

The SPG, tasked to formulate Strategic Policy is, in the words of the cabinet 'the principal mechanism for inter-ministerial coordination and integration of relevant inputs in the formulation of national security policies.' It can be convened by the NSA or the Cabinet Secretary and consists of the three Chiefs of the Armed Forces and all pertinent Department Secretaries. Although it is the in-house policy formulation group and is serviced by the NSCS, it rarely meets and has hardly formulated any strategic policy. This is also the only body where the service chiefs as members can have a say in policy formulation. As the practice has been to formulate policy through the CCS route or the NSCS route, the views of the armed forces are consequently filtered through the MoD.

The NSCS's role is that of a security integrator, as it can provide a platform for inter-ministerial consultations. In the policy formulating process, the inter-ministerial consultations are always the most challenging, as turf battles and ministry-centric tunnel vision have to be often dealt with by identifying the national security imperative as its beacon. Inter-ministerial disagreements are also sought to be resolved through mechanisms like GoM and Committee of Secretaries. While there may be some weight in the criticism in some quarters that the contribution of the NSCS in policy formulation is sub-optimal, it is not entirely true. An acceleration in the functioning of the NSCS necessitates an improvement in the quality of its human capital which is, however, an issue, that not only encompasses the whole of government, but especially pervades the national security system.

Human Capital Problem

It is ironic that despite a very large educated population base in the country, there are chronic shortages of officers across the governmental system. Large-scale shortages have prevailed for more than a decade in the Civil Services especially the Indian Foreign Service (IFS), Indian Administrative Service (IAS) and the Indian Police Service (IPS). For over two decades the Indian Army has faced a shortage of 10,000–12,000 officers which tantamount to over 20 per cent from its authorized strength. Major shortage of personnel, at the level below officers, has continued to exist in the state police forces. In addition, the dearth of specialized skills essential in the wide-ranging activities in government domains has had an impact on the National Security System, which is a major sub-system that is impacted by the qualitative deficit.

The national security system at the central government level includes the MHA, MoD, MEA, Intelligence Agencies and NSCS amongst its main components. In 2001, the GoM had identified the need for personnel with specialized skill sets to staff these organizations. The GoM had therefore recommended the creation of a group of civil and armed services officers who will form the backbone of human capital of the National Security System. They were to be specially trained to provide analytical skills at various levels in the domains of intelligence, strategy and policy formulation and rotated within the ministries and departments dealing with national security. Unfortunately, this important recommendation despite approval by the Union Cabinet has not been implemented, due to 'cadre management problems' and has, instead been substituted by a weak and diluted system of training capsules.

Generalists continue to populate the relevant national security ministries and departments of which the NSCS is a prime example. Despite flexible recruitment rules and special dispensation for an eight-year tenure, it is not uncommon to find a person from the Ordnance Factory Services doing the job of an intelligence analyst—an area of alien interest to him.

As he does not undergo an institutionalized training process, he has to learn on the job and is, therefore, ill-equipped to deliver the goods. There is also a dearth of suitably qualified and experienced national security professionals in the country as a whole since Strategic studies/Defence studies has been a neglected subject at the university level.

The government has acknowledged the neglect of strategic studies, as a subject, in India's University system. It had appointed a committee under the late Air Commodore Jasjit Singh to examine the issue. The Human Resource Development (HRD) Minister approved the committee's recommendations in 2011. But as of date, except for some initial meetings conducted by the University Grants Commission (UGC), there has been no progress on the ground. It is understood that much effort has been expended on the issue of whether the subject is to be nomenclature as strategic studies or defence studies! In 2013, the author had suggested to the HRD minister that strategic studies in India would get a fillip, if it is included as a subject in the civil services examination. But such a move requires commonality of syllabus across all universities—a key recommendation of the Jasjit Singh Committee. It would not be surprising, that this would be another case of a government-approved reform remaining unimplemented, which is also particularly the case, in the arena of defence reforms.

Defence Reforms

It has been widely acknowledged that a reformation of India's Defence system to improve its functional efficiency and effectiveness in delivering the public good of national defence is the need of the hour. While several reforms were approved and implemented post the GoM report of 2001, the key reform of Chief of Defence Staff (CDS) was not and some approved recommendations such as specialized training for key MoD staff and the integration of service headquarters with the MoD were diluted in their implementation.

It is therefore not surprising that the only document that provides strategic and political guidance to the armed forces, does not actually originate from the MoD, but is, instead, written at the Headquarters of the Integrated Defence Staff (IDS) which services the Chiefs of Staff

Committee (COSC). It has the highest security classification and is called the Raksha Mantri's (RM's) Directive. In practice, the draft is initiated at the IDS, examined by the MoD, which also carries out inter-ministerial consultations. It is finally approved by the RM and issued to the IDS with suitable modifications. It does not have CCS approval. So the fact of the matter is that the base document on which India shapes its hard power does not have approval at the highest political level.

Such approval is difficult to obtain, because a National Security Strategy does not guide the base assumptions of the RM's Directive. As noted earlier, a formal National Security Strategy document has so far not found political approval. But the fact that the RM's Directive has been commented upon by the stakeholders including the NSCS, presumably gives it some amount of authenticity regarding the role of military power in India's security. It is however understood that the existing document lacks specificity. Therefore, when coupled with the absence of a CDS or some other such entity, the RM's directive is amenable to service-centric interpretations, especially when the armed forces have not evolved a military strategy that will guide and shape the growth of military power.

The Strategy Deficit

Since the RM's Directive is the only document that supposedly provides some political guidance to the armed forces, military strategy should be its derivative. Ideally, the COSC should evolve a military strategy, which should preferably be approved by the CCS. But no military strategy has ever been evolved. Instead, there is the Long-Term Integrated Perspective Plan (LTIPP). The planning function is thus carried out in a strategy-free context.

The LTIPP has a fifteen-year perspective and is best described as a compilation of the wish list of the three services wherein, based on the RM's Directive, each service has identified for itself the equipment and organizations it must procure and create in the next fifteen years. While it is quite naturally service-centric and lacks an integrated interpretation of the RM's Directive, another major lacuna is that the LTIPP does not enjoy any financial support; therefore the planning process is disconnected from the resources required to support it. In brief, the LTIPP is a shopping list that the country cannot afford and is bereft of direction to build integrated military capability aligned to policy.

Based on the LTIPP, Five-Year Defence Plans are made to facilitate phasing of the hard power development process. The lack of financial support encumbers its implementation, which in practice is therefore dependent on the ability of a service to navigate the byzantine bureaucratic procurement processes. For several years, the major concern of the MoD was to somehow fully expend its capital budget before the end of the financial year. It comes down to a simple exercise of 'file pushing'; the service which is able to 'push its file' first, gets to procure their requirements. The Indian Navy, being a smaller service, has in comparison, been relatively successful in the implementation of their 'wish list'. The Air Force has been struggling to replace their fighters, transport and helicopter fleet and being largely dependent on imported equipment, have, because of government to government deals, managed to procure the C-130 and C-17 transport aircrafts. The Army, on the other hand, has not been able to make any major procurement in the last five years, despite the fact that most of its capital stock in terms of guns, tanks, mechanized vehicles, air defence guns et al., are in need of replacement.

Procurement priorities for capability building are virtually non-existent. Since 2010–11, the committed liabilities on purchases already underway, have consumed most of the capital budget, making prioritization of acquisition, a dire need. However, prioritization is also difficult to establish because in the absence of a CDS, the existing inter-service structure cannot arbitrate inter-service differences; a factor that is compounded by the weakness of our defence industrial base.

Absence of a CDS

The creation of the post of a CDS has remained an unfulfilled agenda of the GoM report of 2000. The government apparently did not accept the recommendation because of an unstated apprehension that it would concentrate too much power in an individual. The stated position of the government was, however, the need for wider political consultations across all political parties, before a decision is finalized. Therefore every six months, for over a decade, the MoD has been reminding political parties that their views are still awaited, without any success—it keeps the MoD's tail clear and has been cited as a rationale for indecision!

But the non-acceptance of the CDS recommendation was also due to inter-service differences on the matter. A group of IAF ex-Chiefs met Prime Minister Vajpayee and conveyed their views opposing the creation of the CDS. The IAF was opposed to the CDS, because, from a service-centric viewpoint it was felt that the existing system of COSC was effective enough. Not stated publicly was the fear that the powers of the IAF chief would be curtailed.

The need for a CDS or a similar appointment was always based on two primary arguments. Firstly, the government must receive military instead of service-centric advice and secondly, the dire need to improve inter-service cooperation—an imperative for preparations and fighting modern wars. The operational imperative for integrated, operational commands, training and logistics structures are well known. Such structures cannot materialize without a CDS. In terms of preparations, prioritization of plan acquisition cannot take place in the absence of the CDS. Today, need for prioritization is acute but virtually impossible, as the existing COSC system simply cannot arbitrate inter-service differences.

The Naresh Chandra Committee in 2012 has also reiterated the need for a Permanent Chairman for the COSC with two-year tenure. This time around, while the three services have been fully supportive of the recommendation, the UPA government did not endorse the recommendation and left it for the BJP government to decide. The issue is still under consideration and it is anybody's guess what the outcome would be.

Without the CDS or any other similar entity in place, India's armed forces will continue to procure military assets that will be suboptimal in terms of creating military power that is aligned to political objectives. The absence of military strategy, CDS and a poor defence industrial base are thus key areas begging for reform. Inaction by the government in these areas is a triple whammy. The tragedy is that even though the government knows what requires to be done, it is unable to do so primarily because of inept execution, which is its bane. The lack of military strategy and CDS, combined with a weak defence industrial base has now created a precarious situation for military effectiveness. The raising of the Mountain Strike Corps is illustrative.

The Mountain Strike Corps

In July 2013 the CCS sanctioned the creation of a Mountain Strike Corps (MSC) which would consist of nearly 90000 thousand personnel, two infantry divisions, two armoured brigades, supporting artillery and rotary assets apart from logistic support units. In terms of personnel strength, the army was adding a navy to its existing strength! The sanction by the CCS was projected as India's answer to the growing Chinese military threat through Tibet. The MSC including the cost of infrastructure to house it would cost over one lakh crores which was to be found from within the envisaged budget allocation. It is to be raised in seven years.

It is the author's case that the raising of the MSC is a reflection of the absence of military strategy, weak joint-service cooperation, and is unsupported by our defence budget and defence industrial base. It is a monumental blunder that will, in the long term, suck a lot of scarce resources and weaken the entire military structure unless there is a significant enhancement in the size of the defence budget—an unlikely prospect in the next five years at least. Worse, it is unlikely to deliver the capability of deterring China.

The Army's rationale for the creation of the MSC was based on the need to deter China by creating an offensive capability that would, when applied across the Himalayas, be able to capture territory. Such capture of territory, it was argued, will provide the political leadership, the bargaining power in post-conflict negotiations. The argument was borrowed from the Western front, where the creation of a strike corps against Pakistan was expected to deliver such bargaining power. The only problem is that when used against the Chinese, such an argument is completely misplaced.

The MSC should have originated from an integrated military strategy that answered the question—how to deter China? The question should have been asked and answered at a joint service forum. More importantly, the answer must be resource-informed. The MSC was never part of the LTIPP. Instead the army unilaterally decides the creation of the MSC as the best deterrence method and presents its case to the CCS for approval.

By the time approval was granted in 2013, a public narrative had built up, that conveyed the notion that the raising of the MSC will provide India with a military instrument that is the best answer to China on the Northern Front. It is a canard that needs to be exposed.

The operational idea that the MSC will be applied across the Himalayas, onto the Tibetan plateau is highly questionable in terms of its feasibility as it is virtually impossible to visualize a situation where the entire MSC can be applied as a cogent force, due to logistics and operational restrictions imposed by terrain and infrastructure support available on our Northern borders. In any case, if the idea of deterrence is based on capturing territory across the Himalayas, then we would require at least two or three such MSCs, as the Sino-Indian border is nearly over 4000 km long. With only one MSC, its positioning would be problematic, because its induction and application can be decided only post a reaction to a major Chinese offensive. The problem is compounded due to the requirement of acclimatization.

The MSC, even if applied across the Himalayas, will always be in danger of being cut off and destroyed, as its logistic support would be based on vulnerable lines of communication as also the fact that China's web of road communications gives it a tremendous ability for lateral movement. The MSC idea privileges the notion of an offensive capability when the Indian Army should be exploiting the defensive potential of the Himalayas and that is the fundamental operational mistake.

The Himalayas are a formidable mountain obstacle system that must be exploited to defend our territory. Any Chinese incursion across the Himalayas exposes its lengthy logistic tail, which is also its vulnerability. India must develop military capability to exploit that vulnerability. The MSC poses a threat against China's strength. Instead India should pose a threat against its vulnerabilities. Such a capability will require special forces, long-range fire power of missiles, air and artillery based on infantry-manned defensive lines deployed to exploit the defensive capability of the mountains.

As any defensive capability must be backed by a limited offensive capability, what is lacking presently is sufficient organic limited offensive capability with the holding corps. So, instead of raising an MSC that would be useless operationally, another four infantry divisions worth are required.

This will provide a division worth of limited offensive capability for each of the holding corps in addition to existing but limited offensive assets. Importantly, it will cater for the entire range of the conflict spectrum from border skirmishes to large-scale conflict. Two armoured brigades envisaged with the MSC is certainly unnecessary as terrain does not permit its use; any armour threat in the mountains is best neutralized from air or infantry-based anti-tank missiles. The catch is, we can neither afford the raising of four divisions nor the MSC, without weakening the existing military structure.

The answer to the lack of resources problem lies in constructing a military strategy that must aim to defend against both China and Pakistan. Much of India's military power is, even today, postured against Pakistan, the lesser threat, in terms of size. Ironically, much of that military power is unusable due to presence of nuclear weapons. The need is for a military strategy that will permit the rebalance of military power from the West to the North. The four divisions should therefore come from the West as it will not only operationally strengthen our capability against China to cater for the small to large scale of conflict, but it will free our resources in the long run to create a naval capability that will be a usable military instrument for projecting power in the Indian Ocean arena. The map of Asia and the Indian ocean on the next page illustrates the point.

The upside down view of the map provides a perspective of geography's endowment to India. The development of India's coastline for trade and commerce is a natural strategic choice. Since relations with China and Pakistan are unlikely to improve appreciably, India must focus on becoming a maritime power as a long-term objective, which, to accomplish means, the development of access and facilities in ports, hinterland connections and a robust naval capability to defend its interests, especially in the Indian Ocean littoral. As naval capabilities are extremely expensive and time-consuming to build, especially given our scarce financial resources, the only solution to do so would be by rebalancing continental land power. However, as such an understanding requires a joint service approach that is not feasible given the already stated prevailing organizational climate. It only serves to illustrate the important fact that India's military power is shaped incidentally, of which, the creation of MSC is a case in point.

Map 1: Asia and the Indian Ocean

Conclusion

Currently, India's hard power is being shaped by bureaucratic inertia instead of a military strategy that ought to bridge the space between envisaged political objectives and national resources available. The RM's Directive that supposedly guides the growth of hard power is neither based on a National Security Strategy, nor does it originate from political imagination. It actually stems from the military itself with the original drafting done by the military, as the MoD civil staff is incapable of originating the document being generalist in experience and skills.

The areas for reform are many—the need for creating a group of national security professionals in government has been identified more than a decade ago. But nothing much has been done about it. Strategic studies should be introduced in the university system, so as to provide an adequate supply of national security professionals. The Indian National Defence University (INDU) must be established forthwith.

The deficit in political guidance is, in contemporary times, compounded by the suboptimal jointness between the three services and the defence budget crunch. It is a triple whammy that has frozen procurement choices and created a dilemma in decision-making. The short-term solution lies in an immediate revision of the RM's Directive that emphasizes the military role in the envisaged geopolitical context. It is a role, which must be met supported by available resources. In the absence of a National Security Strategy document, the RM's Directive must be subjected to an intense inter-ministerial evaluation and then approved by the CCS. A better-informed document may provide more than a modicum of political guidance to shape India's hard power.

However, the downstream problem of a crystallizing military strategy cannot be resolved without the appointment of a CDS or any other equivalent entity that can provide military advice in contrast to service-specific advice, evolve a joint military strategy, harmonize inter-service differences and, at the same time, mitigate the prioritization of acquisition problem.

Undoubtedly, due to the changing character of warfare, reforms in India's defence domain should remain persistent. But the pace of execution witnessed, despite identification of reform measures, is indeed a snail's pace. It is a pace that the country can ill afford. Only political will can overcome the inertia that characterizes India's defence reforms.

CHAPTER VII

The Theory and Practice of Civil-Military Relations

S Kalyanaraman

An effective defence policy must not only secure the country from external threats but also do so within the available economic means and by least sacrificing other national objectives and social values. For crafting such a policy, an optimal institutional mechanism to suitably order civil-military relations and effect coordination among the political, military and bureaucratic establishments is an absolute imperative. That is so because the institutional mechanism of civil-military relations ultimately determines the nature of the decisions made with respect to defence policy and how these decisions are embedded within the larger ambit of national policy.

Defence policy broadly involves decisions on three main sets of issues. The first set of issues is quantitative in nature, namely, the size of the armed forces and the proportion of national resources that needs to be devoted for military needs. The second set of issues is qualitative in nature and includes the organization of the armed forces, their composition, deployment pattern, chain of command, and complement of weapons and equipment. And the third set of issues relates to the employment of the armed forces—when and under what circumstances they will be used and the strategy they will adopt to achieve the goals set by the political leadership.[1]

Theory of Civil-Military Relations

An automatic consensus on these issues is unlikely to ensue between the political and military leaderships on most occasions. That is because of the different perspectives from which each approaches the issue of national security. Given the military's singular role as the sword arm of the nation, its leadership naturally places greater emphasis upon the ways and means of overcoming security threats. As the representatives of the people who have bestowed upon them the authority to govern, political leaders are not only responsible for safeguarding national security but also for attaining other equally important economic and social objectives as well as preserving the legitimate political order and the constitutional foundations on which it rests.

In effect, two imperatives shape defence policy decisions and the military institutions that ultimately result from them. One is the security imperative stemming from threats and challenges in the external environment. And the other is the social imperative flowing from the dominant forces, ideologies and institutions in the domestic environment. An over-emphasis on either imperative is undesirable. A principal role for the economic, social and political factors in shaping and controlling the armed forces would render them incapable of effectively performing their task and thus imperil national security. But a predominant role for the security imperative in determining the size and role of the armed forces would compromise the attainment of other economic and social objectives and may even make it 'impossible to contain' the resulting military institution within the political order.[2] In other words, both the civilianization of the military and the militarization of politics and society are suboptimal choices.

It is the interaction between the security and social imperatives and, by extension, the interaction between civilian and military leaders charged with addressing these imperatives, that is 'the hub of the problem of civil-military relations.' Because, reconciling these imperatives, that is, achieving both security and development within the existing political order, calls for 'a complex balancing of power and attitudes' between civilian and military leaders.[3] In other words, it requires an optimal ordering of civil-military relations and translating it into an organizational structure that enables effective coordination between the stakeholders.

An optimal order of civil-military relations has to establish a balance between two central necessities. Firstly, it must ensure that the role of the armed forces within the political order is minimized and the military leadership subordinated to the civilian authority. And secondly, it must enable the armed forces to emerge as the most powerful coercive arm of the state and the military leadership to retain its professional expertise in directing, operating and controlling the violence that the armed forces may be called upon to apply. In effect, a balance must be maintained between minimizing the role of the armed forces in politics and society and maximizing their professional competence in the application and 'management of violence.'[4] That is, a balance between 'a military strong enough to prevail in war' and one that is at the same time prevented from employing the 'overwhelming advantage in coercive power' it enjoys to overthrow the political order or make excessive demands on national resources or dictate the course of foreign policy. In a nutshell, establishing and maintaining a civil-military balance involves reconciling 'a military strong enough to do anything the civilians ask with a military subordinate enough to do only what civilians authorize.'[5]

But how is this balance to be established and maintained? Samuel Huntington, who formulated the first formal and still dominant theory of civil-military relations, prescribed the ideal of maintaining the armed forces as an autonomous professional institution for this purpose. Referring to this mode of civil-military relations as 'objective civilian control,' he contended that such a step 'is most conducive to the emergence of professional attitudes and behaviour among the members of the officer corps.' Professionalism would, in turn, de-ideologize the officer corps with respect to contending political views among civilian groups within society, thus rendering it 'politically sterile and neutral' and consequently willing to 'carry out the wishes of any civilian group which secures legitimate authority within the state.' In effect, objective civilian control would militarize the military and make it 'the tool of the State.'[6]

In practice, Huntington's prescription has been understood as meaning that civilian 'interference or meddling in military affairs' must be avoided since it would undermine military professionalism and thus the ability of the armed forces to effectively perform their task.[7] Therefore, the leadership of the armed forces must be given 'as free a hand as possible in military matters.' Civilian leaders should not ask too many questions, let alone give orders, 'about tactics, particular pieces of hardware, the design of a campaign, measures of success,' etc.[8] This interpretation of objective civilian control is best captured by Moltke the Elder's contention during the Franco-Prussian War of 1871 that 'once war was declared the statesman should fall silent until the general delivered the victory.'[9] In effect, it meant that policy stopped when war began.

American Practice of Civil-Military Relations

But such a contention militates against the Clausewitzian understanding of war: that war has its own grammar (how it is waged) but not its own logic (why and for what purpose it is waged); that 'war is simply a continuation of political intercourse, with the addition of other means'; that 'war in itself does not suspend political intercourse'; that 'the main lines along which military events progress, and to which they are restricted, are political lines that continue throughout the war into the subsequent peace'; that divorcing war from political intercourse would lead to 'something pointless and devoid of sense'; 'that the political view ... [cannot] wholly cease to count on the outbreak of war'; that since 'war is part of policy, policy will determine its character'; and that while policy 'will not extend its influence to operational details' such as determining 'the posting of guards or the employment of patrols,' political considerations 'are the most influential in the planning of war, of the campaign, and often even of the battle.'[10]

Huntington's ideal of objective civilian control has consequently never been practised by Western political leaders in the manner in which he envisaged it. Great wartime leaders such as Abraham Lincoln, Georges Clemenceau, Winston Churchill and David Ben-Gurion did all those 'improper things' that the ideal of objective civilian control warns against. While these leaders did not dictate to their military subordinates or act like generalissimos, they did 'coax or bully, interrogate or probe' their generals. And they 'treated military advice as just that—advice, not a course of action to be ratified with no more than formal consideration.' In effect, these great political leaders held what Eliot Cohen has described as 'an unequal dialogue' with their generals. It was a dialogue because 'both sides expressed their views bluntly, indeed, sometimes offensively, and not once but repeatedly.' And it was unequal because 'the final authority of the civilian leader was unambiguous and unquestioned.'[11]

Both during the Cold War and post-Cold War years, American civilian leaders continued their intrusive monitoring of the US military, although the level of intrusiveness varied across administrations. According to Peter Feaver, the single biggest factor that enabled such intrusive monitoring was the steady increase in the size of the civilian bureaucracy in the office of the president, in interagency mechanisms such as the National Security Council, and in the Office of the Secretary of Defence. For instance, the strength of the civilian component of personnel in the Office of the Secretary of Defence increased from less than 1,000 in 1948 to more than 3,000 in the late 1960s and subsequently stabilized between 2,000 and 2,500 during the late 1980s and 1990s.[12] At the same time, congressional oversight over the US military also increased, thus adding another layer of intrusive civilian monitoring. This is most evident from the fact that '[t]he portion of the defense budget requiring authorizing legislation, one measure of congressional micromanagement, climbed from 0 per cent in 1962 to essentially 100 per cent by 1983.'[13]

Organizational Structure of Civil-Military Relations in the United States

A key element in practising objective civilian control and thus maximizing both military professionalism and national security is the establishment of a balanced organizational structure of civil-military relations within the defence department. Huntington contended that only a balanced organizational structure would ensure 'a greater degree of specialization' in the performance of the department's three distinct functions. These functions were: the professional military function, the administrative-fiscal function, and the policy-strategy function. The professional military function involves advising the political leadership 'on the military implications of proposed courses of action' as well as on what the armed forces need for implementing the policies adopted on the one hand and directing the forces to implement national policy on the other. The administrative-fiscal function includes 'representing the interests of economy and efficiency, advising on fiscal, budgetary, and management matters, and administering "civilian" activities such as supply, procurement, construction, non-military personnel and the budget.' And the policy-strategy function consists of 'balancing the professional military and administrative-fiscal viewpoints, formulating the departmental recommendations on force levels and the military budget, and defending departmental views before outside groups.' In Huntington's view, each of these essential functions is best performed 'by a distinct unit' in the civil-military matrix: the formulation of policy and strategy by the Secretary of Defence; the provision of professional military advice by the leadership of the armed forces; and the management of administrative-fiscal affairs by 'a separate set of officials, civilian or military.'[14]

In fact, it was precisely such a conception that drove American political leaders in the 1950s to divest the military of the policy-strategy and administrative-fiscal functions that it had acquired during the Second World War. And they did this through the National Security Act of 1947, the amendments made to it in 1949, and the defence reorganization effected in 1953. In addition, these reforms also led to the Joint Chiefs of Staff being divested of other additional responsibilities that they had acquired including the provision of overall advice to the president on national security policy, coordination of defence research and development as well as national intelligence, and control over the nuclear weapons programme.[15]As a result, in the post-Second World War era, the Joint Chiefs were restricted to the purely military function.

These and other reforms that followed—the Defence Reorganization Act of 1958 and the Goldwater-Nichols Act of 1986—also introduced two key innovations. The first of these was the appointment of a Chairman of the Joint Chiefs of Staff (JCS) and his subsequent elevation as the principal military adviser to the political leadership. And the second was the creation of unified theatre commands and the conscious removal of both the Chairman of the JCS and the Service Chiefs from the chain of command running from the President to the Secretary of Defence to the combatant commanders.[16]

The reduction of the military leadership's role to the purely military function resulted in the Comptroller's Office emerging as the focal point of the administrative-fiscal function. As 'the preeminent representative of the civilian demands for economy and efficiency,' the Comptroller's power actually flowed from 'the identification of civilian control with budget control.' This power of the Comptroller was legally sanctioned by Congress in the 1949 Amendments to the National Security Act and it was subsequently reiterated in the Goldwater-Nichols Act. In effect, the Comptroller's Office became 'a significant counterweight' to the Joint Chiefs within the Department of Defence.[17] The other consequence of reducing the role of the military leadership to the purely military function was the empowerment of the office of the Secretary of Defence, which gradually emerged as the centre for crafting policy and strategy.

Features of US Civil-Military Relations

The principal conclusion that flows from this overview is that the American practice of civil-military relations is best described as a modified form of objective civilian control. This modified form has four main features. Firstly, political leaders have consciously exercised their authority over the military particularly by assuming monopoly over the policy-strategy function. Secondly, they have intrusively monitored the military especially through the civilian component of the bureaucracy as well as by empowering the Comptroller's Office in the Department of Defence to ensure economy and efficiency in the use of national resources for military purposes. Thirdly, they have expressly allocated purely military functions but also a wide degree of autonomy to the military leadership for the purpose of fostering military professionalism. And finally, to enhance military effectiveness, they have enforced coordination among the armed services by establishing unified commands and empowering the Chairman of the Joint Chiefs of Staff to the required extent.

What has determined this practice of civil-military relations and its organizational structure is the acute concern felt by the political leaders of the world's oldest democracy and largest economy about three issues. Their first concern has been regarding the undue accretion of coercive power in the hands of the military leadership and the challenge that this may pose to the political order and social values. Indeed, the theory of civil-military relations that Huntington developed drew its inspiration from democratic theory, which is primarily 'concerned with devising ways to ensure that the people remain in control even as professionals conduct the business of government.'[18] The second concern of American political leaders has been about the defence budget crowding out expenditure on social and economic goods. From Eisenhower's emphasis on a balanced budget and his decrying of the military-industrial complex to Obama's call for paring down defence expenditure, balancing the budget and focusing on nation-building at home, this issue has been a continuous concern. Finally, the third concern of America's leaders has centred on professionalizing the military and restructuring its command system to ensure greater military effectiveness.

Civil-Military Relations in India

Two and a half of these three concerns have also dominated the thinking of India's political leaders on civil-military relations and its organizational structure. Firstly, they have consistently taken the view that defence and development must go together and that the one cannot come at the expense of the other, especially given India's low human development indices. For instance, in the immediate aftermath of independence, Jawaharlal Nehru called for building 'an economically strong and well-balanced India with a strong enough defence apparatus.'[19] But at the same time he also warned that the defence apparatus should not simply come to mean the possession of an army, navy and air force. Instead, these spearheads have to necessarily rest on a broad industrial and technological base and a sound economy.[20] This emphasis on defence and development going together has persisted till date. Early last year, P Chidambaram, the then Finance Minister, emphasized the importance of not only sustaining a high economic growth rate for building up India's 'comprehensive national power' but also of embracing 'the twin goals of prosperity and security.'[21]

Secondly, Indian political leaders have been acutely conscious about subordinating the military to civilian authority. Expressly articulating this concern during a discussion in Parliament on General Thimayya's resignation, Nehru asserted that 'civil authority is and must remain supreme.'[22] And thirdly, while Indian political leaders have sought to foster professionalism by granting considerable autonomy to the military leadership, they have also been at the same time concerned about too much power accreting in the hands of the military leadership. This concern is especially evident from their continuing reluctance to approve the appointment of a Chief of Defence Staff, which position is widely acknowledged as necessary. But this reluctance has prevented greater inter-Service coordination as well as financial savings that could potentially flow from the rationalization of roles, missions, training and support systems among the services.[23] The persistence of these concerns is clearly evident from the manner in which Indian political leaders have practised civil-military relations and the organizational structure that they have evolved for this purpose.

Two different assessments prevail on the mode of civil-military relations that India has practised. One view holds that with the exception of the period when the Forward Policy was adopted towards China, India has practised the Huntingtonian ideal of objective civilian control in terms of the political leadership not interfering in military operational issues.[24] And the other contends that India has actually practised subjective civilian control by interfering excessively in military affairs.[25] Neither is, however, an accurate description. The fact is that while civilian leaders have indeed granted a wide degree of internal autonomy to the armed forces, they have not at the same time given military leaders *carte blanche* during the course of various wars and conflicts. Further, they have also treated military advice as just that, not a course of action to be automatically endorsed.

For instance, in November 1947, during the course of operations to rescue Jammu & Kashmir, the political leadership set aside the advice given by Lt Gen Dudley Russell, then commander of the Delhi and East Punjab Command, that an immediate advance be undertaken towards Muzaffarabad. Instead, the Army was instructed to send a relief column to the besieged town of Poonch, where not only the State Force garrison but also 40,000 non-Muslim refugees remained trapped. In effect, as SK Sinha concludes, driven by humanitarianism, 'political considerations outweighed military requirements.'[26]

Similarly, during the 1965 War, the Air Force was prohibited from undertaking offensive retaliatory action against East Pakistan. This prohibition flowed from two political considerations articulated by then Defence Minister YB Chavan. One was the need to avoid 'wasteful escalation' along a secondary front, and the other was the imperative of not provoking China.[27] At the same time, political leaders not only advised the Navy to play a defensive role but also expressly instructed it 'not to operate beyond the latitude of Porbandar.'[28]

More recently, the Kargil conflict of 1999 saw political leaders expressly prohibiting the army and air force from undertaking operations that involved crossing the Line of Control.[29] Another telling example of close political management of military developments occurred during the course of Operation Parakram, which saw the military being mobilized for the express purpose of coercing Pakistan into cracking down on anti-India terrorist groups in its territory. At the height of this coercive diplomatic exercise, Lt Gen Kapil Vij was removed from the command of 2 Corps because he reportedly ordered some elements of his armour formations to move from their concentration areas to strike areas.[30] Further, that the political leadership did not simply endorse the military options given by the military leadership during this crisis with Pakistan is clearly evident from what Prime Minister Vajpayee said at that time during the course of a conversation with the prominent journalist Shekhar Gupta. According to Gupta, Vajpayee said:

> Everybody wants to go to war, particularly the armed forces, they really want to thrash Pakistan.... But I am asking the chiefs, when the history of this war is written, what name will be given to it? The war of destruction of Pakistan, liberation of Kashmir, annihilation of the Pakistani army, what? We must have a clear objective before we go to war. We can't launch what history would merely call a war of anger.... The problem with a war is, how you start it, when and where you start it, is in your hands. But how it will end, and when, is never in your control. That is why the decision to go to war is never taken lightly or in anger.[31]

It is thus evident that Indian leaders have exercised a modified form of objective civilian control. This practice has had four distinct features:

1) Conscious subordination of the military to civil authority including by reducing the pre-independence status enjoyed by military leaders.
2) Grant of a wide degree of autonomy to the military leadership in internal affairs.
3) Reluctance to carry out reforms that may unwittingly result in an all-powerful and assertive military leadership, and

4) Intrusive monitoring of the military by the civilian bureaucracy in general and the Finance wing of the Ministry of Defence in particular.

Formal Subordination of the Military

Formal subordination of the military to civilian authority began with the formation of the interim government in September 1946. The handover of British power to Indian hands necessitated a change in the colonial system of civil-military relations. In the colonial system, the Commander-in-Chief of the Indian Army 'dominated the defence apparatus' because of the authority he enjoyed over all the three Services as well as because of his position as the War Member of the Viceroy's Executive Council.[32] In this system, ultimate civilian control lay in the hands of the Secretary of State for India, the British Cabinet and the British Parliament. With the transfer of power, this system had to be necessarily altered and formal civilian authority over the military vested in Indian hands.

Consequently, as a first step, a civilian leader assumed the position of Defence Member (Defence Minister equivalent) in the interim government. At the same time, the commander-in-chief was stripped of his formal authority over the other two services, which then emerged as independent entities under their own chiefs. This latter measure was actually recommended by Lord Ismay who essentially devised independent India's organizational structure of civil-military relations.[33] It was, however, only after the adoption of the Constitution that civilian authority over the military was fully formalized. The Constitution made the President the supreme commander of the armed forces and vested responsibility for national defence with the cabinet as a whole. The Cabinet, in turn, discharges its responsibility for defence through the Ministry of Defence headed by the Defence Minister.[34]

Formal subordination of the military to civilian authority did not stop there. Subsequent years saw the position of the military leadership being consciously downgraded 'both administratively and socially.' In 1955, the designation of the three service chiefs was changed from Commander-in-Chief to Chief of Staff. According to Lloyd and Susanne Rudolph, this 'reflected some nervousness concerning the military's potential role' in political affairs and 'a consequent desire to "trim their tails".' Other measures adopted to reduce the status of the military leadership included the abolition of the entitlement of lieutenant general rank officers to gun salutes and placing the army chief at the 25th place in the Warrant of Precedence behind the Comptroller and Auditor General, chief justices and members of the Planning Commission.[35] All these measures were designed with a single intent in mind: to reduce the high pre-war status and position enjoyed by the military leadership in the colonial government hierarchy and thus their salience in the democratic political order.

Internal Autonomy to the Military

The importance given by the political leadership to fostering professionalism has been evident since independence. It is because of the felt need for this imperative that the political leadership refrained from retaining in the armed forces any officer who had chosen to join the Indian National Army under Subhash Chandra Bose during the Second World War. This decision 'not only cemented the loyalties of the old officers to the new regime but also strengthened the idea that professional competence, not political initiatives, was the first requirement of the Indian Army.'[36] That this imperative can be ignored only at a high cost was tellingly brought home during Defence Minister Krishna Menon's tenure, which ended with the disastrous military performance against China in 1962.

Since then, the imperative of fostering professionalism and avoiding politicization has led political leaders to grant a wide degree of autonomy to the military leadership. They rarely, if ever, ask questions about the doctrine that each service chooses to employ or stress upon in performing its role. Similarly, civilian leaders do not attempt to dictate to the leaders of the armed services the force structure they should develop. Given that political leaders have generally refrained from probing the military leadership on these larger aspects that directly relate to strategy and doctrine, it is only natural that they also do not interfere in issues relating to training, military education and even appointments up to a certain rank.[37]

Reluctant Reformers

Even as they have granted a wide degree of autonomy to the military leadership on internal Service matters, political leaders have been reluctant to fundamentally reform the organizational structure of civil-military relations. The structure designed by Lord Ismay at the time of independence has remained more or less the same, although marginal changes have been effected in it from time to time. Thus, at the apex level, the Defence Committee of the Cabinet was successively renamed as the Emergency Committee of the Cabinet, the Cabinet Committee on Political Affairs, and the Cabinet Committee on Security. The Defence Minister's Committee ceased to exist and it was replaced by the system of Morning Meetings chaired by the Defence Minister. At the apex level, only the Chiefs of Staff Committee remained unchanged. At the same time, some new committees were established to foster greater coordination among civilian and military officials, the most prominent of which was the Committee for Defence Planning and its replacement, the Directorate General of Defence Planning Staff.[38]

Even the post-Kargil reforms did not fundamentally alter the organizational structure of civil-military relations. The National Security Council and its associated offices—the National Security Advisor and his Secretariat, the Strategic Policy Group and the National Security Advisory Board—have been constituted as an additional layer for inter-agency coordination. And the new agencies that were established—Headquarters Integrated Defence Staff and the Defence Intelligence Agency—to foster coordination among the Services have not been allowed to function by the Services themselves.[39] In effect, nothing much has changed especially given the political leadership's reluctance to institute measures that may excessively enhance the power of the military leadership.

Nothing illustrates this reluctance more than political discomfort with the very idea of a Chief of Defence Staff (CDS). The idea of an Indian CDS began to be advocated first in the 1960s after Lord Mountbatten, then serving as Britain's Chief of the Defence Staff, sent a note in this regard to the Government of India. According to RD Pradhan, who was then serving as Private Secretary to Defence Minister YB Chavan, this idea did not find favour with the political leadership with Nehru simply observing 'Seen, No comment' on Mountbatten's note.[40] The idea was again mooted by the Chief of the Army Staff General Krishna Rao in June 1982 and it was even echoed by some Opposition leaders in Parliament during the parliamentary debate on the defence budget in March 1983. But once again, the government in power and its Defence Minister (R Venkataraman) rejected the need for such an office because of concerns about too much power accreting in the hands of one general officer.[41]

These concerns have continued till date. In the year 2000, the Vajpayee government appointed a Group of Ministers led by LK Advani to recommend reforms to the national security system. One of the principal recommendations of this Group of Ministers was the appointment of a Chief of Defence Staff.[42] Yet, when the reforms were instituted, a CDS was not appointed apparently because of the inability to forge a political consensus on the issue. This situation did not change during the next decade as well. According to a statement made by former Defence Minister AK Antony in Parliament in August 2013, the government was still in the process of consulting various political parties on the appointment of a CDS.[43] Even the latest recommendation by the Naresh Chandra Task Force on National Security that, instead of a CDS, a Permanent Chairman of the Chiefs of Staff Committee be appointed was rejected by the government which appointed the task force in the first place. Indeed, the Cabinet Committee on Security consciously refused to consider all major proposals of the Task Force relating to higher defence management.[44]

Political reluctance to appoint a CDS has only been reinforced by opposition from the air force and navy because of concerns about being dominated by the army. In addition, top military leaders from all three services are themselves reluctant to approve of a measure that would considerably reduce their own power and role. For their part, civilian bureaucrats are equally reluctant to support this measure because it is likely to empower the military at its expense.[45] Thus, overall, there is no single agency within the state apparatus that actually favours far-reaching reform of the organizational structure of civil-military relations. Instead, during all these years, support for the appointment of a CDS has been limited to a handful of individuals in the services, the civilian bureaucracy, the political establishment, and the security studies community.

Intrusive Bureaucratic Monitoring

The fourth feature of civil-military relations is the intrusive monitoring of the armed forces by the civilian bureaucracy. As early as 1967, two committees established by the Administrative Reforms Commission highlighted this issue by stating that civilian power over the military should not be interpreted to mean bureaucratic control.[46] Nothing much has changed in the last forty-seven years. A recent commentary by a retired Chief of the Naval Staff notes that 'each case emanating from the SHQ is required to be steered through multiple layers of bureaucracy that exist in four departments of the MoD as well as its Finance Division. Queries are sequential, repetitive and often raised to prevaricate; and every file movement takes weeks, if not months.' As a result, force modernization has been thwarted and combat readiness affected.[47]

In effect, driven by concerns about the military emerging as too powerful an institution in what is still a young and poor democracy that is often described as 'the world's greatest example of functioning anarchy,'[48] India's political leaders have consciously sought to keep the military contained and constrained through an intrusive bureaucratic monitoring process.

This daily process of what is often seen as over-intrusive bureaucratic monitoring has led to two related conclusions. Exasperated commentators have repeatedly asserted since the 1960s that civil-military relations in India are characterized not by civilian control but by bureaucratic control. And since what prevails is bureaucratic control, there is an absence of dialogue between the political and military leaderships.[49] That such interpretations do not accurately capture the reality is clear from the experience of General VP Malik, the Chief of Army Staff and Chairman of the Chiefs of Staff Committee during the Kargil conflict. He notes:

> The CCS met on an almost daily basis till the second week of July 1999. Besides the Prime Minister and other CCS members, the meetings were attended by the National Security Advisor, the Cabinet Secretary, the three Service Chiefs, the secretaries of the Defence, Home, Finance and External Affairs ministries, heads of Intelligence Bureau and R&AW, and the Secretary, NSCS. Sometimes, for specific purposes, special invitees were called in.... It was a refreshing change in the decision-making process, both at the political level as well as at the armed forces level: open and direct. The political leadership received views of the Service Chiefs first-hand. After discussions, the concerned executive authorities, including the three Chiefs, received directions from the Prime Minister. The National Security Advisor, who was always

accessible and a very effective trouble-shooter, facilitated this process creditably. All these developments led to an integrated approach to 'war management' with the political, economic, diplomatic, media and military aspects meshed cogently.[50]

Conclusion

India's practice of civil-military relations has four distinct features. These features are the product of three major concerns that have dominated the thinking of the political leadership: the need to ensure that defence and development go hand in hand; the imperative of subordinating the military leadership to civilian authority; and three, not empowering the military leadership in any manner that might contribute to their assertiveness. These concerns have motivated American political leaders as well. Indeed, these concerns are endemic to all democracies—rich or poor, young or old. That is because the theory of civil-military relations itself is based on democratic theory and its most fundamental principle, namely, ensuring that the people have ultimate control over the government.

Nevertheless, there is indeed a case for undertaking calibrated reforms of the civil-military organizational structure to ensure greater military effectiveness and efficiency in the use of national resources for military purposes. The most crucial in this regard are the appointment of a Permanent Chairman of the Chiefs of Staff Committee as recommended by the Naresh Chandra Task Force and the creation of a specialist administration cadre to man the security bureaucracy as recommended by the NN Vohra-led Task Force on Internal Security (2000) and accepted by the Group of Ministers in the following year.

NOTES

1. Samuel P Huntington, *The Soldier and the State: The Theory and Politics of Civil-Military Relations*, Dehradun: Natraj Publishers, 2005 Indian edn., p. 1.
2. Huntington, *Soldier and the State*, p. 2.
3. Ibid.
4. Ibid, pp. 11-13.
5. Peter D Feaver, *Armed Servants: Agency, Oversight and Civil-Military Relations*, Cambridge, MA: Harvard University Press, 2003, pp. 1, 2, 4, 5.
6. Huntington, *Soldier and the State*, pp. 83-4.
7. Feaver, *Armed Servants*, p. 18.

8. Eliot A Cohen, *Supreme Command: Soldiers, Statesmen, and Leadership in Wartime*, New York: The Free Press, 2002, pp. 4-5.
9. Cited in Hew Strachan, *The Direction of War: Contemporary Strategy in Historical Perspective*, Cambridge, UK: Cambridge University Press, 2013 Kindle Edition, p. 30.
10. Carl von Clausewitz, *On War*, trans. and eds., Michael Howard and Peter Paret, Princeton, NJ: Princeton University Press, 1976, pp. 605-7.
11. Eliot A Cohen, *Supreme Command: Soldiers, Statesmen, and Leadership in Wartime*, New York: The Free Press, 2002, pp. 5, 208-9.
12. Feaver, *Armed Servants*, pp. 121-4, 193. But it must be noted that, at the same time, the number of military personnel servicing this office as part of the Joint Chiefs of Staff (JCS) also increased over these years. While the strength of the JCS staff was at first limited by the National Security Act of 1947 to 100, this figure was later revised to 210 under the National Security Amendments of 1949 and again to 400 by the Defence Reorganization Act of 1958. But when this strict limitation was lifted by the Goldwater-Nichols Act of 1986, the strength of JCS staff rose dramatically to reach nearly 2,800 by 1996. For the strength of the JCS staff between 1947 and 1958, see Rajneesh Singh, *United States Reforms to its Higher Defence Organization: Lessons for India*, Monograph No. 41, New Delhi: Institute for Defence Studies and Analyses, July 2014, pp. 16, 21, 23, http://www.idsa.in/system/files/monograph41.pdf. And for its increased strength between 1986 and 1996, see Feaver, *Armed Servants*, p. 197.
13. Cited in Feaver, *Armed Servants*, p. 127.
14. Huntington, *Soldier and the State*, pp. 428-9.
15. Ibid, pp. 431-4.
16. For a useful overview of these reforms, see Rajneesh Singh, *United States Reforms to its Higher Defence Organization*, pp. 11-39.
17. Huntington, *Soldier and the State*, pp. 431, 437-8. Also see Section 107 of *Goldwater-Nichols Department of Defence Reorganization Act of 1986*, http://www.nsa.gov/about/cryptologic_heritage/60th/interactive_timeline/Content/1980s/documents/19861001_1980_Doc_NDU.pdf.
18. Feaver, *Armed Servants*, p. 5.
19. Nehru's speech at the Industries Conference, New Delhi, 18 December 1947. Reprinted as 'Production, The First Essentia'l, in *Jawaharlal Nehru: Selected Speeches Vol. 1: 1946-1949*, 6th edn., New Delhi: Publications Division, Ministry of Information and Broadcasting, Government of India, 1996, p. 96.
20. Nehru's intervention in Lok Sabha debate, 21 March 1956, reprinted as 'True Meaning of Defence,' in *SWJN-SS*, Vol. 32, eds., HY Sharada Prasad and AK Damodaran, New Delhi: Jawaharlal Nehru Memorial Fund, 2003, p. 283.
21. P Chidambaram, 'India's National Security—Challenges and Priorities,' *K. Subrahmanyam Memorial Lecture*, 6 February 2013, http://idsa.in/keyspeeches/IndiasNationalSecurityChallengesandPriorities.
22. Cited in Srinath Raghavan, *War and Peace in Modern India: A Strategic History of the Nehru Years*, Ranikhet: Permanent Black, 2010, p. 269.
23. BD Jayal, 'Management and Delivery of Joint Military Capabilities,' in Anit Mukherjee, ed., *A Call for Change: Higher Defence Management in India*, Monograph No. 6, New Delhi: Institute for Defence Studies and Analyses, July 2012, p. 63.
24. PR Chari, 'Civil-Military Relations in India,' *Armed Forces & Society*, Vol. 4, No. 1, November 1977, p. 13; Srinath Raghavan, 'Civil-Military Relations in India: The China Crisis and After,' *Journal of Strategic Studies*, Vol. 32, No. 1, February 2009, pp. 172-4.

25. VK Nayar, 'Civil-Military Relations,' *Journal of the United Service Institution of India*, CXXXVIII, 574, October-December 2008.
26. SK Sinha, *Operation Rescue: Military Operations in Jammu & Kashmir 1947-49*, New Delhi: Vision Books, 1977, pp. 31-2. The quotation can be found on p. 32.
27. Defence Minister YB Chavan's instructions, as cited in RD Pradhan, *Debacle to Resurgence: Y. B. Chavan: Defence Minister (1962-66)*, New Delhi: Atlantic Publishers, 2013, p. 255.
28. BC Chakravorty, *History of the Indo-Pak War, 1965*, Chapter 10, p. 287, http://www.bharat-rakshak.com/LAND-FORCES/Army/History/1965War/PDF/1965Chapter10.pdf.
29. VP Malik, *Kargil: From Surprise to Victory*, New Delhi: HarperCollins, 2010 paperback edn., p. 139.
30. S Kalyanaraman, 'Operation Parakram: An Indian Exercise in Coercive Diplomacy,' *Strategic Analysis*, Vol. 26, No. 4, Oct-Dec 2002, p. 485.
31. Shekhar Gupta, 'Narendra Modi: Getting his foreign policy right,' *India Today*, 4 September 2014, http://indiatoday.intoday.in/story/shekhar-gupta-narendra-modi-foreign-policy-china-atal-bihari-vajpayee/1/380924.html.
32. Chari, 'Civil-Military Relations in India,' p. 7.
33. SK Sinha, *Higher Defence Organisation in India*, USI Papers No. 7, New Delhi: United Service Institution of India, 1980, p. 6.
34. NN Vohra, 'Civil-Military Relations: Opportunities and Challenges,' *USI National Security Lecture*, 6 December 2013, http://idsa.in/resources/speech/CivilMilitaryRelations_NNVohra.
35. Lloyd I Rudolph and Susanne Hoeber Rudolph, 'Generals and Politicians in India,' *Pacific Affairs*, Vol. 37, No. 1, Spring 1964, pp. 9-10. The quoted phrases can be found on p. 9.
36. Rudolph and Rudolph, 'Generals and Politicians in India,' p. 8.
37. Anit Mukherjee, 'Civil-Military Relations and Military Effectiveness in India,' in Rajesh Basrur et. al., eds., *India's Military Modernization: Challenges and Prospects*, New Delhi: Oxford University Press, 2014.
38. Laxman Kumar Behera, 'Defence Planning in India,' *Journal of Defence Studies*, Vol. 4, No. 3, July 2010, pp. 127-8.
39. For a critical review of post-Kargil reforms, see Anit Mukherjee, *Failing to Deliver: Post-Crises Defence Reforms in India, 1998-2010*, IDSA Occasional Paper No. 18, New Delhi: Institute for Defence Studies and Analyses, 2011.
40. Remarks made as Chairperson in seminar on 'The Need for Institutionalised Coordination Between the Indian Political Leadership and Military Leadership,' *The Nehru Centre*, Mumbai, 29 November 2014.
41. Jerrold F Elkin and W Andrew Ritezel, 'The Debate on Restructuring India's Higher Defence Organization,' *Asian Survey*, Vol. 24, No. 10, October 1984, p. 1069.
42. *Reforming the National Security System—Recommendations of the Group of Ministers*, New Delhi: Government of India, 2001, pp. 100-03.
43. Defence Minister's Response to Question in Parliament on 19 August 2013, http://idsa.in/resources/parliament/QUESTIONNO168CHIEFOFDEFENCESTAFF.
44. Pranab Dhal Samanta, 'Govt rejects Chandra panel proposal for a four-star general,' *Indian Express*, 3 May 2014, http://indianexpress.com/article/india/india-others/govt-rejects-chandra-panel-proposal-for-a-four-star-general/99/.
45. Arun Prakash, 'Defence Reforms: Contemporary Debates and Issues,' in Anit Mukherjee ed., *A Call for Change*, pp. 31-2. Also see, Sinha, *Higher Defence Organisation in India*, pp. 16-21; Elkin and Ritezel, 'The Debate on Restructuring India's Higher Defence Organization,' pp. 1069-85.

46. Sinha, *Higher Defence Organisation in India*, p. 14.
47. Arun Prakash, 'Civil-Military Dissonance: A Chink in India's Armour,' *Third K. Subrahmanyam Memorial Lecture*, 20 January 2014.
48. John Kenneth Galbraith, 'Rival Economic Theories in India,' *Foreign Affairs*, Vol. 36, No. 4, July 1958, p. 590.
49. Anit Mukherjee, 'The Absent Dialogue,' *Seminar*, No. 599, July 2009, http://www.india-seminar.com/2009/599/599_anit_mukherjee.htm.
50. VP Malik, 'Higher Management of Defence and Defence Reforms: Towards Better Management Techniques,' in Anit Mukherjee, ed., *A Call for Change*, p. 42.

CHAPTER VIII

Forging an Indian Security Consensus: Political and Military Challenges

VR Raghavan

Introduction

Civil-military relations form an essential component of a nation's security system. The interplay of responsibilities between the political and military establishments of any nation is a principal component of its military security policy. This policy should aim at developing a system of civil-military relations that will maximize military security at the least sacrifice of other social values. In the words of Huntington, such an objective involves a complex balancing of power and attitudes among civilian and military groups[1] and nations that develop such a balanced pattern of civil-military relations have a great advantage in the search for security. In the extant literature on civil-military relations, analysts have sought to explain the ways in which a nation can achieve the optimum balance that Huntington mentions. The premise of many theories is that the problem of civil-military relations is one of choice between civilian control or civilian supremacy over the military.

Transcending the view that the problem of civil-military relations is merely that of civilian control or separating military from politics, Andrew Cottey states that the challenge today is more of state capacity-building and bureaucratic modernization.[2] The security environment in a globalized world requires a strategically effective military providing advice to a strategically informed and competent civilian leader. Such an environment requires a high degree of harmony among national defence elites, as is argued by Sir Michael Howard that 'neither institutions nor men can fulfil their purposes...save in an atmosphere relatively free from mistrust and tension between soldiers and civilians.'[3] Furthermore, Janowitz asserts that 'civilian leadership includes not only the political direction of the military, but the prevention of the growth of frustration in the profession, of felt injustice, and inflexibility under the weight of its responsibilities.'[4] Therefore ideal relations between civil and military groups would be a combination of Huntington's 'objective civilian control'[5] and Janowitz's model of civilian leadership.

Indian political and military leaders have been conscious of the need for civilian control of the military, as well as the dichotomies that have emerged in the enabling institutional structures for such control. India has had to fight a number of wars since independence and the disadvantages of insufficient synergy between the political and military leadership have been known. In peace, the long preparation for national security requires an integrated endeavour by all organs and ministries and the synergy deficit in these efforts has been an expensive shortcoming. The integration of civilian industry and research capacity with defence needs has not been possible due to the compartmentalized functioning of the Ministry of Defence (MoD). To its credit political leadership had constituted a number of expert and high-level Committees and Study Groups to analyse the problem and make recommendations. Most notable amongst them were those set up after the Kargil War in 1999 and the Naresh Chandra Group in 2011. The first even led to a Group of Ministers deciding on the corrective measures to be initiated.

Politico-Military Coordination during India's Wars

It is a paradoxical truth that at the time of independence, some sections of the ruling elite considered the armed forces to be an anachronism in a peace-loving country like India. The Indian military was also viewed in some political quarters as an instrument of colonial rule. But this sentiment soon changed when the army and the air force had to be extensively used to consolidate the Indian State through operations in Jammu and Kashmir (J&K), and in states like Hyderabad and Goa. The nature of civil-military relations in India was affected by various significant developments. These included the immediate aftermath of the partition—unprecedented communal carnage and internecine riots, exploding population, threat of external aggression and massive refugee migration into the country—and the wars that the country fought in 1948, 1962, 1965 and 1971. The first war over Kashmir in 1947–8 was a test for the higher defence control and strategic thinking in the country. The higher direction of the war was firmly with the civilian leadership who not only laid the operational priorities but also restrained tactical movements on the ground. Decisions were taken by the DCC and military goals were extremely limited amounting to just 'repulsing the invaders.'[6] The operations were thus limited to the tactical level and there was no larger strategic analysis of the critical issues in the significant military operations in the State of J&K. There was no larger strategic objective of denying routes of ingress or pulverizing the capacity of the adversary to strike back.[7] After the war, civil-military relations were governed by the attitude that civilian and economic development instead of defence preparedness was crucial for the nation. Governance and foreign policy of the new nation were subsumed in developmental priorities at the national level and by non-alignment in the international power play. Subsequently, Ayub Khan's coup in Pakistan had led to an increased anxiety in India's political leadership about the political role that the armed forces could play. The insufficient interest in defence matters and understanding of the role of force in the pursuit of national interests was a result of such anxieties on the part of the political leadership. While being accountable to the elected representatives in the Parliament, the decision channels of the armed forces were subjected to increasing scrutiny of the civil servants. This overriding role of the bureaucracy became and remains a major issue of contest between the civil and military leadership in the country.

The war with China in 1962 revealed the dysfunctional higher defence control in India and was a watershed in India's approach to defence and strategic affairs. No study on Indian civil-military relations would be complete without appraising the developments in the country surrounding that war and the changes in its aftermath. The Indian defeat brought to fore the importance of the hitherto neglected relationship between the political and military leaders and set the trend towards greater operational freedom which Indian armed forces enjoy till date. In the late 1950s, Krishna Menon had been appointed the new Defence Minister while General Thimayya became the Chief of Army Staff. The established civil-military hierarchy came under gravest threat during this period. While in the years post 1948 Indian politicians showed remarkable maturity in not politicizing the army, the infamous Krishna Menon–Lt Gen BM Kaul nexus unearthed the friction between an apolitical army and the politico-bureaucratic establishment.

The flawed civil-military relationship resulted in the civil and political leadership denying itself the insight in the military implications of an adversarial relationship with China. In its turn the military leadership could neither foresee the consequences of a foreign policy without military underpinnings nor question the merits of military demands made on it by a political leadership devoid of military understanding. The lost strategic opportunities that could have been obtained by resolving the boundary issue with marginal accommodations of Chinese claims were a consequence of the flawed civil-military dynamic. As a result, the costs of sustaining a decades-long boundary conflict with military and economic consequences could also not be assessed.

One of the major shortcomings of this period was the military high command not being integrated with the political high command. The latter worked in the belief that the military should do as directed and not be involved in strategic planning. Perceptions of the military leaders were not accepted or were disregarded when deciding on major foreign policy choices. The military defeat at the hands of China was the outcome of an avoidable dissonance in the politico-diplomatic strategy on the one hand and the military capability on the other. Diplomacy of the time was neither coordinated with military capability nor adapted to military necessity. As has been said by George Schultz 'military provides the umbrella under which all diplomacy is conducted' and equally by the views of former US

President John F Kennedy that 'Diplomacy and Defence are not substitutes for one another. Either alone would fail.' [8]

Post 1962 and 1965 there was a massive expansion of the Indian armed forces. The Indian Armed forces were poorly equipped with arms and equipment of the Second World War vintage. Indian military commanders were new to commanding large forces. Most of the operations thus far, were tactical in nature and did not help in building experience in war fighting capabilities against modern armies, involving major military force deployment. This too had begun to change. The defence expenditure as a percentage of gross national product doubled between 1961 and 1965.[9] The Indian Army virtually doubled in size and expanded from a largely plains force into a two-front army, one for the Himalayas and one for the plains, and its employment became as diverse as the country's landmass.[10] In the process the armed forces ascended a learning curve and developed expertise in combat, especially in high altitude and extreme cold climate. The armed forces now had a high degree of operational freedom even as strategic choices were made exclusively by the political leadership.

The politico-military debacle in the war against China had galvanized civil-military relations. YB Chavan, with no defence background, was brought in as defence minister. He combined brilliantly with Prime Minister Lal Bahadur Shastri to evolve a new working arrangement for the conduct of the 1965 War. Chavan's diary of the war is an eloquent account of how he improvized a civil-military relationship based on his subtle handing of the chiefs of army, navy and air force.[11] This experience had largely set the stage for the arrangement which became a powerful dynamic in the 1970s. The planning and conduct of the 1971 India-Pakistan war in which the Indira Gandhi-led political leadership completely trusted the operational judgement of General (later Field Marshal) Manekshaw remains the Indian role model of wartime civil-military relationship. The persistence on waiting for the right time and the execution of the 'defence in the West–offence in the East' strategy led to one of India's most remarkable victories. The model of civil-military relationship adopted in this war set the basic pattern of civil-military cum strategic-operational relationship dynamic in India. However, civilian control turned into civil service control of defence services in the two decades which followed.

The Kargil conflict of May-June 1999 was a strategic and tactical surprise for the Indian political and military leaders. The need to fight a limited conventional war in the shadow of nuclear weapons forced an interactive phase in political and military coordination. After the attack on the Indian Parliament in December 2001 the Army was mobilized on the border. This in turn led to a strong international involvement in the strategic management of India–Pakistan tensions. The politico-military coordination for the standoff left much to be desired. The civil-military situation, in the words of K Subrahmanyam, reflected a system where 'politicians enjoy power without any responsibility, bureaucrats wield power without any accountability and the military assumes responsibility without any direction.' The positive development after Kargil was the political leadership's choice to constitute the Kargil Review Committee Report and the Group of Ministers' Report. Both these were emphatic in highlighting the inadequacy of institutional structures for political–military coordination and recommended a series of corrective measures.

The creation of the Integrated Defence Staff (IDS), the National Security Council Secretariat, the devolution of financial powers to the armed forces and a greater emphasis on inter-agency coordination were some of the positive steps initiated. These changes have, however, been rendered ineffective in practice. The IDS still remains without its logical head of Chief of Defence Staff (CDS), leading many to question the role and function of the IDS. The post of a CDS is essential in providing an institutional link between the political leadership and the armed forces in terms of higher direction of war as well as the agency for institutionalized contingency planning. The CDS can provide a coordinated strategic and operational guidance to the three services in their interaction with the political and bureaucratic leadership. Such a post can ultimately help civil-military relations by coordinating and commanding inter-service operations, deploying strategic forces, honing the military into integrated theatre commands, eliminating duplication of resources, and maximizing strategic advantages. More importantly, the CDS, as a principal military advisor to the government, will coordinate the three Chiefs in developing a joint military strategy for national security planning. The CDS or the pragmatic alternative recommended by the Naresh Chandra Group of a full-time Chairman of the Chiefs of Staff Committee is as much a political necessity as a military one. The establishment of this post has, however, been ignored and bypassed, leading to lack of jointness in operational planning and insufficient strategic guidance. The lack of an integrated political–military approach in a nuclear environment makes strategic decision-making even more prolonged and directionless.

The second important recommendation of the Kargil Committee and the Group of Ministers related to restructuring the Ministry of Defence (MoD). This required the ministry to change from a purely civil service ministry to an integrated one combining civil service and defence services' officers working together. This was intended to obtain a qualitatively superior functioning. The result after more than a decade after Kargil is of the MoD now being called the integrated ministry, without any change in its composition.

Politics of Internal Security Challenges

India faced internal security (IS) challenges of insurrections, insurgencies, and demands for separation from the national mainstream almost since independence. The longstanding IS conflicts were supported by foreign powers both in the North East and in J&K. Large numbers of the army formations had to be stationed in these areas of unrest. The involvement of the army in such large numbers in a democratic setup created unique problems of the civilian government and military working together in disturbed areas. Their respective jurisdictions, powers and authority had all to be re-worked within the constitutional and legal framework of the country. The impact of these measures on civil-military relations was significant. It led to continuing friction between the elected governments and the military. Political leadership in J&K and states in the North East have found it necessary to retain a military presence as part of governance structures for decades. Yet the same political leadership finds it difficult to cope with the need to provide legal cover for military operations. Questions on Armed Forces Special Forces Act (AFSPA) and other operational demands on the army are still not resolved. In some states AFSPA is made part of the electioneering discourse. India has on its hands internal security operations which are to be carried out against elements equipped with capacities requiring use of military force in all its forms. A range of campaigns combining regular conventional, irregular, guerrilla, terrorism and Peoples' War are being waged against India in a seamless scenario. Politico-military coordination in such circumstances demands unique management skills which require structures and politico-military processes unique to Indian conditions. The need for institutional arrangements for political-military coordination has not been met either in Delhi or in the state capitals. Consequently, while the armed forces and the Army in particular are subjected to misplaced criticism, the wars against the State continue over decades.

The National Security Council Experiment

When the Kargil crisis erupted the NSC was criticized for being unable to play a leadership role both before and after the conflict. This failure in the light of the Kargil crisis renewed the debate on the NSC's utility and effectiveness. This led the government to appoint the Kargil Review Committee (KRC) under the chairmanship of K Subrahmanyam to review the failures in the national security apparatus. Criticizing the lack of a structured institutional mechanism to address national security issues the KRC noted that 'An objective assessment of the last 52 years will show that the country is lucky to have scraped through various national security threats without too much damage, except in 1962. The country can no longer afford such ad hoc functioning.'[12] Even with regard to the NSC, the problem of civil-military relations remains one of a general wariness on the part of the civil and bureaucratic leaders towards the armed forces and the subsequent hesitancy in giving a greater role to the three services in national security planning. The establishment of the NSC led the armed forces to hope that they could have a greater role in security planning and policy recommendations. However, the armed forces continue to remain out of the decision-making process of the NSC. In the NSC, the Chiefs of Staff are members at the bureaucratic level and the armed forces are represented by the Defence Minister at the apex. The NSC was supposed to be the central body for the formulation of national security strategies, thereby providing the basis for the formulation of national military strategies by the military hierarchy. However, without the involvement of the armed forces at the decision-making table it is unclear how the NSC could play this role optimally.

Civil-Military Interface Today

Civil-military relations in India cannot be defined as turbulent or volatile, nor do they represent a system where the civilian leaders continuously push and the armed forces remain docile. Indian civil-military relations represent situations where there is a constant effort to find equilibrium through adjustments, even while the risk of a weak political leadership overreacting to tensions remains. A tense and wary relationship between the civil and military leaders will remain an avoidable consequence of the existing politico-military institutional relationship.

Two important aspects in balanced civil-military relations and effective national security planning that flows from it, are strong political direction and continued interaction and dialogue between political and military leaders. Strong political leadership results in steadfast decisions and effective direction of the armed forces. It will also effectively balance the institutional relationship between the military and civil services. In contrast, a weak political leadership will be unable to take decisions and leave defence and security-related issues undecided for years together. It also results in the political executive relying more on the civil service for its decisions. The Siachen glacier provides a useful example. The United Progressive Alliance (UPA) government had early in its first tenure, come under strong suggestions from the US to settle the Siachen glacier dispute. It was the US view that a concession on Siachen would strengthen Gen Musharraf's hands to deal with other issues affecting Pakistan. This in effect required the Indian Army to demilitarize the glacier area. The Indian Army, bearing a massive trust deficit with the Pakistan Army, balked at the idea. It insisted on Pakistan agreeing to authenticate the positions of both armies on maps before a pullout could begin. Pakistan was unwilling to do this. When faced with some informal but persistent push from the Indian political leadership, the Indian COAS made a strong public case of his reservations on a pullout from Siachen during a media interaction. This brought about a public response in favour of the army's position which in turn led to the political leadership abandoning the idea of concession to Pakistan.[13] A stable majority government led by the energetic Mr. Modi has taken charge in Delhi in 2014. Despite being viewed as sympathetic to reforms and change, the government has not indicated any sign or urgency towards implementing the key recommendations regarding the MoD.

The second aspect is the importance of continuing interaction between the political leadership, senior bureaucrats and the military both in war/ crisis as well as peacetime. The sociological, organizational and institutional divides between the politicians, bureaucrats and the armed forces are a reality. The bridging of these rests in the political leaders' domain and only effective political leadership can bring this about. This is a not a problem unique only to India. Eliot Cohen, for example, argues for the idea of an 'unequal dialogue' between political and military and leaders. 'A dialogue in which both sides expressed their views bluntly, indeed, sometimes offensively, not once but repeatedly and unequally, in which the final authority of civilian leader was unambiguous and unquestioned.'[14]

All major nations after attaining civilian control have usually undertaken reforms to enhance the effectiveness of their armed forces. This step in India has yet happened only imperfectly. No doubt there have been incremental reforms over the years, but for the most part the armed forces have been either excluded or barely consulted even on thematic issues such as strategic planning and threat assessments, international security issues, development of nuclear weapons and their delivery systems. The reforms essentially should not be directed at the civilian establishment alone but also the military establishment which require periodic reassessments and appraisals. While the civilian bureaucracy should be reformed to deal with integration of the MoD, reforms concerning the armed forces should address the issues of reorganizing, and reforming their joint operations' capacity in the era of cyber and information wars. The substantive reform measures recommended by the Group of Ministers after the Kargil campaign offer the example. One of the key recommendations of the Naresh Chandra Group was to appoint a permanent Chairman of the Chiefs of Staff Committee. This was pragmatic dilution of the longstanding clamour for a CDS. This measure would have provided the essential institutional mechanism of politico-military coordination. The three services have strongly endorsed this sensible measure. The UPA government and its RM stalled this measure. The CDS or the Chairman of the Chiefs of Staff Committee is as much a political necessity as it is a key military organizational reform. The strong political leadership of Mr. Modi should have no difficulty in forcing this issue. The second major recommendation of the Group was on integrating the MoD by cross-posting of service officers with civil servants. This is the norm in all democracies and states with large defence forces. The MoD in India has vehement objections to this since it will open up the Ministry's functioning to the user services. The issue is in the domain of the political leadership which can demand compliance if it so desires. The fact that the political executive is unwilling to exercise its authority is indicative of its opposition to reform the current suboptimal MoD system.

In the pursuit of balanced civil-military relations, such reforms would in turn make way for the principle of shared responsibility, where there is space for alterations in rules and norms as per the demands of the times. The Indian experience in the managing civil-military relationship, six decades since independence, has been marked by episodes of doubts and misgivings. That both the civil and military have struggled but found the required balance in the relationship is proof of the maturity of the Indian democratic processes. The reality of dynamic but continuing tension in this relationship is also proof of systemic shortcomings. Civil-military relations will thus never be wholly free from tensions and episodic peaks and tangles which have the potential to reach crisis levels. India's political establishment has chosen to follow an unusual paradigm in which policymaking is assigned to the bureaucracy, while strategy is crafted by diplomats, and matters impinging on grand strategy, like nuclear deterrence and ballistic missiles remain in the hands of scientists and technocrats. Uniquely amongst major powers, India has not seen it fit to entrust its armed forces with any role in national security decision-making.[15]

In the era of instant communications and 24/7 media, every household is aware of the smallest crisis and governments will be hard put to deny or obfuscate on security failures. In the age of cyber wars, international terrorism, satellite-based command systems, the need is for a government system working as a whole instead of in intellectual and procedural silos. The requirement of the new era of warfare and new threats to security is not for civilian control but for politico-military cooperation with the civil service acting as facilitating agency. There is need for a national consensus on security management as a national effort, instead of operating it as patron-client arrangement.

National Security Inertia

The causes of political and civil service unwillingness to modernize the MoD and introduce the recommendations of Expert Committees and Groups are rooted in historical, cultural and organizational beliefs of political and bureaucratic privilege or gains. This has led to actions that are self-evidently needed in national security interests being opposed or sidelined due to unfounded fears and unstated prejudices. While its deep-seated belief in civilian control over the armed forces is strong and well-founded, Indian political leadership has also not found the time or capacity to define national security aims and objectives. There has been a marked reluctance to announce national security strategy through defence white papers or national strategy documents. The political leadership has found it expedient to use the rhetoric of nationalism instead of the grammar of strategic discourse to state its position on security. It has chosen always to work the defence forces through civil service functionaries, instead of working directly with military leaders on key issues of national security. As a consequence, political leaders and civil service have given primacy to procedures over outcomes. The maze of precedents and regulations are used to mask the unwillingness to implement modern security measures. As a consequence, 'The Defence Ministry, in effect becomes the destroyer of the cutting edge of military's morale; ironic considering that the very reverse of it is their responsibility. The sword arm of the state gets blunted by the state itself.'[16]

The political executive is well aware of the serious flaws in national security apparatus and institutions. It assuages its sense of guilt and the criticism from the public, by forming expert committees and groups, tasked to find ways to improve things. The valuable recommendations of experts are however never implemented, or, at best put into effect as token actions. This in spite of Parliamentary Sub-Committees pointing out the failures of implementation of the government. The process of appointing committees of experts has in itself become a policy recourse to conveniently bypass the need for action. An important but underplayed cause of this unwillingness to change the system is of the longstanding but unfounded suspicion of the defence services attempting to get more power. A former Defence Secretary, himself a veteran military officer, has analysed the reasons for it. After listing them, he writes, 'Added to this is the constantly lurking fear of the military usurping more than the legal share of power.'[17] The limits of the military's legal powers have not been stated, but they cannot be other than what is stated in the Constitution. On the other hand, analysts have another view and one of them has written, 'While we worry that the military might stray into the civilian sphere, there is a growing sense that the balance is being damaged by civilians...they have not sufficiently involved the military in issues where military advice and involvement is proper and vital....'[18]

The Kargil Review Committee had made the telling observation on the place of defence forces in Indian democracy. It said, 'India is perhaps the only democracy where the Armed Forces Headquarters are outside the apex government structures...what we need is a National Defence HQ. Most opposition to change comes from...a reluctance to move away from considerations of parochial interest. The status quo is often mistakenly defended as embodying civilian ascendancy over the armed forces, which is not the real issue. In fact locating the service headquarters in the government will further enhance civilian supremacy.'

National security management reforms are as much a political necessity as a defence forces' need. It is clear that only the elected political executive has the power and mandate to influence, direct and enforce the institutional reforms needed in national security management, through political initiatives and consensus building. Major economic, legal, labour and civil society reforms have been undertaken in India which have led to the country being seen as a rising power and a net security stabilizer in the international arena. Threats to Indian security in the coming decades will be varied and complex. These are best handled through institutional structures which allow political–military coordination and not with the existing civil service-led MoD. A major effort will be needed to modernize the system through a new security consensus. National security reforms await the sagacity and vision of its elected political leaders.

NOTES

1. Samuel Huntington, *Soldier & the State, The Theory and Politics of Civil Military Relations*, Dehra Dun: Nataraj Publishers, 1985.
2. Andrew Cottey, Timothy Edmunds and Anthony Forster, 'The Second Generation Problematic: Rethinking Democracy and Civil Military Relations,' *Armed Forces and Society 36*, Fall 2002, 32.

3. Sir Michael Howard, *Soldiers and Governments: Nine Studies in Civil-Military Relations*, London: Eyre and Spottiswoode, 1957, 22.
4. Morris Janowitz, *The Professional Soldier: A Soldier and Political Portrait*, New York: The Free Press, 1960, p. vii-ix.
5. Objective civilian control [involves] the recognition and acceptance by [civilian leaders] of an area of professional competence and the autonomy of the military. Samuel Huntington, 'Reforming Civil-Military Relations' in Larry Diamond and Marc F Plattner, *Civil-Military Relations and Democracy*, Baltimore: Johns Hopkins University Press, October 1996.
6. Jaswant Singh, *Defending India*, London: Macmillan, 1999.
7. *Ibid.*
8. VR Raghavan, 'Strategic Culture: A Military Perspective,' in NS Sisodia and C Uday Bhaskar (ed.), *Emerging India: Security and Foreign Policy Perspectives*, New Delhi: IDSA, Promilla and Bibliophile South Asia, 2005, p. 21.
9. Sunil Dasgupta, India: The New Militaries, in Muthiah Alagappa, (ed.), *Coercion & Governance : Declining Political Role of the Military in Asia,* Stanford University Press, 2001.
10. Jaswant Singh, *op.cit.*
11. RD Pradhan, *1965 War: The Inside Story-Defence Minister Y. B. Chavan's Diary of India-Pakistan War*, New Delhi: Atlantic Publishers, 2007.
12. Kargil Review Committee, *op.cit.*
13. Author's personal interaction with top political and military leadership.
14. Eliot Cohen, *Supreme Command: Soldiers, Statesmen and Leadership in Wartime*, New York: Free Press, 2002, p.209.
15. National Security Reforms: Ten Years After the Kargil Committee Report; Admiral (Retd) Arun Prakash, *USI Journal,* October-December 2012.
16. Jaswant Singh, *Defending India,* New Delhi: Macmillan India, 1999.
17. Shekhar Datt, *India's Defence & National Security,* New Delhi: Har Anand Publishers Private Ltd, 2014. Chapter on Changing Higher Defence Organisation.
18. Kanti Bajpai, 'Re-booting India; Be Civil to the Military,' *Times of India*, 6 March 2011.

CHAPTER IX

The Role of Intelligence in Defence Preparedness

V Balachandran

Introduction

Intelligence was always used as an important instrument for anticipating, assessing, planning, and operationalizing national security situations like waging wars for expanding territorial boundaries, resisting foreign aggressions and quelling internal rebellions. Struggles to push boundaries were common before the Western World adopted the Westphalian system (1648), which indirectly came to respect territorial integrity of 'Nation States.' Intelligence in different forms was used even in pre-Biblical days. The first recorded case of intelligence used for a country's defence came from the writings of Herodotus, the fifth-century BC Greek historian. He said that the independent Greek states were saved from Xerxes' surprise attack in fifth century BC due to an advance coded alert from a Greek spy who had observed the huge mobilization by Xerxes. As a result, the Greek states were able to formulate their resistance plans in advance and also inflict a crushing defeat on the huge Persian fleet near Athens on 23 September 480 BC.[1]

Unlike military doctrines for waging regular wars which had some amount of similarity between strategies of different countries, operational philosophy of intelligence had always assumed unorthodox characters which differed from country to country and from context to context. This is because intelligence was used to confuse the enemy and penetrate their ranks from time immemorial. Also, the concept and definition of security had always varied with the rulers' policies. Caleb Carr, well-known American military historian says that the Roman Republic, which followed a policy of inclusive justice to those conquered including giving citizenship even to the slaves, had a 'profound taste for revenge against enemies' exemplified by the razing of Carthage in the third century BC. They felt that 'Punitive Wars' including massive civilian casualties were necessary for preserving their security.[2] To some extent this unorthodox definition of security prevails even now. Intelligence has to set up an unconventional architecture to implement these policies. USA feels that its security lies also in Afghanistan, Iraq, Far East or Pakistan. The former Soviet Union believed that they had to spread Communism for its security. France blew up Green Peace 'Rainbow Warrior' in 1985 since it was threatening Mururoa Atoll security. Libyan dictator Gaddafi wanted to eliminate his opponents for his security. Pakistan's ISI openly told India in a back-channel talk that it had to support terrorism in India for its security. Israel sincerely believes that it has a right to bombard Palestinian civilian houses to protect its security.

Evolution of Intelligence Organizations

Intelligence was mostly military-oriented till the early twentieth century. The concept of civilian-dominated intelligence came only in the twentieth century with England taking the lead. Allen Dulles, father of modern US intelligence says that 'in the craft of intelligence, the East was ahead of the West.' Sun Tzu wrote the first written manual of intelligence ('The Art of War') for an organized intelligence service in the fifth century BC, when the West was still employing oracles to predict future security situations. The traditional Chinese methodology of employing five types of agents ('native, inside, double, expendable and living'), resembles the modern practice of employing locals, penetration, double, and disinformation agents. Dulles says that Mao Tse-tung practised these teachings during his successful campaigns.[3] Surprisingly, Francis Dovornik in his *Origins of Intelligence Services* says that the Romans whose domination extended through Italy, Western Europe, Adriatic, Greece, the Mediterranean, and the 'Near East' did not have an organized intelligence service.[4] At the same time Egypt, Babylonia, Assyria and Persia had established intelligence services to defend their countries and to safeguard the security of their dynasties. Dulles feels this was because the Greeks (in the days of democracy) and Romans (in the days of the republic) conducted their governments 'openly, policy made more openly, and wars usually planned and mounted openly.' Julius Caesar (100 BC–44 BC) had set up an intelligence service which however did not prevent his own assassination. In the second and third centuries the Roman emperors (Hadrian onwards) utilized 'Frumentarii' (Wheat Collectors) for collecting intelligence from even among their followers.

West Europe knew very little of the East Europe during the Middle Ages due to inadequate intelligence collection. Due to faulty intelligence assessments, they also consistently weakened the Byzantium without knowing that it would have provided a bulwark against Eastern invasion. As a result they could not prepare their defence against repeated attacks from the East, first by Attila, the Hun (AD 440–AD 452) and later by Mongols (thirteenth century). 'They underestimated the Turkish threat during the period when the Ottomans were consolidating their power.'[5] The same attitude was adopted by the Church and the Kings about the East during the Middle Ages despite inflow of information through voyagers like Marco Polo and Italian merchants. Historians say that during the Crusades (1095–1291) intelligence was used for knowing the defences around Constantinople and Jerusalem.[6] The Crusades were followed by the Inquisition (1229–1826) which used their vast networks of informants to find and denounce suspected heretics and political dissidents. From 1542 onwards the Pope centralized their information network but shifted the focus to scrutinizing the actions of Europe's monarchs and prominent aristocrats.[7] Even now the Vatican is reported to have the best sources of strategic information.

Meanwhile the Italian city states were the first to establish permanent embassies abroad during the early Renaissance. Milan was the first to establish its embassy in other city states. Tuscany and Venice also set up their missions from the fourteenth century onwards. Dulles says that the envoys of Venice were 'especially adept at obtaining strategic intelligence.'[8]

In 1455 Milan sent their first representative to the French Court. Gradually this practice spread to other European countries. In 1487 Spain sent their envoy to the Court of England. By the sixteenth century this became a common practice especially after the Peace of Westphalia (1648).

The need to have separate foreign and internal intelligence arose with the rise of nationalism and religious struggles in the sixteenth and seventeenth-century Europe, especially after the adoption of the Westphalian system (1648). Henry VIII set up a large secret police under Thomas Cromwell to locate Catholic cells who threatened the English monarchy. Sir Francis Walsingham, Queen Elizabeth's Secretary of State (1530–90) excelled in the role as her spymaster. He practised all the modern techniques of intelligence like infiltration, deception, interception of mails, cryptology and crypto-analysis. His notable contribution was creating a professional intelligence system in England instead of using ill-trained volunteers or soldiers. He was perhaps the first to employ linguists, scholars, authors, engineers and scientists for collection and analysis. His major achievements were unearthing the Babington Plot to foist Mary, Queen of Scots to the English throne and collection of advance intelligence on the Spanish Grand Armada's invasion by King Phillip of Spain. The first was a penetration operation while the second was what is now called 'Third Country' operation through which he obtained intelligence from Italy which had close relations with Spain. In a way he might have set up the tradition of having civilian intelligence agencies which is practised by most countries now. In the late eighteenth and early nineteenth centuries separate organizations were set up in Europe to deal with the growing internal dissidence and the problems of external issues threatening national security.

Unlike India, America used intelligence operations during their struggle to end the colonial rule. George Washington, while leading the Continental Army, created intelligence cells to monitor the movements of British forces. In 1775 the Continental Congress created the Committee of Secret Correspondence to gather intelligence from England, Ireland and Europe to help their war of independence. In January 1790 George Washington asked for funds to finance intelligence operations. The seeds of the modern US policy of parliamentary control over intelligence agencies and the Congress controlling even secret funds were planted as early as the eighteenth century. During the American Civil War (1861–5), both the

Union and Confederate commands had their own intelligence units. The Union forces set up the first professional intelligence force by creating the Bureau of Military Intelligence in 1863. This was disbanded after the end of the Civil War. However, some elements of this Bureau were drafted in 1865 when the US Secret Service was established which now protects the US President but which was originally created for checking currency counterfeiting. The first peacetime intelligence organization was set up under the US Navy in 1882 to collect intelligence on foreign navies. In 1885 a similar organization was created under the Army. The first American president to use intelligence for strategic territory expansion purpose was Theodore Roosevelt who stirred up a 'revolution' in Panama to justify its annexation in 1903.

Intelligence Organizations in the Twentieth and Twenty-first Centuries

In 1886 the Russian Czar set up an intelligence and security service known as 'Guard Service' to control the growing labour unrest after a failed assassination attempt on Alexander II. This later became 'Okharna' under Alexander III. It had its foreign offices in Warsaw, Paris and London. However, some of their 'Penetration' operations like printing leftist literature to infiltrate such organizations boomeranged on them, which in fact spurred the leftist movement. Gradually labour unions controlled covertly by Okharna, originally set up by its chief Sergey Zubatov, which were meant to wean workers away from leftist influence, started becoming more militant. It resulted in the 'Bloody Sunday Massacre' on 22 January 1905 at St. Petersburg when troops fired upon the demonstrators killing 96 and injuring more than 300. This was an important milestone in the Russian Revolution. Another mistake done by Okharna was in promoting the Bolsheviks who were considered as relatively harmless against more militant leftists. Roman Malinovsky, their agent became a leading Bolshevik leader, winning over Lenin's confidence. However, despite such crucial agents in place, Okharna could not anticipate and prevent the 1917 (February–November) revolution. Part of the reason was that they had also to watch the German attempts of destabilizing Russia by funding the leftist revolutionaries. Okharna's headquarters was burnt down during the 1917 February revolution.

However, the 'Okharna threat' to England was taken seriously by London according to Christopher Andrew, official historian of the British domestic intelligence service who wrote *The Defence of the Realm—The authorized history of MI-5*. The German and Russian threats to England and colonies were responsible for the creation of their organized intelligence services in 1909 when Capt. Vernon Kell (South Staffordshire Regiment) and Capt. Mansfield Cummings (Royal Navy) established a 'Secret Service Bureau' (SSB). Capt. Kell (known as 'K') was in charge of counter espionage while Capt. Cummings ('C') dealt with foreign intelligence. In 1916 the SSB became part of the Military Intelligence. The internal wing was designated as MI-5 while the external arm was known as MI-6. In 1931 MI-5, later known as Security Service (SS) became independent and was placed under the Home Secretary.

William Melville, Special Branch superintendent who did some investigation work from 1903 for the Military Operations Directorate, forerunner of SSB, was partly responsible for sensitizing the British colonies about the 'Okharna' threat. Melville reported that 'Okharna' had agents 'throughout the whole world.' Rachkovsky, its chief was operating in great opulence when British intelligence was starved of funds. Rudyard Kipling fictionalized this challenge through *Kim* (1901), described to be the 'finest of all spy novels.' He popularized the expression 'The Great game' dealing with the Russian threat to India and Afghanistan although the concept might have originated through Bengal Light Cavalry intelligence officer Arthur Connoly (1807–42).

In USA the Army's G-2 looked after the intelligence functions since 1903. In 1942 the Counter-Intelligence Corps (CIC) and Naval Intelligence (ONI) performed these functions. Former Secretary of State Dean Rusk recalled in 1941 that G-2 had very little background papers in their 'Far East' section, of which he was in charge, on that vast part of the world a year after the war in Europe started. All they had were a tourist handbook on India and Ceylon, a 1924 military attaché's report from London on the Indian Army, and a drawer full of clippings from the *New York Times* collected from World War One![9]

The Pearl Harbour attack (1941) led to the setting up of the Office of the Strategic Services (OSS) under Col. Donovan, a distinguished lawyer who had seen action during World War I. OSS began as a 'Research &

Analysis Organization' as part of the Library of Congress, handpicking some of the best historians and scholars to give strategic assessments. In 1942 the name was changed into OSS when it began activities like the British Special Operations Executive (SOE) behind the enemy lines. After the War, President Truman disbanded OSS in 1945 and handed over the intelligence functions to the War & State Departments. However, the compulsions of the Cold War led to a re-thinking. A New York businessman, Ferdinand Eberstadt, was commissioned to give a draft outline for creation of a civilian intelligence agency. As a result the National Security Act was passed in 1947 creating a National Security Council (NSC) and the Central Intelligence Agency (CIA). NSC was charged with the responsibility of coordinating all intelligence work while the Central Intelligence Agency (CIA) under a Director was charged with a national intelligence mission. The National Security Agency (NSA) was created in 1952 for consolidating signals intelligence while the Defense Intelligence Agency (DIA) was launched in 1961 after the ill-fated Bay of Pigs fiasco. In the same year a National Reconnaissance Office (NRO) was started to consolidate all imagery intelligence.

Till 9/11 there was no domestic intelligence agency in America. The Federal Bureau of Investigation (FBI) under Department of Justice was looking after domestic security threats including extremism. The CIA was mainly looking after threats from abroad. The Watergate affair (1973–4) caused a serious setback to intelligence agencies, especially the CIA although the latter's role was only 'tangential involvement in Watergate primarily through the activities of former employees, and in the preparation of a psychological profile of Daniel Ellsberg,' although later revelations confirmed that the CIA had refused President Nixon's cover-up operations.[10] The media started speculating that the CIA was doing domestic intelligence. The Rockefeller Commission (1975) instituted by President Gerald Ford under Vice-President Rockefeller reported that the CIA was involved in domestic mail opening and had kept files on 3,00,000 US citizens and organizations over dissident activities. After such severe churning, CIA stabilized under President Reagan who had alleged that the Democrats had impaired intelligence efforts. The Congress also supported these efforts, despite the Iran-Contra scandal which had defamed the National Security Council and intelligence organizations.

The Gulf War (1991) under President George Herbert Walker Bush saw heightened intelligence efforts. 'Never had so much information been conveyed so quickly from intelligence systems to war fighters with such devastating effect. The accuracy of US precision-guided weapons astounded the world. The war also highlighted the need for the United States to expand its own efforts to link intelligence systems with combat systems and to train military personnel to use these systems effectively.'[11] 'The Joint Intelligence Center was established during the war with representation from the key intelligence agencies and provided a model of providing crisis support to military operations. Indeed, a permanent National Military Joint Intelligence Center was established shortly after the conflict at the Pentagon and later at all unified commands.'[12]

9/11 provided another opportunity for intelligence reforms. Intelligence Reform & Terrorism Prevention Act 2004 created a Director of National Intelligence (DNI) to 'focus, guide, and coordinate all the United States' 16 intelligence agencies to better provide timely, tailored intelligence support to a wide range of users with different, and often competing, requirements. The National Security Act sought to unify US military and foreign intelligence efforts, but it did not envision or provide for today's requirement to integrate intelligence and law enforcement.'[13] A National Counter-Terrorism Center (NCTC) was established which integrates intelligence from the 16-member national Intelligence Community (IC). They work closely with the Department of Homeland Security's (DHS) intelligence structure, created after 9/11. The pivot of this system is 72 'State Fusion Centers' to continuously update State Police and local security agencies on inputs from NCTC. The CIA, in addition to using human and technical intelligence also deploys their secret Special Operations Group (SOG) to hunt down overseas terrorists manually or by using UAV predators. The exact number of the people killed during the drone strikes is not known. A Chatham House paper of 2013 has put the figure between 2967 and 4533 in Pakistan, Yemen and Somalia through 405 strikes during 2004–12.[14]

In England the three national intelligence agencies (Secret Intelligence Service or SIS known as MI-6, Security Service or SS, called MI-5 and Government Communications HQ or GCHQ, Communications Intelligence organization) underwent reforms towards the close of the twentieth century. The Security Service Act of 1989 (SS), The Intelligence Services Act of 1994 (SIS and GCHQ) and The Regulation of Investigative Powers Act of 2000 gave legal founding to these organizations. The Anti-Terrorism, Crime & Security Act 2001 passed after 9/11 further amended the laws governing these organizations prescribing their charter, accountability, supervision and parliamentary control.

India

There are two versions on the origin of our Intelligence Bureau. One is that the 'Thughee Department' of Col. (later General) William Sleeman, which was set up in Jubbulpore in 1829 with 7 assistants and 300 Nujeebs (soldiers) to hunt down and prosecute Thugs was, after the suppression of Thughee in 1848, merged with the British Indian Government's Intelligence agency. During this period Sleeman had launched prosecution against 4,500 Thugs of whom 504 were hanged, more than 3,000 given life sentence and only 250 acquitted. Mike Dash, eminent British historian says: 'The department thus survived for a further half a century, being abolished, with the empire itself, only in 1947. As late as the latter years of the Second World War, the Government of India's intelligence agency—then based at Simla—was popularly known as the *Thagi Daftar*: The Thug office.'[15]

The other story is that the intelligence department founded by Sir Charles Metcalf MacGregor, Quarter Master General of the British Indian Army located in Simla after the Second Afghan War (1878–80), became the Intelligence Bureau (IB) after 1947. In 1909 an Indian Political Intelligence (IPI) office was opened in London to watch the growing freedom movement in India. IPI used to control the Indian IB. Chritopher Andrew, the official historian of Security Service (MI-5) says: 'During the 1920s the Service's most active imperial liaison had been with the Delhi Intelligence Bureau (DIB or IB), whose diminutive London office, Indian Political Intelligence (IPI), was situated inside MI-5's headquarters.'[16]

The late BN Mullik, father of Indian intelligence says:

> Prior to 1947 the Intelligence Bureau worked purely in the field of internal intelligence; foreign intelligence was looked after by the British from London. Even in the internal field the IB mostly worked in the

> field of collation, assessment and dissemination and did little work in the field of collecting intelligence, which was the most difficult process. For this the IB depended almost entirely on the State Special Branches. Hence the IB staff at headquarters and at State capitals was very limited and composed mostly of police officers with previous Special Branch experience. And the top posts in intelligence, either in the Centre or the states, were held mostly by the Britishers because few Indians could be trusted; and so few Indians had any experience in the higher fields of intelligence. [17]

The 1962 China War underlined the need for a separate foreign intelligence agency and hence an organization known as 'Research & Analysis Wing' of the Cabinet Secretariat was created in 1968. A Joint Intelligence Committee (JIC) was functioning in the Cabinet Secretariat even before our independence on the same lines as its counterpart in England. However, with the creation of our National Security Council in 1998 this was merged with the National Security Council Secretariat. After the Kargil War (1999) a Defence Intelligence Agency (DIA) was set up.

Thus we have a textbook situation in which all intelligence agencies are in place. One of the unique features of the Indian system of intelligence is that very little is known officially on their working. No law exists on their charter. Codification of their activities would have given protection to their intelligence operations and ensured better accountability. The present CBI case of IB officers being 'involved' in the 2004 Ishrat Jahan fake encounter case during an intelligence operation could have been better handled and their activities could have been examined in the background of that special law. However, in the absence of any such law the IB's charter was left vague resulting in different interpretations. We still believe in a policy of needless secrecy which has been abandoned by almost all other democracies including even the newly independent countries like South Africa, which have codified the creation and working of their intelligence agencies. The National Strategic Intelligence Act (1994) gave the mandate for the new intelligence setup while The Intelligence Services Act (1994) created the National Intelligence Agency (NIA) for domestic intelligence and South African Secret Service (SASS) for external intelligence, which included external military intelligence too. The NIA and SASS were formed on 1 January 1995 merging the four separate agencies of the Apartheid era.

Impression of 'Intelligence Failures'

Intelligence is knowledge or foreknowledge of events around us to enable policymakers take adequate and timely decisions. Intelligence is not mere collection of information. It is a long and often tedious process of bare facts becoming policy inputs and ground action through an alchemic process—collection of facts, analysis, evaluation, assessment and dissemination to the consumers by the agencies, then arbitration by a higher body like National Security Council to plug gaps in intelligence, reporting to the policymakers (Cabinet), policy adjudication by the Cabinet, policy implementation by different ministries, review and accountability at the end. This is called the 'Intelligence Cycle.' If any one of these steps is missed an impression arises about 'Intelligence Failure.'

However, not all intelligence undergoes such transformation. At the district or state level bare facts are presented by the district or state intelligence organizations leaving the onus of assessment to the senior officials on labour agitation, communal riots, or agrarian crisis. These are 'law and order-oriented intelligence' of short duration, but time-sensitive. In all such cases the political masters expect intelligence agencies to compete with news agencies in delivering information. This is not possible while assessing strategic intelligence.

Intelligence is of two types—'current intelligence' (what happens around us) and 'estimative intelligence' (what is likely to happen). Both current and estimative intelligence can be 'strategic' (long-term, affecting the country as a whole) or 'tactical' (limited and short-term, both in time and area). Estimative intelligence is like a jigsaw puzzle and often difficult as inputs or trends might come from different sources, thereby testing the competence of the analysts to piece them together to form the picture on a strategic canvas.

Open and clandestine sources feed intelligence. It is often found that 90 per cent of what we need to know, even military intelligence is available openly if one cares to read. But it is the secret 10 per cent that has to be dug out by intelligence agencies through clandestine operations which is crucial to plug the missing gaps. Open sources are media including technical journals, diplomatic contacts, trade, war games and air shows while clandestine sources are HUMINT (spies), SIGINT (signal intelligence), IMINT (imagery intelligence) and MASINT (measurement and signature intelligence).

National intelligence agencies are usually divided into 'Production' and 'analysis' divisions. Production desks are field officials and their supervisors who run agents. On special occasions even outsiders are enlisted into field intelligence work. Technical divisions assist production desks by obtaining technical intelligence. Analysts who are expected to be area specialists anatomize this 'raw' intelligence and conceptualize a 'big' picture for policymakers. Scientists, economists, code breakers and military specialists assist this analysis.

Intelligence Cycle

Security intelligence is collected on a parallel track by major central agencies including military intelligence, not to speak of the Customs, Enforcement Directorate, State Police and paramilitary outfits. Till 9/11 most countries used to collect intelligence on a parallel track without anybody taking a holistic view. Information available with any odd organization would assume importance and become actionable only if conveyed immediately to the concerned 'action' department for further action. Also, the service receiving the information has to initiate prompt action. The US National Commission, which enquired into 9/11 incidents, found such failures on the part of CIA and FBI. Sometimes absence of vertical or horizontal dialogue even within an organization leads to failure in taking cognizance of inputs as seen with FBI which ignored the Phoenix and Williams Alert Memos of July 2001 from field stations about 9/11 terrorists. The US National Commission on 9/11 (Kean-Hamilton) said: 'The most important failure was imagination. We do not believe leaders understood the gravity of the threat.' But in common parlance, all these are treated as 'Intelligence Failures.'

The process of 'Stitching the Seams' of intelligence inputs is known as 'Intelligence coordination,' which is sometimes mistaken for 'Intelligence arbitration.' Intelligence coordination is merely placing together intelligence collected by different agencies for reporting to policymakers. A higher responsibility is 'Intelligence arbitration' wherein the arbitrator coordinates, asks questions, directs the intelligence agencies to fill in the gaps, tries to evolve a total picture for the highest policymakers and monitors implementation. We have two models of such work in India. The late RN Kao as Senior Security Adviser to Indira Gandhi had initiated a system of weekly meetings of Central Agencies to pool intelligence. However, this was given up after he demitted office in 1985. A second practice was started by PC Chidambaram, former Minister of State, Internal Security, in the wake of the 2 October 1986 Rajghat shooting incident to integrate intelligence on the Prime Minister's (PM's) security. In 1998 our National Security Council in India was created, which among other roles, was to be the Intelligence arbitrator since JIC was incorporated within it.

Intelligence coordination and arbitration are daunting tasks not merely because of the difficulties in nudging different agencies to cooperate. The Kean-Hamilton Commission found nine instances of serious negligence in regard to advance action to prevent 9/11 of which seven were failures in intelligence integration. The Kargil Review Committee also had referred to the lack of interagency coordination. How does one deal with this? Our three-tiered National Security Council (NSC) with its Secretariat (former Joint Intelligence Committee) which was set up in November 1998 was meant to be an expert body to function as a think tank, intelligence arbitrator, policy adjudicator, decision-maker and performance monitor. In fact this writer had, through an article in *The Times of India* (1 April 1998), warned that the proposed NSC would become dysfunctional unless we enacted a law on its role. Otherwise 'we may create yet another organization which will waste the taxpayers' money.'[18]

Unfortunately this is exactly what happened. The NSC could neither integrate intelligence nor give strategic advice to the Cabinet on the Kargil War since it met only on 8 June 1999, a month after the Pakistani incursion was noticed.

Case Studies of some Serious Security Situations[19]

In making the following observations, I am merely giving my assessments on the intelligence process and its integration for policymaking, and not on the military measures, or on the historical aspects of the situations:

1962 Indo-China War

A common impression persists even now that intelligence had failed before the hostilities. Two reasons are responsible for this. First, the statement of the then Defence Minister, the late YB Chavan in Parliament on 2 September 1963 giving a summary of the Henderson Brooks Report (HB) led to an impression that intelligence had failed. What many people have not realized was that Chavan's statement was merely on the military intelligence and not on the Intelligence Bureau's (IB) intelligence reports. This was made clear as early as 1970 by the late K Subrahmanyam who wrote a review of Neville Maxwell's book *India's China War* for *Hindustan Times*.[20] On the other hand the book *My Years with Nehru—1948-1964* by the late BN Mullik who was then the Director, IB states that the Bureau had reported the following Chinese steps:

(a) May 1962: 7 divisions of PLA on Northern border
(b) June 1962: 'Aggressive designs' –May happen in September/October
(c) August 1962: Enemy moved troops from rear bases to the border, built new roads, reserves and doing propaganda
(d) September 1962: 8 divisions on border. Could also move 4 more divisions from Lhasa, Shigatse, Chamdo, Nagchuka, etc., at short notice.
(e) Propaganda in Tsona area opposite Kameng on Tibetan and NEFA tribesmen: China 'would drive away' Indians who had 'occupied' Chinese territories.
(f) 8 September 1962: China occupied Thagla Ridge-Nayamkachu River, surrounded the Dhola post of Assam Rifles.[21]

The second reason for this impression was due to the leak of HB report to Neville Maxwell who incorporated some portions in his book, especially the proceedings of a meeting convened by Prime Minister Nehru on 2 November 1961 to discuss India's 'Forward Policy,' wherein the Director, Intelligence Bureau was reported to have assessed that the 'Chinese would not react.' But the HB report had clearly stated that they had not seen the original record of this PM's meeting and had gone by the Army's version. As a matter of fact the terms of reference of HB dated 14 December 1962 excluded any Cabinet Office files and not even the office of the Chief of the Army staff from their enquiry. They had said: 'In this process, a number of loose ends concerning Army HQ could not be verified and have been left unanswered. The relationship between the Defence Ministry and Army HQ and the directions given by the former to the latter could, therefore also not be examined.'

On the other hand, the late Mullik had given this version in his book on this meeting: 'Unless all the vacant spaces on our side of the frontier were occupied by Indian troops or police there was every danger of the Chinese surreptitiously coming and occupying them.' He added that our 'Forward Policy' was likely to bring us into conflict with the Chinese.[22]

The late K Subrahmanyam supports this possibility in his above quoted piece: 'But the intelligence reported by the IB was consistently played down by the Army Headquarters. PVR Rao who was defence secretary from November 1962 to January 1967 and therefore had intimate knowledge of both 1962 and 1965 operations has categorically stated in his book *Defence without Drift* that the allegation that in 1962 and 1965 operations intelligence failed was a canard.'[23]

In fact a similar thing had happened in the Yom Kippur war (first phase) during 6-25 October 1973 in which the combined Egyptian-Syrian forces launched a surprise attack on an unprepared Israel destroying 102 Israeli aircraft and killing 2,812 Israeli soldiers on the holiest day of Judaism. It led to the resignation of Prime Minister Golda Meir and Defence Minister Moshe Dayan. Mossad had repeatedly warned of the impending attack which was rejected by the then Defence Intelligence Chief Gen Eli Zeira. A commission headed by the then Chief Justice of the Supreme Court Shimon Agranat had found fault with the processing of intelligence and the mindset of Gen Zeira. As *The Times of Israel* remarked as late as 1 November 2013: 'Zeira, long considered the face of Israeli hubris on account of his refusal to accept that Egypt and Syria might dare wage war on Israel, told the commission on 27 November 1973, during his first hearing, that the IDF's 'Military Intelligence Directorate made a mistake in its estimation regarding war. That's a given... Zeira's certainty about Egypt's intentions, and the way it shaded his interpretation of the facts on the ground, has led a generation of intelligence officers to read and study the Agranat Commission's report as a cautionary tale.'[24]

Unfortunately, our military officers have had no chance to read the Henderson Brooks Report and learn from the mistakes since the Government of India has refused to release it.

1999 Kargil Attack

The Kargil Attack by Pakistan (February-April 1999 to July 26 1999) is yet another instance of 'Intelligence failure' in popular parlance. However, the Kargil Review Committee[25] led by the late K Subrahmanyam (KRC) had acknowledged that 127 intelligence reports were received since August 1997 of which 45 were important alerts provided by RAW (11), IB (9), Brigade Intelligence Team (8), BSF (2) Intelligence & Field Security Unit (2), etc. The KRC had mentioned that intelligence was neither coordinated nor arbitrated since several alerts were not shared and no action to fill in the gaps was taken to get an overall picture. For example, RAW had reported in September 1998 about the assembly of intruders in Gultari but neither the Army, nor JIC thought of asking ARC to do an aerial survey to get an overall picture between October 1998 and May 1999. RAW also did not think it necessary to ask ARC to do that. The Commission had faulted the JIC process in not pressing the constituents for more information. For example, in a National Security Council Secretariat (NSCS) meeting on 14 May 1999, BSF and IB reported that 300 intruders had infiltrated while Director General of Military Intelligence (DGMI) and RAW had no information. No attempts were made by NSCS to task the other agencies for getting more information. In their conclusions the KRC remarked, echoing the 9/11 US National Commission on 9/11 attacks: 'Pakistani intrusion in Kargil Sector came as a complete and total surprise to Indian Government, Army, International agencies and J&K Government....There is no mechanism for tasking the agencies, monitoring their performance and reviewing their records to evaluate their quality.... There are no checks and balances in the Indian intelligence system...No system of regular, periodic and comprehensive briefings at political level or COS". (COS-Committee of Secretaries)

This writer had published two pieces in *The Times of India* on 15 July 1999 and 21 September 2000 on what had gone wrong with our system of intelligence assessment and integration even after creating our National Security Council. My piece of 15 July 1999 had started like this: 'In the din of conflicting sound bytes after the Kargil aggression, a fact largely overlooked is the apparent sidelining of the National Security Council, which could meet only on 8 June 1999, a month after the incursion was formally noticed. Evidently, the Indian bureaucratic system has once again managed to devitalize an institution, which was set up with great fanfare to anticipate and manage such crisis.'[26]

Conclusion

(a) History reveals that Intelligence organizations working on parallel tracks cannot guarantee national security and defence preparedness unless there is a high-powered coordinator to tie up the loose ends to prevent clues from 'slipping between the cracks.'

(b) Despite setting up a high-profile National Security Council with a big secretariat, India has not been able to do satisfactory intelligence integration to anticipate security threats.

NOTES

1. Simon Singh, *The Code Book*, Fourth Estate, London, pp. 4-5.
2. Caleb Carr, *The Lessons of Terror*, Little Brown, London, pp. 18-19.
3. Allen Dulles, *The Craft of Intelligence*, West view Press, Boulder & London, pp. 13-14.
4. Chapter 'Intelligence in the Roman Empire,' in a rare book reproduced by the Virginia Military Institute (www.vmc.edu).
5. Allen Dulles, op. cit., p. 17.
6. *Encyclopedia of Espionage, Intelligence, and Security*-Vol. 1, p. 418.
7. Ibid.
8. Allen Dulles, op. cit., p. 17.
9. *Commission on the roles and capabilities of the United States Intelligence Community-1995*, (Harold Brown Report), Appendix A, p. A-5.
10. Ibid., p. A-15.
11. Ibid., p. A-23.
12. Ibid.
13. Mike McConnell, *Foreign Affairs*, July-August 2007.
14. http://www.chathamhouse.org/sites/files/chathamhouse/public/International%20Affairs/2013/89_1/89_1Boyle.pdf0
15. Mike Dash, *Thug: The true story of India's Murderous Cult*, Granta, 2005, p. 253.
16. Christopher Andrew, *The Defence of the Realm—The Authorized History of MI-5*, p. 137.
17. BN Mullik, *My years with Nehru 1948-1963*, Allied Publishers, New Delhi, 1972, p. 208.
18. V Balachandran: 'A defunct Defence: Toothless NSC will not do,' *The Times of India*, 1 April 1998.
19. I had given a lecture at the Centre for Police Research, Pune on 20 April 2013. There were about 9 so-called instances of 'Intelligence failures' in history beginning with the

1941 Pearl Harbour Attack to the 26/11 terror attacks on Mumbai in 2008 and I had argued that in all such cases advance intelligence was available but could not be converted into policy and action due to the failure of institutional infrastructure.

20. K Subrahmanyam, 'Neville Maxwell's War,' Book review, *Hindustan Times,* 18-25 October 1970.
21. BN Mullik op.cit., Chapter 17 and 24.
22. Ibid, p. 215.
23. Ibid.
24. 'New Yom Kippur War testimony details the failures,' *The Times of Israel,* 1 November 2013.
25. 'From Surprise to Reckoning,' *Kargil Review Committee Report,* 15 December 1999.
26. V Balachandran: 'No strategic Canvas: Undermining the National Security Council,' *The Times of India,* 15 July 1999 and 'Intelligible Intelligence: An alchemy of Collation and Coordination,' *The Times of India,* 21 September, 2000). Also see: *Intelligence Management—A new Paradigm,* Indus Source Books, Mumbai 2014.

III. CAPABILITIES

CHAPTER X

Future of Defence Technology and India's Priorities for Self-Reliance

Amitav Mallik

Backdrop

India, with its long history of dominance by foreign rulers was exposed to many a weakness as it became an independent nation in 1947. It was very natural for such a nation to first concentrate on human development and infrastructure-building. Paradoxically, the war with China in 1962, although humiliating, was a blessing in disguise for India that became acutely aware of the need for robust capabilities for defence and security. In the five decades since then, India has made impressive progress and is now recognized as an emerging world-class democratic power with its own techno-military capacities. This has been possible because of India's clear focus on 'Self-Reliance' (SR) on all issues of critical importance to India's national security including defence, economic progress and societal stability.

This has been achieved despite the geo-political reality of hostile neighbours on both sides with a history of boundary disputes, and also an unfriendly attitude of the advanced group of Western nations that would have preferred to see India as a subservient ally and not as an independent leader of the developing countries' group. India therefore faced serious technology denials and export restrictions that were politically motivated during the ensuing Cold War between the two superpowers. The story of India's many struggles through the decades of difficulties to the present status of imminent third largest economy with its own strengths in technology and human capital is a history that India can be proud of.

Yet there is a feeling that India could have done more, particularly in SR in defence technology and systems, where India continues to depend heavily on imports and thus has become the world's largest buyer of defence equipment. It would indeed be ideal if India could become self-reliant for every need of the defence forces down to every sub-system and component of defence equipment. But in today's fast globalizing world, there is a need for realistic introspection and a revised understanding of 'Self-Reliance.' Avoiding dependence on imports for critical defence technologies that could be denied in times of conflict, is clearly the first priority for SR because such vulnerability is not acceptable for any powerful independent nation. Hence India's focus has been on areas such as missile systems, electronic warfare, avionics, C^3ISR (*Command, Control, Communication, Intelligence Surveillance & Reconnaissance*) systems and ICT (*Information-Communication Technology*) advances, etc. This is besides the indigenous capability in space technology, cyber warfare and in nuclear technologies. The success story of India in short five decades, needs no elaboration.

However, there is one area of high dissatisfaction within the Indian armed forces, particularly the Army, about indigenous defence technology and production capabilities not meeting the defence requirements on time and within projected cost. While this is indeed a problem that requires to be addressed seriously, there is also a need for understanding the rapidly changing perceptions of defence and security in the modern globalizing world and examining the priorities for SR in the future. In a world that is getting increasingly integrated and inter-dependent, the threat of all-out war involving large armies and conventional equipment is fast receding. Armed forces the world over are getting leaner and sharper with higher focus on technology capability. It is in this context that India needs to re-evaluate the SR priorities for the future. This paper presents some thoughts on such a realignment of SR for the country.

Defence Technology in India—Looking Back

Starting from scratch on 26 January 1951, the Indian Republic has made many impressive advances in short six decades. Since the economic liberalization in 1991 India has achieved very promising results in technology and economy, seeds for which were sown during the first few decades of the young nation. The country produced superior calibre of software engineers at the turn of the century, earning for the first time an identity of a technological power in the world. The world also saw the historic unveiling of project 'Shakti' on 11 May 1998 at Pokhran which caused sharp international reaction at first but eventually gained grudging acquiescence and even some respect over time. Indigenous missile technology strides have created the much needed deterrence capacity in the nuclear neighbourhood and space technology advances have provided not only many modern technology advantages to Indian people, but also the backbone for defence and security in space for the nation. The indigenous Prithvi-Agni series of missiles, the Brahmos supersonic cruise missile, successful missile defence tests, the 'GLSV' launch vehicle, Indian Air Force acceptance of LCA and many such first-time successes in cutting-edge technology have added to the global recognition of India as a potential advanced technological power of the future.

However, sixty-five years after gaining independence, India continues to struggle with a rather paradoxical situation, where a few pockets of excellence create cheer in the midst of overall hollowness in several areas due to the short-sightedness and un-professionalism of its educated elite class of people who wield power and influence. And yet these very people do exceedingly well once they are outside India. There must be something wrong in the way we in India perceive patriotism and professionalism when it comes to long-term important issues like technology and security. A closer examination can show that the reason can be found in the marginalization of the institutions for the benefit of individual ambitions and even greed. While some compulsions of coalition politics are perhaps understandable, bureaucratic delays and absence of accountability for inaction have led to major hurdles in implementations of good plans and projects which often remain on paper without action. These cause a major loss to the nation while politicians and those in power multiply their assets manifold every five years.

India, with a long history of technology denials by the Western alliance of advanced countries has always been keen to achieve a high degree of Self-Reliance in Defence Technology. The SR Index is often defined as the ratio of the expenditure on the indigenous part of the defence procurement to the total expenditure on all defence acquisitions in a financial year. Measured by such yardsticks, the SR in Defence often rates very poorly at about 30 per cent where the balance 70 per cent needs for conventional arms and equipment come from imports. Imports continue to be the preferred choice of the user Services. Indigenous research and development (R&D) and production agencies have difficulty in competing with the global defence industry because indigenous defence technology lacks the historical technology depth as also the scale advantage of the global leaders. This often leads to failure in winning the cost-time-performance race with global competitors.

The SR in conventional defence systems can be much higher if the user Services show genuine commitment to indigenous options and engage with the R&D and production community in the country. This has indeed happened in many cases with the Navy and the Air Force, but the traditional Army has been rather reluctant to participate in the pursuit of self-reliance, preferring to import the majority of its modernization requirements. The Defence R&D results are often very promising but productionizing the R&D success into systems and equipment acceptable to user Services becomes formidable because user acceptance tests are often mired in a mindset that aspires only for foreign-made systems.

It would be prudent to acknowledge that advanced countries selling their technology and defence products will always protect their 'Know-How' and offer yesterday's technology at tomorrow's prices. Strangely, this often seems to be acceptable to the user Services who risk ending up getting low-grade products from top-class suppliers. The buyer (India) also ends up paying for the R&D cost amortized by the seller country.

An exception to the above scene is that the areas of critical technologies for defence and security technologies are fiercely protected under one or the other technology control regimes. In almost all such areas India has made tremendous progress despite all hurdles. This is where 'Self-Reliance' really matters the most and the world has come to applaud India for the intelligent choice in utilizing its limited budgets for its security. In the area of conventional arms and equipment, the drive for SR has failed to catch momentum since the early days of import substitution, mainly because imported options from glossy magazines are always more attractive and available. This is not to say that SR in conventional defence systems is not important or to absolve the inefficiencies or often dismal performance of Defence R&D or Production agencies in the country. But one must recognize the reality that SR in conventional arms and equipment can happen only if all stakeholders including user Services are genuinely committed to SR in this part of the defence modernization.

Fortunately, forces of globalization are changing the very definition of SR and now investing resources and time in creating indigenous options for what the country can afford to buy competitively from overseas, may no longer be a wise decision. Now the focus of SR in Defence technology must change to developing technology maturity in emerging advanced technology areas to become a smart buyer who can always get the best value for its money. This is indeed what the science and technology base in the country has achieved today for India, opening up new potential for trade and commerce across a wider spectrum of dual-use technologies including defence and space sectors. For India the 'buy options' for several latest technology equipment are much wider today mainly because of the technology maturity acquired within the country which has changed the image of India from being a target country for technology denials to a progressive country worthy of international partnership in pursuit of many high-tech endeavours.

The focus of SR thus has been on critical technology and products that cannot be imported and as already discussed, India has done fairly well on that count. Besides these absolute sensitive technologies where India has achieved recognized independent capabilities, in many other dual-use areas India has now chosen the option of 'Buy & Make' which would allow indigenous industry to benefit from all defence acquisition exchanges through the 'off-set' programmes to build new capacities for rapidly catching up with contemporary technology and systems. Here again, overall SR performance can improve only with a higher level of professionalism across developers, producers and users. With changing perceptions of security and defence the choices for most desired technology are changing fast and hence there is a need to realign the older perceptions of SR for routine military guns and platforms.

Now with a majority Government in power at the Centre, which is committed to decisiveness, efficient governance and rapid progress, India can look forward to a bright future in Defence technology with higher level of self-reliance in areas where it matters most. With positive leadership, one can also expect sharp improvement in professionalism across disciplines, and enhanced performance of the nation as a whole.

Changing Perceptions of National Security

Concepts of 'Defence and Deterrence' are going through a paradigm shift in response to forces of globalization and interdependence. As the line between the military and civil technologies gets thinner, diffusion of dual-use including military technology is becoming unavoidable. Shared concerns of global problems such as—asymmetric violence of terrorism, possibility of use of biological or radiological agents by terrorists, crippling energy shortages, non-reversible environmental degradation—these are creating major shifts in security perceptions of nations and societies.

Thanks to new technology options for deterrence via coercion to prevent war, and prohibitive cost of war, the threat of full-scale war between states has reduced significantly. Changing security perceptions are now shifting emphasis to protecting national assets, national interests and human well-being. Major threat perceptions are now dominated by religious fundamentalism, economic disparities and competition for techno-economic superiority. Long-term threats include issues of energy shortages and concerns of inevitable climate changes that will impact the economy and security of nations in the future.

Traditional threat perceptions in respect of weapons of mass destruction (WMD) proliferation and regional territorial conflicts going out of reach of negotiation still remain relevant in many parts of the world. With technology evolving continuously, controlling proliferation of sensitive high technology from reaching wrong hands will pose serious challenges. Present strategic security concerns include implications of Missile Defence shields, increasing militarization of outer space, and possible misuse of advance dual-use technologies for unfair or dangerous designs.

Easier access to high technology for the rogue-state or non-state actors is also emerging as a major common security concern. Real and present dangers are now perceived from common enemies of global peace and stability such as Islamic fundamentalists, organized crime and international drug-trafficking networks. Technological advances have made it possible for non-state groups to use the same tools to enhance their capabilities that States use for security and defence. As modern society gets increasingly dependent on sophisticated technology, the perceptions of vulnerabilities also grow exponentially and information flow and control is emerging as the new currency of power. Cyber security will be a major challenge as it impacts vulnerability of societies. Future threats are perceived more from 'Weapons of Mass Disruption'—the new class of WMD.

Technology sophistication has enhanced the capacity of an individual to cause greater damage to societies or nations. Intentions now dominate 'Threat Perception' much more than capabilities. Peace-loving societies and nations will have to build wider and deeper cooperation to combat common threats and address common concerns. These new types of dangers can include pandemics spreading across continents, computer viruses paralyzing global nodes of communication and control, climate change impacts creating unprecedented refugee movements across national boundaries, etc. These represent real threat scenarios where conventional military might may be of little relevance.

In the changing patterns of new concerns and asymmetric threats, nations will have to gear up for a complex security environment with diffuse threats. This is a more serious matter for India with its open, diverse society that is on a rapid growth curve with major goals to be achieved in demanding timeframes. Any derailment will be devastating for India.

Emerging Technology Trends and Security Implications

Cruise missile technology has become extremely reliable and lethal while it is also becoming more cost-effective than ballistic missiles and increasingly accessible. This is a major threat for future conventional conflicts. Major improvements can be expected in its range, accuracy and weapon delivery flexibilities. Unmanned Aerial Vehicle (UAV) is now far more versatile with satellite-based control and robotics-assisted combat missions. Extended range and accuracy of these combat drones provide a very low-cost option for precision attack on specific small targets such as a group of terrorists. The technology, however, can be very useful against enemy strategic targets in times of war.

Advances in technology and easier access to dual-use modern technologies have added new complexities where the traditional nuclear-missile deterrence may no longer work for the full spectrum of threats. As already noted, globalization and economic interdependence has reduced the threat of major wars, except for specific conflict-prone zones in developing regions. Propagation of democratic values and human freedom has further sharpened the focus on human security. The integrating forces of information and communication technology (ICT) have increased interconnectivity and mutual awareness among nations.

However, several regional tensions continue to simmer, fuelling the race for techno-military superiority. In the backdrop of such international security dynamics, India today faces many complex and interdependent challenges in protecting its national interests. India also has to push ahead with its momentum in techno-economic progress, without which its national security as well as the foreign policy priorities could get seriously compromised.

Internationally, ICT is proving to be a double-edged sword—extremely useful in all walks of life and yet very difficult to control its misuse by anti-social elements. Commercial and security interests are often in conflict due to the very nature of the Internet and open dual-use applications. Nano-Technology and Bionics are ready to usher in a new generation of sensors, controllers, miniaturized systems with 'Cognitive Intelligence' to create fiction-like autonomous capabilities. On the one hand, these can greatly enhance the capabilities of a single soldier, while on the other hand this can also make foot soldiers redundant to a large extent!

Control of outer space and space defence capabilities are becoming increasingly important for all space-faring nations and all modern military strategists. As dependence on space systems continue to grow the vulnerabilities also grow steeply and the counter-space technology race will get pretty fierce among leading nations. 'Directed Energy Weapons' (DEW) with instant speed-of-light velocity targeting capability and space-based smart systems with built-in redundancies when under attack, may decide the power balance equations for the twenty-first century.

Given the diffuse and asymmetrical nature of future threat, advanced nations will have to form a consortium for cooperative security while at the same time engaging in serious economic competition for progress and power. This becomes the new age of 'Co-Optition'—a term being used to define cooperation and competition co-existing among same nations.

Energy competition and growing dangers of climate change due to global warming will probably dictate the security and survival issues in the future when Nature's fury may threaten to annihilate the human race irrespective of the colour of the skin or riches. The increasing gap between 'Haves and Have-Nots' may create such tensions that can compromise most of human aspirations for progress and peace. Technologies and strategies required for dealing with such unprecedented threats will be very different from the tanks or guns of today. Globalization is an inevitable force of change, erasing boundary lines not just between countries but between industries as well. It suggests a borderless world in which China could make Apple iPhones or the leading US auto export could be a German BMW made in South Korea.

Globalization also blurs boundaries between defence and commercial industries, vastly diluting the sources of technological innovation and placing them well beyond the control of any individual government or entity. Google's recent acquisition of Boston Dynamics, a DARPA-funded Organization that develops some of the world's most innovative robots, is an example that served Pentagon an unsettling notice.

Cyber crime and attacks, proliferating weapons of mass destruction, black market in the arms trade, sophisticated smuggling methods and a range of other capabilities provide unparalleled power and influence to illegitimate regimes, crime syndicates and super-empowered individuals.

In the years to come, the convergence of emerging trends in the technological, geopolitical and business environments threatens to profoundly disrupt the global defence industry. These trends are pulling governments and the industries that support them in multiple directions to an extent that calls into question the underlying strategic basis of military technological advantage.

Redefining SR in Defence and Security

Technologies that are critical to the existing requirements for Defence include:

1. Microwave and mm wave Intg. Circuits
2. Fly-By-Wire Flight Control technology
3. Advanced Gas Turbine Engines
4. Ram Rocket and Hypervelocity missiles
5. Atmospheric Re-entry technology
6. Infra-Red Search and Track technology
7. Advanced Inertial Nav Systems
9. Smart Materials and Structures
10. Advanced Unmanned Systems
11. Artificial Intelligence and Robotics
12. Encryption and Cyber Security technology
13. Sat defence & Counter-space technology

Technologies that would be vital for new capabilities for Defence and Security may include:

a) Smart Weapon sub-systems
b) Sensors and Active Arrays
c) Intelligent Terminal Guidance
d) Supersonic and Hypersonic Propulsion
e) Satellite based Comm. & Intell.
f) Advanced Radars and Stealth detection
g) Ceramics and Metal Matrix Comp.
h) Advanced VLSI Devices and ASICs
i) Photonics and Integrated Optics
j) High-Power Lasers and Microwaves
k) Software and Info System Tech.
l) Renewable Energy Technology

SR in these technologies can be achieved only when indigenous know-how and competence is backed with in-country availability of all critical materials and components as well as the necessary integration and test facilities for some of these highly complex advanced systems.

In the complex matrix of achieving SR, the role of Defence R&D is clearly to provide the 'critical technologies' for Defence needs and to build the 'core competence' for enriching the technology base in the country. An effective long-term 'SR Implementation Plan' therefore must advocate selective investments in 'critical technologies' that would help realize the SR objectives specific to the nation's needs, both in the short term and the long term.

The long-term SR Plan for Defence Systems would thus require that while the relative benchmarking for technology maturity gets enhanced at the various R&D labs and production centres as an evolutionary process, there should be a renewed focus on creating 'core competence' in new and revolutionary technology areas as well.

For a futuristic SR Policy Defence R&D must concentrate only on futuristic enabling technologies, much like the DARPA model and take Industry partners for 'Co-Innovation.' Routine production, performance upgrades and Test and Evaluation (T&E) activities for user acceptance should be coordinated by Defence PSU and MOD with close coordination with Defence services.

High degree of SR in defence technology and equipment has been a very critical issue for India in the past. Initial emphasis was on 'Export Substitution' and 'Licensed Production' of equipment, sub-systems and components for priority defence systems. Major programmes were initiated to build indigenous technology and systems that were under strict denials. India has done well to achieve success in most such initiatives. SR in technologies of high impact for defence and security will always remain a defining aspect of 'Techno-Economic' superiority of a nation over its adversaries.

With major changes in security perceptions and international interdependence, SR in conventional defence systems and equipment, while important, will not be the real game changer in future. India is no longer a target for technology denial/export controls because India has demonstrated convincing technology maturity in key areas of defence and security. Security perceptions have changed to new types of threat and new domains of threat. Conventional war can no longer achieve the desired politico-military gains for even the powerful nations. In the new emerging scene, information is getting more powerful and resources are getting more scarce. Future conflicts will therefore likely be resolved by balance of 'Comprehensive National Power' equations.

Missile Defence and Security of Outer Space—Issues and Concerns

Unique advantages of speed, range, accuracy and assured strike has made ballistic missiles with nuclear weapons the ultimate deterrence. At the same time, technology advances for higher accuracy, reliability and lethality have made missiles more valuable even for delivery of conventional smart weapons. Warhead improvements, faster speeds, 'Precision Delivery' technologies for 'Fire & Forget' missiles' and mobile launch capabilities have added highly effective stand-off capabilities. India's threat perceptions include 'missile capabilities' of all nations with reach to Indian territory. Hence India has established a 'Triad' of deterrence for bolstering its security. India has two immediate nuclear neighbours with hostile intent and history of war; hence missile defence is a very essential component of India's security.

Cruise Missiles, shoulder-fired Stinger missiles and anti-ship Harpoon missiles represent serious threats to major military assets at low cost to the enemy. Phenomenal proliferation of missiles by supplier nations, both by numbers and technological sophistication has enhanced the accessibility and utility of missiles for many aspirants including non-state groups.

As seen in the Middle-East conflicts, use of missiles is quite effective to offset weakness in direct conventional warfare capabilities. 'Missile Defence' technology is a high priority for all advanced countries that can afford it. Advanced technologies for 'Missile Defence' will inevitably spread to other nations, adding new dimensions to regional security dynamics.

Missile Defence—Indian Capabilities

Indian R&D advances for missile defence includes tracking and destroying hostile missiles using both the KEW (Kinetic Energy Weapons) and DEW (Directed Energy Weapons). While the indigenous IGMDP (Integrated Guided Missile Development Programme) started in 1983 has provided India with indigenous missile capability across most ranges of tactical and strategic applications, R&D for DEW-based Missile Defence/Space Defence commenced in 1998.

India's ballistic missile defence (BMD) programme is a two-tiered system consisting of PRITHVI Air Defence (PAD) for 50-80 km Exo-Atmospheric altitudes, and the Advanced Air Defence (AAD). For lower altitude interception, AKASH missile and DEW systems are being developed. The first BMD system was tested on 27 November 2006 at an altitude of 40-50 km. With this India became the fifth country to have ABM (after US, Russia, China and Israel).

The BMD test on 6 December 2007 saw successful interception at 15-km altitude. The BMD test on 6 March 2009 was with Long-Range Tracking Radar (LRTR) and the two-stage BMD Interceptor hit the targeted missile at 75 km altitude. Given short flight times in a possible Indo-Pak conflict, India's BMD focus must concentrate on short-range, quick-reaction Missile Defence with hyper-velocity missiles and speed of light DEW (Directed Energy Weapons).

Few countries in the world face the level of missile threats that India faces. Missile flight times are 8-15 minutes for ranges of 600–1200 km. India has successfully tested its missile defence systems in endo and exo-atmospheric altitudes at various ranges and profiles as witnessed in recent tests on 14 March 2010, 26 July 2010 and 6 March 2011. The Indian BMD system is very close to being operationalized with increasing capabilities in a phased manner.

Use of satellites in the military-critical loop makes them easy targets. Thus survivability of satellites and security of outer space is closely linked to the reliability of missile defence systems. Hence India is developing space defence systems and technologies on high priority along with missile defence systems for anti-satellite applications. Mini and Micro Satellites with ASAT capabilities along with DEW for space defence will be required.

Security of Outer Space

The outer space, *'The Province of all Mankind'* is common to space explorations, satellites, ballistic missiles as well as future missile defence systems. As of today, there is 'Unanimous Agreement' among all nations, on 'Peaceful Use of Outer Space' including for defence support systems. Low Earth Orbits (LEOs) are most used by the modern civilization that depend on hundreds of satellites for providing key support to worldwide communication, remote sensing, global finance management, health support across continents, Maritime navigation as well as several areas of military operational support including weapon delivery.

LEO satellites and manned spacecraft thus already face the dangers of collision with manmade debris that can cause a chain reaction of collisions with catastrophic effects. Missile defence technologies have significant A-SAT capabilities with serious implications for the deterrence value of missiles. Deployment of ASAT systems—whether missiles, micro-satellites or DEW—in space can introduce a new complexity for space security and sustainability. Space debris from manmade space objects has also increased to alarming levels that can pose threats to all satellites and space missions of future.

Most space missions of the past have been motivated by national security considerations. Space control and space dominance are now stated doctrines of powerful nations. India with predominant focus on civilian space applications must now concentrate on military space capabilities including counter-space technologies to protect its interests in space. India also needs to engage with other space powers in formulating the future norms and conventions to keep the outer space free of any weapon race.

Non-Conventional Threats to National Security

Energy and Environment Dilemma

Energy security or energy independence is a major imperative for India. Over 70 per cent of India's imports are energy-related presently and this could grow to 90 per cent in the near future unless proactive remedial actions are put in place. Primary energy demand has increased five times in the last two decades and the present energy basket mix is about 54 per cent coal + 5 per cent oil + 10 per cent N-Gas + 21 per cent hydro + 3 per cent nuclear and balance only 7 per cent from renewable. While recent gas finds in the KG basin are promising for building strategic reserves, the nuclear energy component can easily be increased to 10 per cent with careful choice of newer safer and available technology.

The dilemma is how to meet the rapidly increasing demand for energy (electricity) without adding to carbon emission of the country. Otherwise increased use of carbon fuels could accelerate the climate change to such levels that all the economic gains achieved through bigger energy use could be nullified by the economic losses in future due to impact of climate change. One part of the solution is to reduce demand through higher efficiency and the other part is to drastically reduce the use of fossil fuels to reduce the carbon emissions despite increased consumption of energy by increasing use of renewable energy sources.

Solar and wind energy have enormous untapped potential. Wind turbines today provide over 65,000 MW and Solar PV has the potential of providing 100s of GW from just the two states of Rajasthan and Gujarat. India's National Action Plan for Climate Change in 2008 included the National Solar Mission with a target to generate 20 GW by 2022. But the actual potential as per industry experts is much larger and the costs are coming down very fast to almost parity with grid tariff. In wind-power generation India is already the fifth largest after Denmark, Germany, Spain and USA. Offshore deployment of wind generators and technology upgrades can add very significant capacities for India.

Energy Security and Climate Change

China and India together have one-third of the world's population. Rapid Economic growth is moving tens of millions of their population into 'Middle Class' with increasing energy demands. India is already the fourth largest contributor to global warming and resultant climate changes. Concerns of global warming and climate change are driving the demand to reduce the carbon emission. Earth is already 1°C warmer and impacts on climate are already visible. The amount of carbon already in the environment is bound to cause more devastation in the coming years.

Energy shortages will create strong differences among societies and nations. Competition for supplies of coal, oil, natural gas and even uranium will get hostile as nations jostle to ensure their own energy security. It is clear that politics of energy will shape the world equations in future. India is the seventh largest in the world and second largest country in Asia. It has land frontiers of 15,200 km and a coastline of 7516 km. Unless clean energy begins to replace carbon-based resources, the impact of climate change on India would be more severe than on many other nations.

Conservative predictions indicate possible winter temperature rise of 3°C by 2050 and 4°C by 2080 triggering irreversible changes to monsoon patterns and causing serious erosion of glacial ice reserves that feed major Indian rivers with fresh water. Changes in river water flow can intensify the existing water dispute within India and also intra-state with Pakistan in J&K and with China in Tibet. Global glacial melting can cause a significant rise in the sea level, submerging vast areas of coastal mangroves and cultivable land. This will cause large population displacement within the country as well as across borders. Mass migration from Bangladesh, Maldives or Sri Lanka can pose a serious security challenge.

Agricultural production will be seriously affected by water scarcity as 80 per cent of water resources in India are used for agriculture. Higher average temperature will also reduce human efficiency and spread diseases. Where climate change coincides with adverse socio-economic conditions, chaos and anarchy can fuel crime, militancy and terrorism. Climate change will also directly affect the efficiency of security forces. Frequent deployment of Armed Forces for civil distress will be detrimental to military preparedness to face direct threats to national security.

Reluctance of the developed countries to help fast-developing countries like India and Brazil in mitigation of climate change effects, can be perceived as use of climate as a weapon. The increasing divide between the rich and poor can push the world politics into escalating conflicts and even war for resources and livelihood. These have serious implications.

Homeland Security and Technologies for Low-Intensity Conflicts

Since full-scale war between nations has huge economic cost, use of mercenary forces to wage low-intensity war is becoming the accepted norm. Hence border surveillance and control has become a critical issue for India. Threat perceptions are changing, getting more asymmetric and unpredictable. This places heavy demand on technical intelligence and human intelligence. Intelligent video surveillance and explosive/metal detectors proved very effective.

Advances in Information & Telecommunication Technologies (ICT), combined with satellite surveillance and GPS has transformed the intelligence gathering, processing and decision support for counter-terrorism. ICT is also very effectively used for detecting rogue financial transactions. Electronics intelligence and counter measures are used for threat forecasting. High-power (HP) lasers and HP microwaves are useful for flushing out hidden insurgents. Flash-blinding and microwave heat-guns are also very useful for non-lethal close combat.

Improvised explosive devices (IEDs) pose a major threat and technology for detection is fast developing in many parts of the world including India. These tools can provide quick access to suspected threat items or areas including buried threats, culvert emplaced charges, and IEDs in other concealed areas. Technologies for explosive detection at all entry and exit points of the country are also a very critical requirement for internal security.

Concluding Remarks

Development and dissemination of technology through increasing trade and commerce have changed significantly in the last two decades because dual-use technologies are now truly interchangeable both for defence and development. Human ingenuity and innovation are now more important issues than mere equipment/systems. Greater awareness of the advantages of modern technologies will intensify the pursuit of 'high-value technology' and competition will increase. Changing patterns of economic progress, global market forces and technology push, can change the security perceptions in favour of collective security. The technology push of the twenty-first century will make it imperative for all progressive nations to tackle the common dangers of 'technology misuse' in a cooperative drive, so as to reap maximum benefits from emerging and maturing technologies for the common good of the mankind.

Perception of India being a potential regional power could now attract adverse attention of other powerful competing nations and also the weak neighbours who may be apprehensive of India's influence. In future national security parameters will include economic strength, energy independence, environmental stability, water management, population and disease control and ethno-religious extremism, etc., all of which will assume larger importance.

The Asian region is expected to assume larger importance than the Western nations as the region is expected to hold 50 per cent of the world population and account for 60 per cent of world GDP. India and China are the two major nations that will emerge as the economic leaders of the world with new responsibilities. India also enjoys a major demographic advantage with over 50 per cent of its population in the under-35 age group. It does not need a genius to understand the enormous potential this scenario offers to India to become a world-class power within the next decade.

India needs to seize this opportunity with a well-planned nation rebuilding movement that will not tolerate incompetent leaders or any nexus between politics and criminal elements. Individual obsession with survival, fear and opportunism can create a 'self-serving' society with very little commitment to national priorities or ambitions. Lack of national pride and lack of professional competence in governance, defence or diplomacy can keep India mired in serious setbacks while the progressive nations stride ahead. The opportunity is so great and the looming cost of inaction is so large, that Indian people will have to put their act together and excel collectively in every sphere of endeavour. Self-reliance and excellence in every sphere will then automatically emerge as the main theme.

Technological innovation, professional competence and economic competitiveness will have to drive this initiative for rebuilding of the nation with integrated and foresighted policy reforms. Future issues of importance to defence and security are likely to be quite different from the earlier concepts requiring massive military strength. Outer space and cyber space have emerged as the new dimensions of future warfare and even the conventional conflicts are likely to be resolved through tactful use of technologies for advance situational awareness and by decisive preventive or punitive actions. Network-centric strategies with autonomous intelligent platforms will change the future battlefield that will be dominated by technology superiority in all dimensions of strategic importance. The world has been witness to the effectiveness of remote delivery of high-precision weapons and surgical strikes against asymmetrical threats from terrorist or rogue elements. These are the indicators of future security technologies where self-reliance and core competence will matter most.

CHAPTER XI

Role of the Private Sector in the Indigenization of State-of-the-Art Systems in the Indian DSTI Base

Deba R Mohanty

Introduction

Recorded history suggests that great powers have invariably possessed sizeable indigenous arms' industries along with robust economic might, apart from other attributes like relative socio-political stability and a competent national administrative structure. A mismatch or imbalance between these two elements—economic might and military capabilities—have invariably led to decline of national power. One of the most important elements of national military might in current times is influenced by the nature and pace of change in military science and technology[1] and the abilities of the national military scientific and technological complex to adapt to such changes and challenges.

It thus becomes all the more important for an established major power or an aspiring player like India to constantly meet the demands of evolving changes in its defence science and technology and industrial (hereafter, DSTI) base and make sure to reduce the gap between the pace of change and domestic industrial capabilities all the time.[2] India has already missed the defence industrial bus for a variety of reasons; it needs double the effort to nurture its domestic DSTI base in order to be counted as a formidable power on the global stage.

This is a challenge and an opportunity. The biggest challenge before the state is to not to get influenced by the might of the military industrial complex, while the related opportunities of military technological development invariably help the civilian economy through spin-offs as well as spin-on. How an aspiring power like India intends to develop its DSTI base and in turn reverse its heavy arms import dependency as well as help the national economy remains a matter of debate. As Indian DSTI base is almost exclusively owned, operated and directed by the national government with negligible contributions from the national private sector thus far. It is not surprising to find that despite encouragement from the government over the last decade or so, the Indian private sector is yet to prove itself as a reliable contributor to the Indian DSTI base. The problem is partly systemic, while lack of will and direction has made it worse.

This paper is designed to examine two specific yet inter-related aspects of Indian defence modernization—location of the Indian private sector in the indigenization of state-of-the-art systems, and in the process its overall contribution to the Indian DSTI base. The scope of the paper being intricately linked to several issues within the larger problem, a set of three fundamental questions will be placed here for further deliberations. First, is the Indian state serious enough to engage its private sector in strategic areas of defence production? Second, is the Indian governmental institutional mechanism in national defence responsive to demands and aspirations from the private sector? Three, and most important, does the Indian private sector possess the capability to deliver in high-tech areas?

The paper, in order to find answers to the above questions, will employ a narrative form of explanations for the very simple reason that neither data from the government sector nor private sector will be either available or sufficient for an academic research or policy paper (both of which rely invariably on primary, secondary and tertiary sources, to say the least). What the paper at best can bring out is a combination, with a hope that it will be of interest to both.

The paper will deal with a brief history of the Indian DSTI base and locate the Indian private sector's role in it. It will also examine the role and capabilities of the Indian private sector in Indian defence R&D efforts. In the end, the paper will make a set of arguments with a focus on future directions for Indian DSTI in general and the role of private industries in particular.

Role of the Private Sector in the Indian DSTI Base

From a rich civilization to a modern independent state, the story of Indian science and technology in general and defence technologies in particular has been consistently inconsistent.[3] Equally important to note is the fact that the private sector has been kept at a long distance from the DSTI ecosystems for the past several decades. Whether the role of the private sector was seen as a hindrance or facilitator has not been debated adequately in India. This is partly because of the fact that the role of the private industry in the Indian DSTI base was not institutionally embedded since the late 1940s, a situation which continues till date.

Documentation of evolution and development in modern Indian defence science and technology by social scientists, especially historians, has been considered herculean in the absence of reliable information in the public domain.[4] Even records of key areas of defence scientific achievements are often times not available in the public domain because of national security exclusivities attached to such programmes. Such is the degree of isolation in the existing structural-institutional and related arrangements related to Indian defence technologies within the larger governance structure that it has not only faced fierce resistance to reforms in institutional mechanisms[5] but also failed largely in meeting the growing demand for contemporary and next-generation technologies by the security forces, thus perpetuating the arms import dependency syndrome. The disconnect between aspirations and reality is evident in almost every aspect of the Indian DSTI base.[6] This is discomforting as well as worrisome. It is in this context that the role of the private sector in contributing to the overall Indian DSTI capacity needs to be examined and deliberated.

While the role of the private sector in the Indian DSTI base has been minimal right from the beginning,[7] the Indian government, in a landmark policy decision in May 2001, decided to open up the defence production sector for private participation. The private sector was allowed to produce any defence item, with foreign direct investment (FDI) up to 26 per cent.[8] Although the private sector was allowed, its participation was subject to obtaining industrial license and security clearance. Both security clearance and licensing have been a major bottleneck for the Indian private companies, who still struggle to meet stringent requirements. However, after the new government has come into power in May 2014, things appear to be a little easier now. The new government has further relaxed norms for industrial licensing and come out with a set of revisions in the industrial licensing policy.[9] Even a rudimentary defence exports policy formulation is in process now, initiated by the Ministry of Commerce as well as Ministry of Defence.[10] Such decisions are considered important for the very simple reason that for the first time the role of the private sector in the DSTI sector has been formalized by the government.

Some changes have occurred ever since this historic decision. For example, till October 2011, more than 200 Letters of Intent/Industrial Licenses (LoI/IL) had already been issued by the Department of Industrial Policy and Promotion (DIPP) of the Ministry of Commerce to various private entities, with a proposed investment of Rs 11,889 crore, and with employment opportunities for 39,129 people. These LOIs/ILs were granted or approved for a wide range of defence products, including armoured and combat vehicles, radars, electronic warfare equipment, warships, submarine, avionics, military aircraft, safety and ballistic products, and armaments and ammunition, among others.[11] In addition to these, the Indian private sector also started participating in various tenders, floated by the MoD, and even started winning a few contracts. For example, Pipavav Defence and Offshore Engineering Company Limited, a Gujarat-based shipbuilder, won an order valued at INR 2,975 crore for building five naval offshore patrol vessels (NOPV) for the Indian Navy. Interestingly, Pipavav won the order against a government-owned shipyard company (Goa Shipyards Limited). In another small yet important tender, a consortium of two Indian private firms—L&T and Ashok Leyland—emerged as the lowest bidder in an INR 100 crore contract for refurbished rocket launchers mounted on specialized trucks for the Army in early 2013.[12]

Other success stories for the Indian private sector in defence procurement tenders include INR 1094 crore Phase I of the MAFI (Military Air Field Infrastructure) project, which was bagged by Tata Power's Strategic Electronic Division (Tata Power SED) in early 2011. Tata Power SED won this project by defeating a government-owned DPSU (BEL) and an international company SelexSistemiIntegrati (a subsidiary of Finmeccanica). The first major success for the Indian private sector in the international arms market came in 2012, when Pipavav secured a major export order valued at INR 1192 crore from an undisclosed West African country for the supply of two Offshore Patrol Vessels. Another Indian company, Samtel Avionics and Defence Systems, signed an INR 500-crore contract with the UK-based Curtiss-Wright Controls Defence Solutions for the supply of high-definition, rugged liquid crystal cockpit displays in September 2012.[13] Ever since the new government has come, a few more projects are being contemplated to be awarded to the private sector companies, for example, like the military transport aircraft (to replace the Avro series), shipbuilding and other armaments.[14] It is important to note that perhaps for the first time, shares of listed Indian companies like Pipavav, Astra Microwave, BEL, resisted increase in the stock market.[15]

Despite some initial success by a select group of Indian companies in recent times, the role of the private sector has historically remained deficient in the Indian DSTI base. Reasons are not difficult to find. While structural and systemic issues for the negligible role of the private sector are explained elsewhere, a set of non-structural and non-systemic issues that have limited the role of the private sector need to be addressed here. First, surprisingly, the Indian private sector had played a visible role in indigenous defence production prior to and immediately after Indian independence. For example, many privately owned defence production companies, like Walchand Hirachand and a couple of shipyards, were taken over by the government. If one looks at the history of the arms industry, the private sector has played a dominant role for the past one and half centuries. Efforts to nationalize arms industries by several developed countries had failed. Arms industrial dynamics are such that states have had to make tough choices to privatize arms industries for sustenance, while bulk of the states that have retained exclusive control over their arms industries are facing numerous problems. As India decided to bring in arms industries under its exclusive control, it has been facing all kinds of systemic, operational and related problems. It is in recent times that India seems to have taken some steps to revitalize its DSTI base through reasonable private participation.

Second, the role of the private sector in the Indian DSTI base has been influenced by contradictory perceptions. For example, even after bulk of the private companies were taken over by the Indian government, players like Tatas were still active participants in defence production since the 1940s and 1950s. However, as the Indian government adopted a socialistic ideology that was politically leaning toward left-of-the-centre approach, which emphasized centralization and nationalization among others, it was but obvious that the Indian DSTI would be structurally and operationally state-owned and controlled. This approach closed the doors for the Indian private sector, which remained an outsider throughout. Contradictory perceptions—that private arms manufacturers would dictate government defence policies even though their role is critical for a robust military industrialization—prevailed and became a dominant mindset over a period of time. Such perceptions were structurally internalized over a period of time as the universe of Indian defence production activities remained within the confines of the South Block.

Third, sensing that the Indian private sector would at best be a component supplier, bulk of the major private companies left the field during the past five decades, except for a few players like Tatas, Mahindras, Godrej and others. Both Defence Public Sector Undertakings (DPSUs), Ordnance Factories (OFs) and Defence Research and Development Organisation (DRDO) treated the private companies as their fiefdom, which led to disappointments among the private manufacturers, who had no choice. In the absence of a structurally defined role for the private sector, bulk of the Indian companies, mostly the MSMEs, had no choice but to survive at the mercy of the DPSUs, OFs and DRDO. Some improvements have been noticed in the last decade, after the government announced a series of reforms in the Indian defence sector. However, plenty of problems still remain to be addressed.

Fourth, questioning the capabilities of the Indian private sector in meeting the demands of the armed forces or leading indigenization efforts in futuristic or state-of-the-art systems is arguably unsound. A section in this paper devotes the role of DRDO and its interaction with the Indian private sector elsewhere. Suffice to add here is that even the R&D capabilities of the government-owned production agencies like DPSUs and OFs are limited. In such a scenario, the role of the private sector need not be questioned, rather a way should be found as to how to integrate the sector within the overall DSTI ecosystem. Instances of the private sector's achievements in current times demonstrate that the sector can graduate from being a component supplier or a previous generation technology producer to the next level.

Defence Science and Technology (S&T) Base (DRDO) and the Private Sector

That India is a weapon merchants' paradise is to state the obvious. Although there is disagreement over figures primarily due to verifiable data, almost 70 per cent of the Indian defence acquisition budget is devoted to imports.[16] Despite tall claims to the contrary to improve the situation, arms import dependency has been a major headache for the Indian defence planners. Consider this: India's defence acquisition budget (hereafter, capital expenditure) has grown from USD 2.1 billion in FY 2002–03 to touch USD 15.4 billion in FY 2013–14.[17] Almost 80 per cent of the budgetary allocations is spent on 'committed liabilities,' leaving about 20 per cent for fresh acquisitions. Most of these acquisitions are from abroad and despite offsets obligations and license production arrangements in place, it is generally accepted that the import component of total acquisitions is to the tune of almost 70 per cent.

Despite having fifty-two scientific laboratories and a strong partnership with about forty academic institutions, fifteen national S&T agencies, fifty public sector units including eight DPSUs, forty OFs; both the DRDO and production agencies have failed largely to meet even the basic demands of the security forces. It appears that DRDO along with defence production agencies are pilloried most for the present state of affairs. Interestingly, two contrasting versions of DRDO's performance are evident in the public domain. One set of literature,[18] authored mostly by former DRDO scientists, cites difficulties like 'triple trap' syndrome,[19] scarce financial resources, difficult isolated environments like technology sanctions, government apathy, dissatisfied end-users, frequent changes in quality requirements, inefficient process innovations by production agencies, etc., while lauding a few pockets of excellence.[20] The other set of arguments, while recognizing such problems, also blames DRDO[21] and production agencies[22] for their overall inabilities in design and development deliverables.

DRDO as the premier defence scientific institution has been working in frontier technologies with claims of considerable advancements been made in the field of aeronautics, armaments, missile systems, combat vehicles, advanced computing and networking, communication, secrecy system, electronics, electronic warfare systems, radar systems, military engineering, life sciences, advanced materials, composites, underwater sensors/weapons and warship technology, etc., and attempts are now being made to meet emerging challenges in these fields.[23] It has constituted four research boards[24] to nurture and harness talent in academic institutions, universities, R&D centres and public and private industry. The boards provide grants-in-aid for collaborative defence-related futuristic frontline research having application in the new innovative systems.[25] When DRDO's design and development efforts lagged behind time schedules, the country had no choice but to fall back on the import option.

DRDO continues to have limited interactions with its counterparts in DPSUs and OFs. It provides technical assistance to these production agencies, which accounts for about 20 to 30 per cent only.[26] DRDO's interactions with academic and research institutions are similarly limited, although it seems to be improving in current times. Its recent academic outreach includes five centres for excellence in areas of explosives and propellants, polymer physics, nanotechnology, opto-electronics, microwave and other areas. DRDO has signed several memoranda of understanding with more than fifty universities and research centres, while more than 200 extramural research projects have been sanctioned to academics and teachers.[27] It has worked with/partnered/allowed sub-contracts to more than 250 private companies on various assignments and projects.[28] Interactions or collaborations with foreign research institutions and private companies are also limited, except for a few partnerships with countries like Israel and Russia.

Structural and Systemic Issues for the Private Sector

At the institutional-organizational level, most of the elements of the Indian national defence sector have witnessed varying degree of changes in the last ten years, especially after the Indian government started accepting and implementing recommendations made by the Group of Ministers on national security management in 2001.[29] Most of these changes or creation of new institutions/organizations were effected within the MoD[30] and a few related to production activities to the Ministry of Commerce. It is interesting to note that when a series of far-reaching reforms' initiatives were undertaken by the Indian government for more than a decade, the Indian private sector's enthusiasm to participate in defence production efforts increased. As stated elsewhere, the private sector received some success in getting a good response from the government sector during the initial years of reforms. However, it would be necessary to explain here as to how things did not work out for the private sector in the last few years. These reasons are mostly structural and systemic, apart from reasons explained elsewhere.

There are three major inter-related structural and systemic problems that have directly or indirectly impacted the role of the private sector in defence production. First, when a particular stakeholder is added to take active part in the Indian DSTI base, it should be integrated structurally within the administrative universe of the particular department or sector. Unfortunately, the Indian private sector's participation has not been formally integrated into the MoD administrative structure. For example, while DPSUs and OFs are administered by the Department of Defence Production or for that matter the DRDO is administered by the Department of Defence Research and Development, no such arrangement has been made for the private sector's integration into administrative mechanisms. Its participation has been informally or indirectly acknowledged through industry forums like CII or FICCI or through bidding processes for selected participants in the tendering process. Second, the role of industry bodies like CII, FICCI, PHDCCI or ASSOCHAM in helping out the Indian private sector is largely confined to interactive meetings between relevant organs of the MoD and industry representatives. Such arrangements need to be formally organized in a manner so as to assure the private sector participants of their future contributions. Third, the MoD administrative processes like offsets facilitation, where the role of the Defence Offsets Management Wing is to facilitate or enable the private sector participants to understand arms procurement directives, need much improvement. In fact, many private companies complain that such important organs are not only under-staffed but their existing knowledge strength is limited.

Needed: A Will and an Action Plan

The role of the private sector in meeting the demands of the armed forces, especially in high-tech R&D and innovation areas is yet to take off. The sector has long been treated as inferior in comparison to the state-owned production agencies as well as DRDO. While DPSUs and OFs have largely failed to improve the indigenous capabilities, many of DRDO's strategic and advanced technology programmes, including technologies that have been matured, faced time delays, leading to technological obsolescence. As Indian armed forces have embarked on a very ambitious military modernization drive, the private sector as well as DRDO's ability to provide the much needed technological backup for manufacturing products, product development, and services will be severely tested in the coming times. Signs of growing gaps between needs/expectations on the one hand and design and development and proven systems on the other are visible, which seems to have put added pressure on DRDO to put its house in order. Expectations from the private sector to take the Indian DSTI base to new heights would also increase in the coming times.

A comparison between what technologies do the Indian armed forces want in the next fifteen-odd years and what the private industry could be able to develop through indigenous or collaborative routes would indicate where the growth of Indian DSTI stands. The Indian MoD recently released a 'Technology Perspective and Capability Roadmap' (TPCR), prepared by the Headquarters Integrated Defence Staff. The document gives an exhaustive list of technologies that the Indian armed forces want in future.[31] Interestingly, DRDO has released a list of critical defence technology areas and test facilities for acquisition through offsets.[32] In both these plans, the role of the private sector would be important. A close look into both documents would reveal that while cutting-edge research efforts need to be undertaken by DRDO in areas like nano technology-based sensors, miniature SAR and ISAR technologies, fibre lasers, technologies for hypersonic flights (propulsion, aerodynamics and structures), high-power lasers, low observable technologies, composite sabot manufacturing technology, etc., some areas like EM rail gun technology, shared and conformal apertures, flexible solar cells technology, carbon fibre, pulse power network technologies, muzzle reference system, precision-guided munitions, etc., can always be carried out by private industries. In many high-technology areas like microelectronics, data fusion, cloud computing, flexible manufacturing, radars, sensors, system integration, robotics, computational fluid dynamics, combat UAVs, microsatellites, hypervelocity projectiles, plasma, technologies, India is much behind its advanced counterparts in the West, Russia and China.[33]

Can India take its DSTI base to the next level of development is a question that needs a comprehensive assessment of the strengths and weaknesses of the Indian defence S&T ecosystem in general and defence industrial capabilities in particular.[34] This is where the state would have to take a firm decision as to how to engage the private sector for maximization of overall DSTI capability. Strengths also lie in India's large young human resources and reasonable ability of the state to devote financial resources for sustenance of both basic and cutting-edge scientific efforts. This is an area where the government would look to the private sector for help.

However, India's weaknesses, most of which are self-created, outnumber its strengths, leading the entire sector to excel in some pockets only. For example, while Indian IT, biotechnology and space sectors are maturing well, their applications in the defence sector are yet to develop fully. Self-created weaknesses also include political apathy, narrow outlook of scientific elites, bureaucratic complexities while the defence technology sector adds resources—both human and material—and denial regimes as prime reasons for its poor performance. Unless corrective measures in the form of a defence industrial and technology vision document as a guiding force, a pragmatic politico-bureaucratic direction, flexibility in structural arrangements with horizontal inter-disciplinary interactions and diffusion on the other, periodic reviews and accountability within the institution and at the higher governance levels are undertaken with seriousness, the story of India's DSTI base is likely to muddle through well into future.

NOTES

1. For an excellent historiography of the role of military technology in national power, see, Barton C Hacker, 'Military Institutions, Weapons, and Social Change: Toward a New History of Military Technology,' *Technology and Culture*, Vol. 35, No. 4, October, 1994, pp. 768–834. Also see, Barton C Hacker, 'Military Technology and World History: A Reconnaissance,' *The History Teacher*, Vol. 30, No. 4, August 1997, pp. 461–87.
2. Most of India's respected scholars focusing on Indian DSTI base have emphasized these points. For details, see V Siddhartha, 'The Triple Trap, Dual Use and Single Reform: Towards Self-Reliance in High Technology', in Satish Kumar (ed.) *India's National Security Annual Review 2011* (New Delhi: Routledge, 2012), pp. 441–9; Amitav Mallik, 'Self-reliance in defence technologies', in Satish Kumar (ed.) *India's National Security Annual Review 2003* (New Delhi: India Research Press, 2004), pp. 166–83; Amitav Mallik, 'Science and technology for a stronger India', in Satish Kumar (ed.) *India's National Security Annual Review 2012* (New Delhi: Routledge, 2013), pp. 379–84; Amitav Mallik, *Indian Science and Technology: A Status Review* (New Delhi: Pragun Publication, 2006).
3. Literature on Indian science and technology is nevertheless growing in recent times. For an excellent historical account on the subject, see, Robert S Anderson, *Nucleus and Nation: Scientists, International Networks and Power in India* (Chicago: University of Chicago Press; 2010). Also see, Dhruv Raina, *Images and Contexts: The Historiography of Science and Modernity in India* (Delhi: Oxford University Press, 2003). Anderson has described the role of the Indian industry in a larger national construct.
4. Most scholars complain of inadequate evidences available in public domain for research on Indian science and technology. See, Anderson, Note 3 and Santimay Chatterjee, MK Dasgupta, Amitabha Ghosh (eds), *Studies in the History of Sciences* (Calcutta: Asiatic Society, 1997). Also see, S Irfan Habib and Dhruv Raina (eds.) *A Social History of Science: Themes in Indian History* (Delhi: Oxford University Press, 2003).
5. Major recommendations made by various important committees on the defence sector have been selectively implemented or even kept on hold by the Indian government due to pressures from affected organizations. For example, creation of a Chief of Defence Staff has been resisted by the Indian Air Force, while nomination of Raksha Udyog Ratna (Champion of Industry) from the Indian private sector to be promoted as system integrators has been resisted by both state-owned defence companies as well as a few large private companies. Importantly, major recommendations on reforms in DRDO, made by the P Rama Rao Committee, have been fiercely resisted by many within DRDO. Interactions with serving and retired members of the armed forces, industry captains and senior scientists from DRDO over the last ten years by the author.
6. The Indian DSTI base consists of DRDO with 50 scientific laboratories, eight large defence public sector units and 40 ordnance factories. The base is also complemented by academic and research institutions and private industries as and when required.
7. In fact, the Indian private sector played a major role in defence production prior to independence. Many of the Indian private companies like Walchand Hirachand, Mazagaon Dockyard and others were privately owned, before they were taken over by the government after independence in 1947.

8. All notifications and guidelines have been included in the Consolidated FDI Policy, brought out by the Department of Industrial Promotion and Policy, Ministry of Commerce, Government of India. For details, see, http://dipp.nic.in/English/Policies/FDI_Circular_01_2012.pdf
9. The Indian government has further relaxed norms and allowed greater private participation in the defence sector. For the announcement, see, http://m.financialexpress.com/news/govt-relaxes-licensing-norms-for-defence-manufacturing/1264579
10. See, http://indiatoday.intoday.in/story/exclusive-centre-notifies-new-defence-export-strategy/1/381240.html
11. For details, see, 'ListofLettersofIntent/IndustrialLicence issued to private companies for the manufacture of Arms and Armament,' available at the official Ministry of Defence website: http:// mod.nic.in
12. Laxman Kumar Behera, *Indian Defence Industry: Issues of Self-Reliance*, Monograph No. 21, July 2013.
13. Behera, Note 12.
14. The MoD recently cleared defence purchase proposals worth INR 80,000 crore. With this announcement, the NDA government has already cleared defence projects worth INR 1,25,000 crore in the last five months. See,http://timesofindia.indiatimes.com/india/Narendra-Modi-govt-clears-defence-projects-worth-Rs-80000cr/articleshow/44935990.cms
15. For details, see,http://www.business-standard.com/article/markets/defence-shares-rally-as-panel-clears-projects-worth-rs-80-000-crore-114102700082_1.html
16. A Self-Reliance Review Committee was constituted by the Ministry of Defence in 1992 to examine all issues related to self-reliance in defence. Recommendations of the Committee led to formulation of a '10-Year Plan for Self-Reliance in Defence Systems,' which envisaged a major coordinated thrust for self-reliance in defence systems. The plan defined the self-reliance Index as the ratio of the indigenous content of defence procurement to the total expenditure on defence procurement in a given financial year. The 10-year plan envisaged raising the self-reliance Index value from 1992–3 estimation of 0.3 to possible 0.7 by the year 2005. This implies that the import content of the defence procurement would be brought down to 30 per cent or less in the next 10 years. However, it is at present hovering around 30-35 per cent, suggesting that import content in arms procurement is still hovering around 70 per cent. See, Defence Research and Development Organisation, 14th Report of the Parliamentary Standing Committee on Defence, Lok Sabha Secretariat, New Delhi, March 2007, p. 3.
17. The Indian defence expenditure stands at USD 37.4 billion in FY 2013–14. The ratio between 'revenue' (salary, pensions and other revenue allocations) and 'capital' (capital purchases including equipment, services and infrastructure, etc.) expenditure roughly hovers around 55:45 respectively for the past ten years. *Defence Services Estimates*, an annual publication from the Department of Defence Finance, Ministry of Defence, Government of India, publishes major heads of Indian defence expenditure. For data on defence expenditure, see, *Defence Services Estimates* for relevant years. Also see, on budgetary allocations for national defence, internal security and related departments, *Union Budget* (for relevant years), (New Delhi: Ministry of Finance, Government of India), available at www.indiabudget.nic.in
18. For example, see, V Siddhartha, 'Technology in future needs of our armed forces", in Satish Kumar (ed.) *India's National Security Annual Review 2001* (New Delhi: Vikas Publishing House, 2002), pp. 227–49; Srinivas Bhogle, "Technology review 2005", in Satish Kumar (ed.) *India's National Security Annual Review 2006* (New Delhi: Knowledge

World, 2006), pp. 235–52; Srinivas Bhogle, 'Technology review: an appraisal of DRDO', in Satish Kumar (ed.) *India's National Security Annual Review 2007* (New Delhi: Knowledge World, 2007), pp. 288–307; Dipankar Banerjee, 'The promise of nanotechnology', in Satish Kumar (ed.) *India's National Security Annual Review 2008* (New Delhi: Knowledge World, 2008), pp. 463–80.

19. Distinguished scientist V Siddhartha has coined this term by arguing that 'what is developed abroad will not suit our requirements, what is suitable for us will be denied to us and what is not denied will be unaffordable.' See, V Siddhartha, Note 13, p. 332.
20. A senior scientist from DRDO has cited a few examples of projects led by DRDO, like integrated network-centric tank (MBT–Mark II), next-generation mobility equipment, advanced versions of hand grenades and explosives and kits, avionics upgrade for LCA, indigenous version of AWACS, missile interceptors, composites, sensors, signal processing, life sciences support systems for high altitude deployment, etc. For details, see PS Goel, 'Technology challenges in national security', in Satish Kumar (ed.) *India's National Security Annual Review 2009* (New Delhi: Routledge, 2009), pp. 403–20.
21. Parliamentary Standing Committee on Defence has severely criticized DRDO for its inabilities in meeting requirements of the armed forces. It has cited several instances of products refused by the armed forces like emergency floatation system for Mi-8, relocatable balloon barrage for IAF and many others; some changed specifications by the armed forces leading to cost overruns include 30mm fair weather towed air defence guns, among others; abandoned projects like air-borne surveillance platforms, cargo ammunition, GPS-based system for replacing fire detection radar, etc.; and also elaborates on at least six major design and development projects that have faced severe cost overruns and delays including LCA Mark II, Nishant, Lakshya, Pinaka, Sambahak, Samyukta and Integrated Guided Missile Development Programme (IGMDP), among others. For details see Note 8.
22. Most of the production agencies have been criticized for not being able to deliver products on time. As recently as in early August 2013, the Chief of IAF, Air Chief Marshal NAK Browne criticized Hindustan Aeronautics Limited for not being able to deliver products like basic trainers, LCA, light utility helicopters and light combat helicopters. See, 'IAF-HAL dogfight over trainers,' *The New Indian Express*, 4 August 2013, available at http://newindianexpress.com/thesundaystandard/IAF-HAL-dog-fight-over-trainers/2013/08/04/article1716645.ece?pageNumber=2 (accessed on 18 August 2013). For criticism on the role of defence production agencies, see, Defence Ordnance Factories, 7th Report of the Parliamentary Standing Committee on Defence, Lok Sabha Secretariat, December 2005, available at http://164.100.47.134/lsscommittee/Defence/14_Defence_7.pdf; Defence Public Sector Undertakings, 9th Report of the Parliamentary Committee on Defence, Lok Sabha Secretariat, March 2006, available at http://164.100.47.134/lsscommittee/Defence/14_Defence_9.pdf (accessed on 18 August 2013).
23. Note 8, p. 1.
24. These include Aeronautics Research and Development Board (AR&DB), Armament Research Board (ARMREB), Naval Research Board (NRB) and Life Sciences Research Board (LSRB).
25. Details on DRDO's mandate, vision, areas of activities and design and development achievements are available on the official website: www.drdo.gov.in
26. Note 8, p. 22.
27. For details, see, www.drdo.gov.in (accessed on 18 August 2013).
28. A list of DRDO-Industry partnership is available at http://drdo.gov.in/drdo/English/IITM/Industry_compendium.pdf (accessed on 18 August 2013).

29. GoM report on national security management was published by the National Security Council Secretariat, New Delhi, in February 2001. The report covered all aspects of national security and made more than 200 recommendations.
30. Most prominent of these organizations include Chief of Integrated Defence Staff (CIDS), Joint Command, Strategic Forces Command (SFC), Defence Acquisition Council (DAC), Defence Production Board (DPrB), Defence Procurement Board (DPB), Defence R&D Board (DRDB), among many others. Direct DRDO representation or participation is factored into most of these organizations, except for exclusive ones like SFC, which may not require its membership. Apart from higher military organizations, the MoD has also announced a series of changes in the production and procurement sectors. The private industry was allowed participation and FDI in defence sector by foreign manufacturers was allowed in 2002. Recommendations of major committees like Kelkar, Prabir Sengupta have been considered while the defence procurement procedure (DPP) has been revised nine times in the last eleven years. Policies like defence offsets, changes related to transfer of technology and many such measures have been undertaken to revitalize the Indian defence production sector.
31. TCPR was released in April 2033 by the MoD. The document is available on the MoD website: www.mod.nic.in. Before TCPR, both the Army and Navy had also released their versions of technology requirements in future. See 15-Year Indigenization Plan, Directorate of Indigenization, Integrated Headquarters of the Ministry of Defence (Navy), 15 October 2008, available in www.ciidefence.com. Also see, Technology Requirements of the Army, available at www.ciidefence.com. Some reflections on future technology requirements can also be found in V Siddhartha, 'The Triple Trap, Dual Use and Single Reform: Towards Self-Reliance in High Technology', in Satish Kumar (ed.) *India's National Security Annual Review 2011* (New Delhi: Routledge, 2012), pp. 441–9; Amitav Mallik, 'Self-reliance in defence technologies', in Satish Kumar (ed.) *India's National Security Annual Review 2003* (New Delhi: India Research Press, 2004), pp. 166–83.
32. The list is available on the DRDO website: www.drdo.gov.in
33. For details, see, Amitav Mallik, 'Science and technology for a stronger India', in Satish Kumar (ed.) *India's National Security Annual Review 2012* (New Delhi: Routledge, 2013), pp. 379–84.
34. The Department of Science and Technology, Government of India, has recently brought out a comprehensive assessment of India's science and technology, including defence technologies. For details see, Compendium on Science Technology and Innovation, available on the S&T ministry official website: http://www.dst.gov.in/Science%20Technology %20&%20 Innovation%20Book.pdf Also see, Amitav Mallik, *Indian Science and Technology: A Status Review* (New Delhi: Pragun Publication, 2006).

IV. APPLICATION

CHAPTER XII

THE CHINESE CHALLENGE

Jayadeva Ranade

At a time when the world is in a state of continuing flux and the economies of the major powers are fragile with vulnerabilities existing in those of the bigger emerging powers in the Asia-Pacific like China, Japan and India, Beijing has accelerated its push for recognition as the dominant power in the Asia-Pacific. This potential shift in the balance of power coincides with the emergence of competing focal points of power in the East. The equilibrium has been disturbed in the past few years by Beijing's assertiveness. This is being resisted by the US, Japan, Vietnam and India, and has also made South East Asian countries nervous. China's sudden assertiveness since the end of 2007 has been prompted by a combination of factors: the global economic downturn; China's considerably enhanced economic and military strength and Beijing's perception that the US as a global power is on the decline. China considers this as an opportune moment for it to regain its self-perceived rightful position on the world stage and alter the status quo in Asia.

The Chinese Communist Party (CCP) leadership is divided on whether to write off the US as the sole world power. One view is that the US is a power irreparably on the decline while the other, which seems to be steadily gaining ground, argues that the intrinsic strength and resilience of the US will ensure its return to the world stage as a stronger, more effective power.

There is consensus, however, that the ability of the US to project power simultaneously in different theatres around the globe is presently constrained, thus offering China a window of opportunity that would last at most between five to ten years. The official Chinese assessment was concisely summed up in mid-August 2014 by the state-owned *Global Times*, a subsidiary newspaper of the official CCP mouthpiece the *People's Daily*. The paper observed that 'The US military has the power to sustain the US dominance internationally, but it is unable to command every country or nation. In East Asia, the US does not have the determination to be fully committed to things that are not in its core interests.'

Undeterred by US actions like the 'Asian Pivot' or Trans-Pacific Partnership (TPP/TPIP),which are intended to convey that the US is not about to cede influence in the Asia-Pacific, Beijing is pressing ahead with efforts to achieve its global and regional ambitions. The continuing tense stand-off with Japan, which is a US ally and East Asia's strongest power, underlines Beijing's willingness to push the envelope in the apparent confidence that the US, Japan and Vietnam will stop shy of confronting it. China's actions in the past few years have dented US credibility as a reliable ally willing to back its partners in the region. China's Ambassador to the US, Cui Tiankai, speaking to a US audience in Washington on 20 February 2014, also reiterated the role that Beijing desires in the Asia-Pacific. He cautioned against 'unilateral interpretations of some international legal instruments, and attempts to impose those interpretations on others.' Adding that while China acknowledges that the US 'is a powerful and very strong country...and will remain so for many years to come,' he said China has 'its roots in the Asia Pacific' and would never succumb to threats or intimidation and 'never shift its priorities.' He said both, the US and China, should work together for peace in the Asia-Pacific.

Policy

China's foreign policy has begun to acquire a sharper and more muscular edge that will impact India, Japan, Vietnam and other countries with which it has territorial disputes. In the intense debate underway in China for the past couple of years on China's international security environment, arguments advocating an uncompromising approach appear to be gaining ground. These are reflected in the views of Tsinghua University Professor Yan Xuetong, a former doctoral tutor of Xi Jinping with reportedly close proximity to him. Notable among Yan Xuetong's views, listed by Dingding Chen in the *Diplomat,* are that: (i) as the probability of conflict with other countries increases, China's foreign policy should directly confront rather than avoid the issue of conflict; (ii) China should try to develop rather than just maintain its 'strategic opportunity period' because waiting for a strategic opportunity period is always passive; (iii) China should begin to shape rather than just integrate into international society because China now has the capacity to do so; and (iv) China should change its non-alignment approach and make efforts to establish a 'community of common destiny.'

Another Chinese scholar Xu Jin from the Beijing-based Chinese Academy of Social Sciences (CASS) also calls for debunking several dominant 'myths' in Chinese foreign policy. Xu Jin lists six 'myths': (i) China should keep a low profile; (ii) China should not seek alliances; (iii) China should not seek leadership; (iv) China will not become a superpower; (v) the Sino-American relationship is the most important one; and (vi) China's foreign policy should serve China's economic development. He believes that all these six 'myths' should be discarded as a new era calls for new ideas.

Important is Xi Jinping's 'China Dream' which envisages: making the Chinese people wealthy; making China a strong nation; and the rejuvenation of China. This muscular aspiration for China spelt out by Xi Jinping at the 18th Party Congress has been adopted by the entire Party and has already entered the lexicon of the CCP. Pertinent to India-China relations is 'rejuvenation,' which implies the restoration to China of its self-perceived rightful international status and recovery of all its territories. The new passports published by China depict its claimed territories, as do its actions in the South China Sea and East China Sea and the expanding claims over Arunachal Pradesh and Jammu and Kashmir.

India

There appears to be a potential for change in the dynamics of the region's geo-politics with the newly elected BJP government in India refashioning the policy towards China. The BJP and its Prime Minister Narendra Modi, have won the hustings with a mandate unprecedented in the last thirty years and are, therefore, not hostage to considerations of state politics in crafting foreign policy. Modi is also a reputedly decisive leader with the capacity to take bold initiatives and the strong political mandate received by the BJP reinforces his ability to do so. This was demonstrated when, coinciding with his swearing-in ceremony, Prime Minister-designate Modi initiated a phase of hectic diplomacy that sought to re-energize some important relationships and highlight India's space for manoeuvre. In the process he has outlined the geographic perimeter of India's neighbourhood of strategic interest and, thereby implicitly identified the areas where India and China's national and strategic interests collide. The tempo wound down in September with his visit to the US and summit with US President Obama which, effectively, also marked the high water point of his diplomacy. Modi has now had summit meetings with the leaders of all three power centres of the Indo-Pacific region, namely the US, Japan and China, and can assess first-hand the potential of each relationship.

China has taken note of these developments. Its media, which closely tracked India's general elections, observed that Modi represents a right-wing political party and noted his utterances on the campaign trail and visit to Arunachal Pradesh. It anticipated that India's stand on China would harden in the event of his victory. Senior researchers in Chinese government think tanks differed, however, and assessed that Modi's statements were actually political posturing and India's policy towards China would remain substantially unchanged. China's leadership began to woo India to prevent the new leadership from drawing closer to the US and Japan as well as seize economic opportunities. Chinese Premier Li Keqiang's telephone call to Prime Minister Modi within three days of his victory emphasizing that 'China is willing to enhance mutual trust' and expressing confidence that India would grow under Modi's leadership, reinforce this. Articles in China's state-controlled media thereafter began projecting that India-China economic relations would improve.

Of particular importance, though, was the tone of a Chinese-language official 'Xinhua' despatch of 29 May 2014, which differed noticeably from other Chinese media reports. This Xinhua despatch asserted that Modi has no option other than economic cooperation with China as India perforce has to recognize China's economic and military superiority in Asia. It stressed that Modi would have to accommodate China, not out of choice or inclination, but out of necessity. While this is arguable, the Xinhua despatch does exhibit China's self-confidence.

China has similarly been steadfast in its opposition to India getting permanent membership of the United Nations Security Council (UNSC). Its aim is to remain the sole Asian permanent member of the UN Security Council.

The visit (8-9 June 2014) by Chinese Foreign Minister Wang Yi soon after Modi's election was intended to engage with India's new right-wing Government and was part of China's strategy of 'Peripheral Diplomacy.' It was clear, including during Wang Yi's visit that China's focus is on economic cooperation with India. It is anxious to find a new market for its huge reserves of surplus cash and another avenue for investment. Clearly reflecting the position of China's leadership, on the question of China's territorial claims on India Wang Yi yielded no ground. At his press conference in New Delhi, he made a carefully worded remark that the issue of stapled visas by China were a 'unilateral,' 'flexible,' 'goodwill gesture' or, in other words, that the status of Arunachal Pradesh and Jammu and Kashmir (J&K) remains disputed. Beijing had, incidentally, hinted at its ability to meddle in India's internal affairs and specifically in J&K, when a Chinese so-called NGO in 2010 invited Hurriyat 'leader' Mirwaiz Umar Farooq to China. Mirwaiz Umar Farooq too had then stated that China has a role in the settlement of the Kashmir issue.

In this context, Chinese President Xi Jinping's visit to India from 17 to 19 September 2014—the first by a Chinese President in eight years—assumes importance. China's new Ambassador in New Delhi and Chinese official media reports described it as 'landmark' and 'historic.' There was anticipation that the meeting between the two powerful leaders, both of whom are politically strong and have a demonstrated capacity to take bold initiatives, could move the India-China relationship forward and add meaningful content to it. Xi Jinping belied both expectations. The intrusion at Chumar in Ladakh that, quite unprecedentedly, carried on throughout Xi Jinping's visit and for many days thereafter, however, cast a shadow over the visit. Xi Jinping's firm grip on the People's Liberation Army (PLA) added to the significance of the timing of the intrusion. It was reminiscent of the intrusion by PLA troops around the time of Chinese Premier Li Keqiang's visit to India in April 2013. At the time, the influential *'Zhongguo Qingnian Bao'* (*China Youth Daily*) on 14 May 2013 also laid claim to Ladakh and accused India of triggering tensions by adopting a 'forward policy.' It stressed that 'Ladakh was unified with China's Yuan Dynasty as part of Tibet in the 13th century' and was 'under the jurisdiction of the central government of China's Qing Dynasty until 1830s.' Stating that it was important for access to Central Asia, it added that 'although it is under Kashmir, Ladakh shares similarities with Tibet in terms of culture, religion, customs, and language, and it has long been dubbed "Little Tibet". The statements read out by Modi and Xi Jinping after their meeting in Delhi on 18 September 2014 also revealed the differences on the border issue. While Modi listed the border issue and solution of the ongoing confrontation in Chumar in Ladakh as the first item, Xi Jinping mentioned it at almost the end and then too made no reference to an early resolution. He merely said that mechanisms exist to sort it out.

The challenge for India is essentially to manage relations with China, a country with which it shares a 4,057-kilometre-long un-demarcated and disputed border, as it pursues its goal of economic growth. The interests of Beijing and New Delhi overlap to an extent as any undue tension or conflagration could derail the aspirations and economies of both countries. The greatest impediment to the India-China relationship achieving its full potential remains the boundary issue despite the agreements signed between India and China since the late Indian Prime Minister Rajiv Gandhi's visit in 1988. These include the: Agreement between India and China on Maintenance of Peace and Tranquillity Along the Line of Actual Control in the India-China Border Areas (1993); Agreement on Confidence-Building Measures in the Military Field Along the Line of Actual Control in the India-China Border Areas (1996); and Political Parameters and Guiding Principles for the Settlement of the India-China Boundary Question (2005). The most important is the agreement of 1993 which states that 'The two sides agree that references to the line of actual control in this Agreement do not prejudice their respective positions on the boundary question,' thus clearly indicating that the two agree that the line of actual control (LAC) is not the border thus obviating the need for incursions from either side to demarcate one's territory. Despite the assurances in these agreements, China's expanding territorial claims on Arunachal Pradesh and J&K and numerous Chinese incursions across the LAC are a source of constant friction in Sino-Indian relations.

A new impediment to improved bilateral relations is Beijing's pronounced emphasis on pushing its new economic agenda, which is trans-regional and would box India into South Asia. Beijing's intention is to focus on the development of economic ties while setting aside resolution of the contentious border dispute till what it deems a more opportune time. This is substantiated by repeated assertions that China will not barter away its 'core national interests.' Two despatches in China's authoritative official news agency Xinhua in August 2011 explicitly declared that burgeoning economic ties are no indication of good bilateral relations which are possible only if China's sovereignty and core national interests are respected.

Beijing's new economic agenda comprises three initiatives, namely the Silk Road Economic Belt, the Bangladesh-China-India-Myanmar (BCIM) Corridor, or the Kunming Initiative, and the Maritime Silk Route. Reliable reports emanating from Beijing reveal that Xi Jinping has taken personal charge of the 'Silk Road Economic Belt' project. This project, which originates in China's southern Yunnan province, envisages an outward westward push through Bhutan, Nepal, Pakistan and the Central Asian countries up to, and possibly beyond, Turkey. India's north east is part of this as well as the BCIM corridor. With their fragile economies and extremely poor connectivity, the north-eastern states will become even more vulnerable in case India accedes to these projects. It would mean allowing the free influx of Chinese goods and nationals with the attendant danger of the latter settling down in these areas.

To reinforce its economic push, in October 2013, China's leaders approved the policy of 'Peripheral Diplomacy' which has obvious implications for India and Japan. The new policy signals that Beijing will intensify efforts for economic engagement with India, including making investments, and accompany this with high-level visits. It additionally envisages a network of sub-regional, regional and 'cooperative' security relationships. China already has an all-encompassing military relationship with Pakistan. The PLA has steadily upgraded ties with Nepal's Army and Sri Lanka and the Maldives have formally agreed to partner Beijing in the Maritime Silk Route. Noteworthy in the context of security arrangements is the precedent set by China and Ukraine on 4 December 2013. The security agreement concluded between the two countries states that 'China promises…to provide security guarantees to Ukraine if Ukraine is attacked by nuclear weapons or threatened by such aggression.' China and Bangladesh also signed a civil nuclear cooperation agreement many years ago, which has remained inactivated.

China's policy of 'Peripheral Diplomacy' for the first time in the history of the People's Republic of China categorizes countries neighbouring China as 'friend' and 'enemy.' It promises huge financial and other benefits—including those flowing from the global influence it exercises—to 'friends' who support China's regional ambitions and warns of sustained periods of pressure and isolation to 'enemies' or countries that oppose China. Chinese commentators point out that the end objective of the policy of 'Peripheral Diplomacy' is to use alternative strategies 'to achieve global leadership.'

Pakistan

Sino-Pakistan relations have played a major role in the policies of Beijing and Islamabad towards India. China, viewing India as a potential challenger in the strategic landscape of Asia, has used Pakistan to counter Indian power in the region, while Islamabad has gained access to China's civil and military resources to balance Indian might in the subcontinent. The China-Pakistan partnership serves the interests of both by presenting India with a potential two-front theatre in the event of war with either country.

China helped Pakistan enhance its military and nuclear capabilities to keep India engaged and focussed on threats emanating from Pakistan, thus, practically freeing itself of any military threat from India. In March 1963, the two countries signed a border agreement that transferred 2,000 square miles of territory in Pakistan-occupied Kashmir (POK) to China. China has, over the years, also made considerable investments in Pakistan's northern areas. The Karakoram Highway built in 1978 and which connects

China's Xinjiang-Uyghur Autonomous Region (XUAR) with Pakistan's Northern Areas, over the 19,000 feet Khunjerab pass well north of the Siachen glacier, has been developed by China into an all-weather road. In return for handing over part of POK, China began selling weapons to Pakistan. Between 1978 and 2008, China sold roughly US$7 billion in military equipment to Pakistan, typically accounting for 40 per cent of Pakistan's total arms purchases in any given year.

More significant has been the transfer of equipment, technology and scientific expertise throughout the 1980s and 1990s by China for Pakistan's nuclear weapons and ballistic missile programmes. A significant development in Chinese–Pakistan military cooperation occurred in 1992, when China supplied Pakistan with 34 short-range ballistic M-11 missiles. Beijing also built a turnkey ballistic missile manufacturing facility near Rawalpindi and helped Pakistan develop the 750-km-range solid-fuelled Shaheen-1 ballistic missile.

In the field of nuclear technology, China helped Pakistan acquire and develop nuclear weapons capability. It built two civilian nuclear reactors at the Chashma site in Punjab province under agreements made before it joined the Nuclear Suppliers Group (NSG) in 2004. In June 2008, Pakistan announced plans to build units 3 and 4 at Chashma, each of 320 MWE and largely financed by China. China had meanwhile consistently opposed the US-India Civilian Nuclear Agreement, finalized during President Bush's New Delhi visit in March 2006, and had at that time warned Washington that it had opened the way for other countries to make similar exceptions. China had also launched a diplomatic offensive to block any changes in the guidelines of the NSG to accommodate India in the field of dual-use technology. Xinhua on 4 March 2008 declared that Beijing wanted India to dismantle its nuclear weapons and sign the Nuclear Non-proliferation Treaty (NPT) as a Non-Nuclear Weapon State. China later signed another agreement with Pakistan in October 2008, together with the assurance that it would further enhance Pakistan's nuclear capability. Latest reports reveal that China has built its largest ever 1 GB nuclear power plant in Karachi with two more planned in the city and another three elsewhere in Pakistan.

South Asia

In recent years China has assertively sought to expand its footprint in South Asia, in the process encroaching on India's strategic space and encircling it. As part of its effort to access the Indian Ocean region and realize its dream project namely, the Maritime Silk Route, China has expanded influence in the Bay of Bengal and Arabian Sea by building ports in Sri Lanka, Pakistan and helping build the Sandia Deep Sea port in Bangladesh. It is additionally trying to enter into arrangements with other Indian Ocean littoral countries. China's Ministry of Defence website retains a posting that announces its intention to acquire a naval base in the Indian Ocean. Pakistan, Bangladesh, Maldives and Sri Lanka have pledged support to President Xi Jinping's initiative as part of the overall Asian Security Plan.

Nepal has acquired greater salience in Beijing's efforts to exercise strategic influence over it. Beijing's effort is driven primarily by its apprehension that Nepal, which has a 1,400-kilometre border with the Tibet Autonomous Region (TAR), could be used as a springboard by 'hostile powers'—shorthand for the US and India—for fomenting unrest inside Tibet. Interesting was the presence of Lobsang Sangay, head of the Central Tibetan Administration, at Prime Minister Modi's swearing-in ceremony in May 2014. China's increasing interest in Nepal is evidenced by the succession of high-level visits from various Chinese departments that Kathmandu has witnessed over the past year. On an average at least two Chinese delegations have visited each month with the tempo picking up since October. Four important Chinese delegations visited Nepal in December 2013 alone. Earlier, China's People's Liberation Army (PLA) had established direct links with Nepal's Army during the visit of PLA Chief Chen Bingde. Interestingly, leaders of visiting Chinese delegations have since the past few years begun interacting with leaders of all political parties in Nepal and, seemingly opting to take on the role of mediator in Nepal's domestic politics, have sought to persuade the various Maoist groups to join forces.

China has also been advancing its interests in Nepal on other fronts. In 2012 had overtaken India with 575 Chinese companies acquiring approval from the Department of Industry (DoI) for foreign direct investment (FDI) compared to 566 from India. India, however, continues to remain the largest FDI investor with FDI from India totalling Rs 37.6 billion compared to Rs 10.6 billion from China. Huawei and ZTE already have a monopoly in the telecommunications infrastructure sector. China's focus, however, is on Nepal's hydropower, tourism and agriculture sectors. Tourism-related sectors like hotels and restaurants are other areas that China is interested in. Bipin Raj Bhandary, head of the FDI section at the DoI, observed that 'most of the Chinese investment is coming in sectors like hotels and restaurants.' Last year alone, Nepal received investment proposals for 24 hotels from China. The increasing number of Chinese tourists to Nepal would be a major economic incentive for Nepal while a tourism industry dependent on tourists from China would give Beijing additional effective leverage over Nepal. Evidence is that by 2013, Nepal's travel and tourism industry directly and indirectly supported an estimated 1,344,500 jobs. Negotiations are additionally underway for direct flights between China and Nepal by a fourth Chinese airline. A good measure of a country's susceptibility to economic pressure is the manner in which Beijing used such leverage to coerce the Philippines to back off during its stand-off with that country over sovereignty of the Scarborough Reef.

During visits to Kathmandu since December 2013, senior Chinese officials have conveyed that as part of 'Peripheral Diplomacy,' Beijing had decided to revise upward the quantum of foreign assistance to developing countries in its neighbourhood and that Nepal and Pakistan will particularly be beneficiaries. Disclosing that both countries have been designated as 'friends,' they said development of the 'New Silk Road Economic Belt' would benefit Nepal. Talks are separately underway for extending the 1200-kilometre Qinghai-Lhasa-Shigatse railway to Kathmandu, agreed to by Chinese Premier Wen Jiabao during his unannounced visit to Nepal in 2012. China has in September 2014 confirmed that the railway will be extended up to Tibet's border with Nepal. Once completed, the railway will alter the geostrategic balance in the region.

Tibetans settled in Nepal are the focus of Beijing's attention and China sees Nepal as important in its continuing efforts to undermine the Dalai Lama's authority and influence among Tibetan Buddhists. A visiting senior Chinese official told a Nepalese journalist 'we visit Nepal because you have Lumbini, the birthplace of Buddha.' Lumbini has, over the past five years, emerged as the centre of Chinese efforts. The Asia-Pacific Exchange and Cooperation Foundation (APECF), a Beijing-based Chinese so-called NGO headed by a provincial cadre and academic of the Chinese Communist Party (CCP)'s United Front Work Department (UFWD), in 2010 unveiled a US$ 3 billion project for the development of Lumbini. Since then at least two other Chinese front organizations including the China Buddhist Association, of which the Beijing-selected 11th Panchen Lama Bainqen Erdini Qoigyijabu, is Vice President, have got involved with plans for redevelopment of Lumbini, which is located inside Nepal barely 30 kilometres across the border with India.

The projects proposed cause obvious discomfort to India as they envisage an international airport, hotels, allocation of plots of land to various Tibetan Buddhist high lamas and sects and a seminary-cum-monastery where all Buddhist monks would be taught by teachers approved by Beijing. This monastery has the potential to make the Indo-Himalayan border belt more vulnerable. Nepal also does not have the skill or manpower to build and manage a world-class airport, which will probably be constructed by PLA personnel. The allocation of plots of land to various Tibetan Buddhist high lamas and sects by Nepal is also done with Beijing's tacit approval and used by China to exert pressure on the Tibetan Buddhist sects to undermine the Dalai Lama. A recent example is the manner in which permission to allow the cremation of Shamar Rimpoche, a Regent of the Karma Kagyu sect, was delayed till Beijing accorded approval. A remark in 2012 by Nepal's then Culture Minister, Dr Minendra Rijal of the Nepali Congress, is revealing. Commenting on the Dalai Lama's exclusion from the US$ 3 billion development project in Lumbini proposed by the APECF, he said the Dalai Lama might visit Lumbini sometime in the future after 'the leadership of China will find ways to deal with His Holiness the Dalai Lama, which will be respectful of the Chinese people.'

The large number of developmental projects in Tibet affects India adversely. Its ecology, environment, climate, glaciers and rivers impact the region around it. Adversely affected will be Pakistan, India's vast Indo-Gangetic belt, Bangladesh, Myanmar, Thailand, Laos, Cambodia and Vietnam. The flows of China's two longest rivers namely the Yangtze and the Huang Ho will also be diminished. The proposed diversion of the

Brahmaputra River, an international trans-boundary river that supports nearly a quarter billion people, has major geostrategic implications for the lower riparian countries. India is the main beneficiary of trans-boundary river flows from the Tibetan plateau and many of its major rivers, including the Indus and Ganges, are fed by the glaciers in Tibet. China has been reluctant to dispel concerns about the proposed plans to divert the Brahmaputra and has been tardy in releasing data of the water flow in the river. The issue was not mentioned by Xi Jinping in his statement during his recent visit to India, though it figured high on Modi's list of concerns.

While there are other important threats that emanate from China, the ones listed above are among the more immediate in terms of current India-China relations. The ability of both sides to contain incidents on the border as the policies of both, India and China change and become firm will be a prominent feature of the region's geo-politics in this decade.

CHAPTER XIII

Pakistan: Capabilities, Intentions and Threats to India

Rana Banerji

Theoretical Premises

India and Pakistan, though emerging from a common colonial past, have followed radically different paths of political evolution, the one developing confidently into a mature Westminster style parliamentary democracy but the other struggling to cope through repeated disruptions of constitutional process and prolonged periods of dictatorial military rule.

Pakistan has been plagued by persisting insecurity about its very identity. Though it came into being as a Muslim majority state, the country consisted of two wings separated by 1000 miles. In between was perceived a hostile India. Events of Partition and bloodshed, the unequal division of military and other assets, and the untimely demise of a charismatic leader like Muhammad Ali Jinnah made the path to statehood very difficult.[1] The inordinate delays and constant bickering over Constitution-making discredited politicians in both parts of Pakistan. They began to be seen in contempt by civilian bureaucrats and Army officers.[2] This led to the Ayub Khan takeover in 1958 and initiated a process enabling the Army to cast itself in the role of arbiter or supreme defender of Pakistan's ideology, integrity and national interests, a dictum it used repeatedly since, to justify or legitimize its interference in domestic politics. The Army increasingly linked itself to Islamic ideology. New research into the Pakistan Army's thinking suggests this occurred not only under Zia-ul-Haq or in the 1960s under Ayub Khan,[3] but even earlier,[4] and it did not conflict with the Army inheriting the British Sandhurstian model in its initial evolution in independent Pakistan.[5] The crutch of Islam was used after every Martial Law takeover. The 1971 war and the emergence of Bangladesh accentuated this insecurity. Though the early 1970s did witness Pakistan's first experiment with democracy, developments in 1977 vividly demonstrated 'the three big refusals' which have plagued Pakistan's constitutional history and politics—(i) the refusal of the Army to accept democratic authority, (ii) the refusal of the Judiciary (at least till 2008) to question the Army's usurpation of power, and (iii) the refusal of the 'mullahs' (Islamic preachers) to allow democratic processes to take root.[6]

In terms of sheer military analysis, six general characteristics of Pakistan's strategic culture have been commonly enumerated:

i) **Opposition to Indian hegemony:** This insecurity is deep-rooted and stems partly from history. It also arises from troubled relations over the Kashmir dispute; it has been a consistent strand—military and civilian political elites are united in this opposition.

ii) **Primacy of Defence requirements:** Pakistan now spends close to $5.5 bn (Pakistani Rupees PRs 450 bn) every year on Defence—it ranks 28th highest in the world and 19th in terms of military expenditure alone. Its army is 5,50,000 strong; the Defence Budget is claimed to be below a ceiling of 4 per cent of GDP; in actual practice, with debt servicing and concealed expenditure under different heads, this amounts to as much as 60 per cent of its GDP.

iii) **Nuclear Deterrence:** Pakistan has waged a determined campaign to acquire nuclear capability after its defeat against India in 1971 and the emergence of Bangladesh. Its nuclear capability is claimed to be India-specific but possession of the 'Islamic bomb' has helped it to gain status and political influence in the Islamic world and in world affairs. The Military has control over nuclear policy. In recent years, Pakistan has rejected 'no first use' and professed intention to deploy 'tactical nuclear weapons' in response to reported Indian doctrinal intentions of 'cold start' to cope with military threats on two fronts.

iv) **Acceptance, but not over-reliance on outside assistance:** Pakistan has consistently sought, and received foreign supplies of modern weapons hardware and military training. The United States has been its main arms provider. In later years Pakistan received missiles and nuclear weapon components from China and North Korea.

v) **Stability on the Western border—quest for 'strategic depth' for conventional and nuclear assets:** This has been a policy objective ever since US help was received to push back Soviet forces from Afghanistan. In recent years, a strategic dilemma has developed as some of the proxy 'non-State actors' have turned inwards to attack bastions of the Pakistan domestic military and police establishment; but the objective of pursuing this strategic depth and excluding Indian influence from Afghanistan still remains.

vi) **Identification with conservative Islamic causes:** The emphasis on Muslim nationalism or 'Islam' as the guiding or rallying force for institutions of State and governance continues to play an important role in shaping national identity and foreign relations; however, it may be important to understand in this context that the military's obsession with India and Kashmir 'is not in origin Islamic, but Pakistani Muslim nationalist' also, over time, because Pakistan became the only Muslim nation to cross the nuclear threshold, its sense of national identity coalesced with its Islamic identity.[7]

Conventional Threats

These strategic imperatives led the Pakistani defence forces to a compulsive quest for conventional parity with India, with the help of generous financial assistance from USA, Saudi Arabia and China. Massive proportions of the budget were appropriated for defence spending, diverting even funds meant for upgrading counter-terrorism capabilities.

Even then, after 1971, the conventional balance remains skewed in India's favour, though not to the extent of a ratio of 3:1 (necessary for complete tactical dominance in battle). Though not exhaustive or entirely factually up to date, some salient points are depicted below:

Chart 1: India and Pakistan Comparative Force Levels

Army: Pakistan (5,50,000)	**India (1,129,900)**
9 Corps, 1 Area Command, 2nd Area Command coming up	13 Corps, 7 Area/Regional Commands
2 Armoured Divisions, 7 Independent Armoured Brigades	3 Armoured Divisions, 8 Independent Armoured Brigades
18 Infantry Divisions, 5 Independent Infantry Brigades	17 Infantry Divisions (Light), 12 Mountain Divisions 7 Independent Infantry Brigades 2 Independent Mountain Brigades
2 Mechanized Infantry Divisions, 1 Independent Infantry Brigade	4 (Rapid) Mechanized Infantry Divisions 1 Armoured brigade 2 Mechanized Infantry Brigades 1 Artillery Brigade
Pakistan	India
Strategic Forces Command (15,000)- Missiles – MRBR, SRBM, LACM- 60	Strategic Forces Command—Missiles- Agni-I, Agni-II, Prithvi I/II, IRBMs, SRBMs, Space-Satellites
2 Artillery Divisions 9 Corps Arty Brigades 5 Independent Artillery Brigades	15 Artillery Divisions 2 Independent Artillery Brigades 3 med Artillery 1 STA/MRL regiment
1 Air Defence Command 3 AD grps 8 AD Btlns 7 Engnr Brgdes	6 Air Defence Brgdes 2 SSM Regts with PJ-10 Brahmos 4 Engnr Brgdes
Air Force	
Pakistan (70,000)	**India (1,40,000)**
5 Commands, 17 Air Bases, 453 combat-capable aircraft	7 Commands, 65 Air Bases,798 combat-capable aircraft
F-16s – 63 in 4 squdrns; JF17s- 29 in 2 squdrns; Mirage III D&E – 70 in 4 squdrns; Mirage III-Rs-10; Mirage V-58 in 4 squdrns; Elint – 2 Falcon 20Fs; AEW&C-3Saab Erieye, 1 ZDK-03; F-7s-127; Trnsprt- 34- Hercules, Cessna, Allouttes, Mi-17s, Falcon 20 E(1)	MiG 29s- 64, Jaguars- 106, Mig 21s -356; Mirage 2000 E & EDs–52; Sukhoi-30s –153; AEW&C- 3 Il 76s; Trnsprt – 217- Il 76s, AN-32s, B-737s, Hercules

Navy

Pakistan (22,000)	**India (59,000)**
Submarines 13 (Tactical 8, SSK 5), Frigates 10, Patrol Craft 12, Mine MCM vessels 3, Amphibious Landing Craft 4, Logistic & support vessels 11	Submarines 29 (Tactical 15, SSK 14), Aircraft Carriers 2, Destroyers 10, Frigates 10, Patrol Craft 61, Mine MCM vessels 8, Amphibious Landing Craft 17, Landing Ships 10, Logistic & support vessels 49
Naval Aviation – 9 Combat-capable aircraft- 3 Atlantics, 6 P-3 C Orions; Helicopters 18;	31 Combat-capable aircraft- MiG 29s, Sea Harriers; ASWs; Helicopters- 127 incl 9 AEW craft & 12 UAVs
Marines 1400	Marines 2200

Basis: ***Military Balance 2012 & Wikipedia;*** accessed August 2015.

Equipment and Holdings

Most of Pakistan's modern military equipment comes from USA and China. A brief description ensues below, about the weapons and equipment profile of the Pakistani Army and the manner in which excessive dependence on US origin supplies have been gradually diversified and dependence on Chinese defence equipment, services and training has increased in all three arms of the Pakistani Defence Forces.

Pakistan Army has about 2,400 main battle tanks—an amalgam of MBT 2000 Al Khalids (240), 320 T-80 UD, 51 T-54/55s, 1100 Type-59, 40-0 Type-69s, 275 Type-85 and 248 M-48 A 5s.

It has 1,266 Armoured Protection Carriers, mostly of M-113 variant (US) and 166 APC (W) s of BTR & UR types.

4,520 Artillery guns include SP 490 155-mm guns (430), 200 M-109/M- 109 A2 guns, 203-mm 60M guns (110).

Towed guns number 1,630, including 105-mm (329), M-101(216) 122-mm guns (570), D-30 (80- from People's Republic of China), Type-54 M-1938 (490), Type-59-130-mm guns (410), 292 guns (155 mm), 144 M-114s, 148 M-198s and 28 M-115 guns (203 mm).

In addition, there are 81-mm and 120-mm mortars and MRL guns.

Other details of aircraft, helicopters, UAVs, Air Defence Equipment and radars, as also equipment with the Navy—submarines, frigates, patrol craft can be found in The Military Balance.

Military Doctrine and Orbat (Order of Battle)

The traditional threat on the Eastern border is tackled through location of Pakistan's main Attack Corps, I Corps at Mangla—this has three Infantry divisions and one armoured division under it, positioned at Jhelum, Kharian and Mangla. After the 2003 ceasefire on the Line of Control, one of these Divisions was temporarily deployed to the Western sector, to assist XI Corps, Peshawar in counter-insurgency (COIN) operations against tribal insurgents in Swat and FATA. The X Corps, Rawalpindi has both offensive and defensive responsibilities, assisted by the Force Command, Northern Areas (FCNA). The second Attack Corps is based in Multan, II Corps—this has Armoured Corps officers heading it usually. It has one Armoured Division and at least two Infantry divisions, as also a relatively newly deployed mechanized infantry division, though relatively peaceful conditions along the international border (IB) permitted deployment of one of the Infantry divisions to the Western sector, under XI Corps. II Corps has to focus on operations in desert terrain across Bahawalpur and into Rajasthan, across the IB. Defensive responsibilities along the eastern border are invested to the XXX and XXXI Corps at Gujranwala and Bahawalpur respectively. The Western sector is looked after by the XI Corps, Peshawar and XII Corps Quetta with V Corps, Karachi having Defensive and Reserve formations, with growing and persistent responsibilities for aid to civilian authorities.

Area Commands

In recent times, the Pakistan Army has accepted the decision to set up Area Commands on the pattern of the Indian Army. Only the Southern Command, coterminous with XII Corps at Quetta is known to have been operationalized though there are reports that there may be two more Commands—Central and Northern. There seem to be differences among the collegiate leadership of Generals on how exactly the division of powers and authority of Corps Commanders versus Area Commanders would be worked out and how Line and Staff duties would be assigned under the changed setup.

The Nuclear Threat

Pakistan acquired nuclear capability clandestinely, through the efforts of Dr AQ Khan mainly and other scientists in the Pakistan Atomic Energy Commission.[8] The clearest exposition of Pakistan's nuclear policy was made after the 1998 nuclear tests at Chagai. Former Foreign Minister Agha Shahi, former Foreign Secretary Abdus Sattar and former Air Chief Marshal Zulfiqar Ali Khan posited a 'counter-strategy' to a draft nuclear doctrine revealed by the Indian National Security Advisory Board (NSAB). They asserted that Pakistan's quest was for 'credible minimum deterrence' and was 'India-specific'; secondly, it was linked to solving the Kashmir issue and third, it was flexible in approach and would be determined by a dynamic threat environment. Further, given India's conventional military superiority, Pakistan rejected India's professed 'no first use' statement as a mere ploy or façade to justify second strike capability and pursuit of massive acquisition of nuclear weapons. Pakistan offered a 'no war pact' instead.[9]

Military Control over Nuclear Policy

The transfer of Pakistan's nuclear weapon-related programmes to military control occurred in stages. Gen Aslam Beg, as Chief of Army Staff (COAS) had given Dr Khan the go ahead to offer nuclear technology know-how to Iran. The Military's control was re-affirmed after Ghulam Ishaq Khan's forced resignation from the Presidency in 1993. Gen Abdul Waheed Kakar, the Army Chief was handed over this responsibility. He delegated this charge to Maj Gen Ziauddin, Director General, Combat Development in the Weapons Directorate, Army Headquarters.[10]

During the March 2012 Nuclear Security Summit in Seoul, South Korea, Pakistan tried to project its nuclear security regimen as a well-defined, robust command and control system comprising the National Command Authority (NCA), the Strategic Plans Division (SPD), and the Strategic Forces Command which exercises control over all aspects of policy, procurement, operations and nuclear security.[11]

Chart 2: Pakistan's Nuclear Command Authority and Strategic Plans Directorate

National Command Authority
(NCA)
(TOP TIER)

Employment Control Committee (ECC)

Development Control Committee (DCC)

Strategic Plans Division (SPD)
(MIDDLE TIER)
DG – Lt Gen. Zubair Hayat

Strategic Force Command (SFC)
(BOTTOM TIER DG – Lt Gen.
Obaidullah Khattak

Nuclear Command Authority 3

NCA Body

Chairman – President
Vice Chairman- PM
Dy. Chairman – (1) Foreign Minister
(2) Chairman JCSC

DCC Body

Head – Chairman JCSC
(Dy. Chair'n NCA)
Members – COAS, VCOAS, CNS, CAS
Head/Rep. of Strategic
Industrial
Organisations (Scientists/
Engineers)
Other Members
Secretary – DG SPD

ECC Body

Head – Foreign Minister
(Dy. Chair'n NCA)
Members - Minister of Defence
Minister of Interior
Minister of Finance
Chairman JCSC
Three Services Chief
Other Members
Secretary – DG SPD

Strategic Plans Division 4

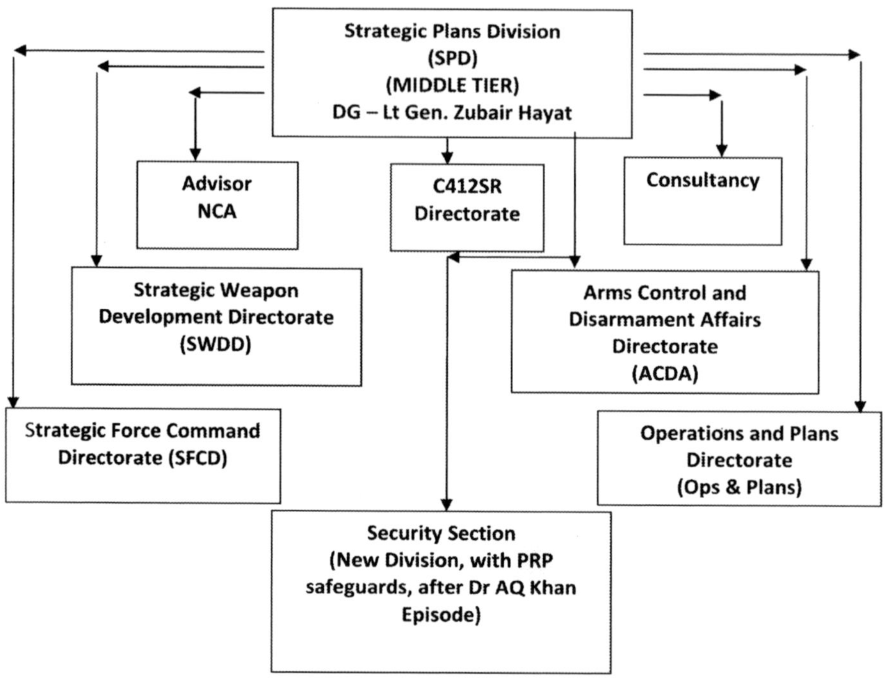

Pakistan has followed both the enrichment route, at the Kahuta nuclear research laboratories, and now the plutonium route, through the nuclear plants built with Chinese assistance at Khushab, in central Punjab. The Kahuta plant has a capacity of 15–45 separative work units (**swu**) and is estimated to have produced 2–3.5 tons of highly enriched uranium (**HeU**) by 2011. The two functioning plutonium reactors at Khushab can produce between 5.7–11.5 kilos of plutonium per year, enough for 1–3 warheads. Pakistan's plutonium stockpile is assessed at 100-160 kilos and its nuclear warhead stockpile is assessed at between 110-130 warheads at present, which may be stored in low readiness, de-mated format at different secret locations.[12]

Pakistan's Missile Development Programme

Pakistan initially relied on aircraft as delivery vehicles for its nuclear weapons.

In the mid-1980s, it procured forty F-16 aircraft from the United States that, when modified could be used for that purpose. Over the past fifteen years, Islamabad has begun placing part of its deterrent on ballistic missiles, dramatically increasing the probability of success of a strike on Indian territory. However, this capability remains limited. With a range of less than 1000 km, the *Shaheen-1* and *Ghaznavi* are more theatre than strategic missiles (though they could reach some of India's cities if placed in the eastern part of Pakistan). The *Ghauri's* range is longer but it is liquid-fuelled, thus less reliable and more vulnerable. Thus planners refer to the solid-fuelled, long-range *Shaheen-2* as the 'mainstay' of the country's future deterrent. If based in Punjab, it could reach the eastern cities of Kolkata, Bengaluru and Chennai.

By the late 1980s, the Pakistan Atomic Energy Commission (PAEC) had begun to import Chinese missiles. A few years later, KRL approached North Korea on behalf of the Pakistani military. Islamabad needed longer range missiles, and China was beginning to be pressed by Washington to limit its ballistic technology transfers. While PAEC introduced the *Ghaznavi* solid-fuelled missile (300-400 km) based on the Chinese M-11, KRL introduced the liquid-fuelled, single-stage *Ghauri-1* (1,300 km and 1,800 km) based on the North Korean No-dong. The National Development Council (NDC), created in 1990 as an offshoot of PAEC, developed the single-stage *Shaheen-1* (450-750 km) based on China's M-9. All these missiles were inducted in the Pakistani armed forces in 2003–04. NDC then developed the two-stage *Shaheen-2* (2,000-2,500 km), now entering service and slated to become the crown jewel of the Pakistani deterrent.

As of 2012, Pakistan may have a total of less than 100 of those medium-range missiles. Pakistan is also developing a large family of theatre or battlefield-range missiles. In the 1980s, SUPARCO developed the Hatf-1 (80 km) and Hatf-1B (100 km), which could possibly be nuclear-armed, but are primarily slated for a conventional role. As of 2012, it had about 100 of those. This family is now being enlarged through the development of a shorter-range missile (*Nasr*, 60 km) and of a longer-range one (*Abdali*, 180 km). The first test of the *Nasr* in 2011 was troublesome, since it was advertised as nuclear-capable which, for a 60 km-range missile suggests more a tactical than a strategic role, aiming to give Pakistan a sub-conventional capability to deter shallow/rapid Indian forays into its own territory.

Pakistan considers that all of its nuclear-armed missiles are of a strategic nature. A few years ago Islamabad began developing two cruise missile programmes, the *Babur* (ground-launched, with possibly other modes) and the longer-range *Ra'ad* (air-launched). Both are heralded as nuclear-capable. There have been unconfirmed plans for a *Ghauri-3* (3,500-4,000 km), which may have been cancelled in favour of a planned *Shaheen-3* (4,000-4,500 km).[13]

Army Strategic Forces Command (SFC)

The Army SFC has an estimated strength of 12,000-15,000 personnel. It is headed by a Lieutenant General and supervises all land-based strategic nuclear forces. Deployed assets include 105 *Hatf I, Abdali/Hatf 2, 50 Hatf* 3 (M-11s from China), up to 10 *Shaheen-I/Hatf* 4 missiles, and up to 25 *Hatf-5/Ghauri-II* missiles. Total surface to surface missiles are estimated to number 190. It is currently led by Lt Gen Obaidullah Khan Khattak.

During the past decade, there have been notable shifts in Pakistan's nuclear doctrine:

i) It has moved away from minimum deterrence to second strike capability expanding its nuclear weapons arsenal to include both strategic and tactical weapons. Their nuclear stockpile may have exceeded India's inventory and are estimated at between110–130 weapons;

ii) There is a deliberate shift from earlier generation enriched uranium weapons toward newer generation plutonium weapons—the newly constructed and functioning Khushab II, as well as reported under construction III and IV reactors, being built with Chinese assistance are not under nuclear safeguards;

iii) Progress has been made in miniaturization of weapons, enabling use in warheads mated to cruise missiles, both air and surface-based (*Ra'ad, Babur* or *Hatf VII/VIII* respectively), though doubts persist about their claimed accuracy during recent test flights. A new generation of short-range tactical missiles, claimed to be nuclear-capable are also being manufactured (*Abdali* or *Hatf II*—range 180 km and *Nasr* or *Hatf-IX*—solid fuel-based, range 60 km, recently tested again, February 2013).[14]

Response to 'Cold Start'/Proactive operations

A mix of old and new threat perceptions, still driven by the existential threat from India continue to prevail over the Pakistani military mindset. Tactical nuclear weapons are said to be a response to India's so-called 'Cold Start' doctrine or its suspected intention to launch quick-response punitive thrusts across the border in case of another major cross-border strike from Pakistan.

Some of these new doctrines were operationalized in a recent military exercise, '*Azm-e-Nau* (2012),' where an effort seems to have been made to practise exaggerated forward deployments or proactive operations, albeit and ostensibly in a defensive posture, to prevent enemy's tactical link-ups. The aim would be to strengthen border outposts with attack resources in advance and deploy 'sub-conventional (tactical) nuclear capability' with a 'credible interface between nuclear and conventional strategies,' to deter enemy advances. The exact details of command and control of these deployed strategic assets have perhaps not been fully or clearly worked out, there being some reports of differences among senior Commanders about the nature and extent of the Line Control of strategic assets, i.e. whether to remain with the SFC or be delegated to the Attack Corps.

Traditional Infantry and Armoured Divisions would be reconstituted as 'multi-role' divisions to facilitate offensive and defensive operations. Composite Battalion Groups comprising all arms—infantry, armour, mechanized units and engineers would be trained to mobilize within two to three hours of orders. Relocation of forward-leaning formations would be buttressed by expanding existing cantonments and constructing new ones, land acquisition for which has already commenced.

Though still stated to be in a formative stage, the implementation of this new military doctrine would remain dependent on funds and the extent of financial support from Pakistan's two main Defence donors, USA and China.

A nuclear component of this new thinking is also evident in recent Pakistani strategic writing, which suggests a shift from 'first strike' to 'first strike plus'; all possibly in the context of an overwhelming, lightning, conventional Indian blitzkrieg into their territory. Pakistan would like to convince India that a nuclear threshold exists, though it may be at a low level. Flexible policy options are touted for four thresholds, which include a pre-emptive response, using low-yield weapons, an early response or a delayed response depending on assessment of threats on its own high-value targets, and finally, an accumulated response when all else is lost.

Asymmetric Threats—Use of 'Non-State Actors'

For a long while now, the Pakistani establishment—including the Army, the Inter-Services Intelligence (ISI), and the bureaucratic and political elite—have believed that the only way to keep India engaged with Pakistan is to compel it to do so through cross-border terrorism and by extending support to non-State actors.[15]

Pakistan started supporting militant outfits in Jammu and Kashmir (J&K) right from 1947. This support was stepped up periodically, to the Jammu and Kashmir Liberation Front (JKLF) in 1989, then to Hizbul Mujahideen (HM) and other, more radical Islamic offshoots like Harkatul Mujahideen (HuM) and Al Badr. The idea that 'liberating Kashmir' was the most legitimate of jihads against the existentialist enemy India has been systematically promoted.[16]

Even before shifting its focus to J&K in the late 1980s and early 1990s, the ISI started supporting Sikh insurgency in India. This was accomplished by taking advantage of contacts with visits of prominent Sikh leaders like Ganga Singh Dhillon to Sikh holy shrines in Pakistan. They were patronized by old Muslim League politicians like Chaudhry Zahoor Elahi, who was close to Zia-ul-Haq. The ISI then took over logistic arrangements to host hardcore Sikh militants like Wasan Singh Zafarwal, Daljit Singh Bittoo, Paramjit Singh Parmar in safe houses inside premises of the Dera Saheb Gurudwara in Lahore. Even now militants belonging to the Ranjit Singh Neeta group continue to be harboured inside Pakistan.[17]

Lashkar-e-Taiba (LeT)

Significant State support was given to LeT from the mid-1990s, enabling it to grow militarily as well as to establish a robust social service apparatus, which the group used to pursue its missionary objectives. LeT won its spurs in J&K, becoming Pakistan's most reliable proxy there.[18] The Musharraf regime subsequently divided militant outfits into 'good Taliban' and 'bad Taliban' based on their controllability and utility, primarily against India. This, despite finding that by the end of the first decade of the twenty-first century many jihadis, especially in the Federally Administered Tribal Areas (FATA) and SWAT were turning against their own establishment.

The LeT has not, however, gone against the military so far. After 9/11, pressures to join the 'global jihad' were strong and LeT developed ties with Al Qaeda and Uzbek militants harboured in the safe havens of FATA and Khyber Pakhtunkhwa (KP). Its leader, Hafiz Mohd Saeed enjoyed considerable patronage from the military top brass and Punjab politicians like Shahbaz Sharif. Viewed through one lens, LeT remains a Pakistani proxy against India; through another, it behaves as a trusted Al Qaeda associate. To segments of the Pakistani populace, it appears through its front the Jamaatud Daawa as a welfare service provider, allowed by the State to so function.[19]

In recent years, safe havens have been extended to Indian Mujahedeen militants who were cultivated initially through contacts in UAE or Saudi Arabia, trained and then infiltrated back into India to function as sleeper cells, for future destabilization modules of violence in different parts of India. This trend too, is likely to continue.

Changing Threat Priorities?

A recent (January 2013) disclosure in the Pak Army's 'Green Book' (internal publication which encourages middle-level officers to cogitate on military doctrines and issues of geopolitical interest), suggests in a chapter entitled 'Sub-Conventional Warfare,' that terrorist organizations and anti-State elements along its western border [not named specifically but alleging to the Tehrik-i-Taliban Pakistan (TTP)] may have replaced India as enemy number one for the time being.[20]

While this could be a valid indication of the beginnings of some introspection or churning of ideas pertaining to the option of asymmetric use of 'non-State actors' against a conventionally superior enemy, it may be dependent on a 'wait and watch' evaluation of the situation across its northern borders even as US and ISAF forces withdraw from Afghanistan.

Tactical peace-making with elements within the TTP continues, despite the ongoing operation, Zarb-e-Azb (Sword of Islam/Prophet) in North

Waziristan and there is no evidence that the Pakistan Military is preparing to jettison groups like the Lashkar-e-Taiba (LeT), 'which remains loyal to and has never attacked the Pakistani State.' [21]

Pakistan's jihadi infrastructure has grown out of a carefully nurtured national narrative—since 1947, Pakistanis have been told that their country is a 'citadel of Islam,' that its destiny is to be an Islamic State, and that its Army is 'the sword of Islam.' This ideological milieu helped religious-political groups exercise greater influence on national discourse than justified by either the size of their membership or votes obtained in Pakistan's sporadic general elections. If the Pakistan Army is serious about eliminating extremism, it must realign itself in the context of Pakistan's domestic ideological polarization. If Pakistani nationalism continues to be defined solely in religious terms and the State rhetoric does not change, current efforts against jihadis in North Waziristan will remain cosmetic.[22]

Pakistan-China Collusion

China has become Pakistan's largest weapon supplier today. Chinese weapons are cheaper than Western weapons. Because of its special relationship with China, Pakistan is able to procure China-produced weapons at favourable prices. Although initially inferior in quality and prone to developing defects while in use, these deficiencies have been rectified or overcome through usage and familiarity, aided by training of Pakistani officials by Chinese technicians.

Modernization of Pakistan's Air Force continues with acquisitions both from USA and China. Of the 426 combat-capable aircraft with Pakistan, 46 are F-16s (A/B variants) while 12 F-16s are C/D variants. One squadron of JF-17 Thunder (built initially by the Chengdu Aircraft Industry Corporation-CAC, China and now being made in joint collaboration with PAF, Kamra at its F-6 Rebuild factory) is already functional while 150 more are on order. The total number of JF-17s with the PAF is estimated to go up to 250. Other aircraft include Mirage III & V, MiG F-7s and Transport aircraft from USA-C-130B/C-130 E, L-100, some AN-26s, Falcon F-20 Elint/EW aircraft & Early Air Warning Saab 200 Erieye (from Sweden), which terrorists attacked in PNS Mehran. In 2008, Pakistan contracted to purchase Chinese-built ZDK-03 early warning aircraft, the first time such aircraft are being sold outside China. Naval acquisitions from China include 24 C-802/CSS-N-8 anti-ship missiles, 4 Jiangwei class frigates and 4 F-22P type frigates ordered in 2006. Two of these, PNS Zulfiqar and PNS Shamsheer are in position, the other two are slated for delivery by end 2013.

However, in the context of asymmetrical use of non-State actors, particularly of the radical Islamic fundamentalist variety, China may have serious reservations regarding Pakistani support for such elements, especially Uighurs finding safe havens in FATA or regions bordering Afghanistan.

In sum, the Pakistan Army is taking steps for war deterrence through a combination of conventional, sub-conventional and asymmetric means to deter India, which will continue to be projected as 'Enemy No 1' by the Pakistani Army in the foreseeable future, even as the domestic threat is contained. Miniscule opinion among fringe Pakistani liberals or intelligentsia, some of them located abroad, suggests beginnings of introspection to change this national narrative, but prospects for internally or externally driven shifts in the Army's strategic culture have not manifest sufficiently.[23] Not much evidence of this change seems visible just yet. Till such time as it does, India can afford no complacency to lower its against persisting security threats from Pakistan and must concertedly devote itself to hone up its Homeland security and defence modernization capabilities under a time-bound programme.

NOTES

1. Shuja Nawaz, *Crossed Swords: Pakistan: Its Army, and the Wars within* (Oxford University Press, 2008), Introduction-Pg xxvii.
2. S Akbar Zaidi, *Military, Civil Society and Democratization in Pakistan* (Lahore: Vanguard Books, 2011), pp. 4-5.
3. Stephen Cohen, *Pakistan Army* (University of California Press, 1984).
4. Hussain Haqqani, *Pakistan: Between Mosque and Military* (Washington DC: Carnegie Endowment, 2005).
5. C Christine Fair, *Fighting to the end: The Pakistan Army's Way of War* (Oxford University Press, 2014), pp. 71-2.
6. Aitzaz Ahsan, *The News, Pakistan*, 2010.
7. Peter R Lavoy, *Pakistan's Strategic Culture* (US Defence Threat Reduction Agency report: 2006). Source:www.fas.org/irp/agency/dod/dtra/Pakistan
8. Feroz Hasan Khan, *Eating Grass: The Making of the Pakistani Bomb* (Stanford University Press, 2013).

9. *'Securing Nuclear Peace,' The News*, 5 October 1999.
10. Feroz Hasan Khan, op. cit.
11. Government of Pakistan, *National Statement on nuclear measures;* 12 March 2012.
12. Bruno Tertrais, *Pakistan's nuclear programme: a net assessment* (Fondation pour la Recherche Strategique, June 2012).
13. Ibid.
14. Shyam Saran, 'Dealing with Pakistan's brinkmanship,' *The Hindu*, 7 December 2012.
15. Sunil Khilnani, Pratap Bhanu Mehta & others, *Nonalignment 2.0: A Foreign and Strategic Policy for India in the Twenty-First century,* (New Delhi: Centre for Policy Research & National Defence College, 2012), pp. 18, para 55.
16. Stephen Tankhel, *Storming the World Stage: The story of the Lashkar-e-Taiba,* (Hachette India, 2011), p.4.
17. R Banerji, 'Pakistan: ISI—An analytical perspective,' *IDSA Defence Journal,* November 2011, Vol. 5. No 4, pp. 6-7.
18. Stephen Tankhel, op. cit. p. 5.
19. Stephen Tankhel, op. cit.
20. *ISPR Press Release*, 3 January 2013.
21. C Christine Fair, 'Lashkar-e-Taiba and the Pakistani State,' *Survival,* ISIS Journal, UK, Vol.93, No. 4 Aug-Sept 2011, pp. 29-52.
22. Hussain Haqqani, 'If the generals have changed their mind' *Indian Express,* 23 July 2014.
23. C Christine Fair, *Fighting to the end: The Pakistan Army's Way of War* (Oxford University Press, 2014).

SELECT BIBLIOGRAPHY

Anderson, Robert S, *Nucleus and Nation: Scientists, International Networks and Power in India* (Chicago: University of Chicago Press; 2010).

Andrew, Christopher, *The Defence of the Realm-The Authorized history of MI-5.*

Balachandran, V, *Intelligence Management-A new Paradigm* (Mumbai: Indus Source Books, 2014).

Basrur, Rajesh, *et al.*, eds., *India's Military Modernization: Challenges and Prospects* (New Delhi: Oxford University Press, 2014).

Behera, Laxman Kumar, *Indian Defence Industry: Issues of Self-Reliance*, Monograph No. 21, July 2013.

Buzan, Barry, *People, States and Fear* (London, 1983).

Carr, Caleb, *The lessons of Terror* (London: Little Brown).

Chakravorty, BC, *History of the Indo-Pak War, 1965* (New Delhi: History Division, Ministry of Defence, Government of India, 1992).

Chatterjee, Santimay, Dasgupta, MK, Ghosh, Amitabha (eds.), *Studies in the History of Sciences* (Calcutta: Asiatic Society, 1997).

Clausewitz, Carl von, *On War*, trans. and eds., Michael Howard and Peter Paret (Princeton, NJ: Princeton University Press, 1976).

Cohen, Eliot A, *Supreme Command: Soldiers, Statesmen, and Leadership in Wartime* (New York: The Free Press, 2002).

Cohen, Stephen, *Pakistan Army* (Berkley: University of California Press, 1984).

Defence Research and Development Organisation, 14th Report of the Parliamentary Standing Committee on Defence, Lok Sabha Secretariat, New Delhi, March 2007.

Defence Services Estimates, Government of India (for relevant years).

Dulles, Allen, *The Craft of Intelligence* (London: West view Press).

Encyclopaedia of Espionage, Intelligence, and Security.

Estimates Committee, 1992-93, 10th Lok Sabha, 19th Report, Ministry of Defence: Defence Force Levels, Manpower Management and Policy (New Delhi, 1992).

Fair, C Christine, *Fighting to the end: The Pakistan Army's Way of War* (Oxford University Press, 2014).

Feaver, Peter D, *Armed Servants: Agency, Oversight and Civil-Military Relations* (Cambridge, MA: Harvard University Press, 2003).

Government of India, Ministry of Defence, Annual Reports, (New Delhi).

Habib, S Irfan, and Raina, Dhruv (eds.) *A Social History of Science: Themes in Indian History* (Delhi: Oxford University Press, 2003).

Haqqani, Hussain, *Pakistan: Between Mosque and Military* (Washington DC: Carnegie Endowment, 2005).

Huntington, Samuel P., *The Soldier and the State: The Theory and Politics of Civil-Military Relations* (Dehradun: Natraj Publishers, 2005 Indian edn.).

Jawaharlal Nehru: Selected Speeches (New Delhi: Publications Division, Ministry of Information and Broadcasting, Government of India, 1996).

Khan Feroz Hasan, *Eating Grass: The Making of the Pakistani Bomb* (Stanford University Press, 2013).

Khera, SS, *India's Defence Problem* (New Delhi, 1968).

Khilnani, Sunil, Pratap Bhanu Mehta & others, *Nonalignment 2.0: A Foreign and Strategic Policy for India in the Twenty-First century* (New Delhi: Centre for Policy Research & National Defence College, 2012).

Kumar, Satish, (ed.) *India's National Security Annual Review 2011* (New Delhi: Routledge, 2012).

Longer, V, *The Defence and Foreign Policies of India* (New Delhi, 1988).

Malik, VP, *Kargil: From Surprise to Victory* (New Delhi: HarperCollins, 2010).

Mallik, Amitav, *Indian Science and Technology: A Status Review* (New Delhi: Paragon Publication, 2006).

Mukherjee, Anit, *Failing to Deliver: Post-Crises Defence Reforms in India, 1998-2010*, IDSA Occasional Paper No. 18 (New Delhi: Institute for Defence Studies and Analyses, 2011).

Mukherjee, Anit, ed., *A Call for Change: Higher Defence Management in India*, Monograph No. 6 (New Delhi: Institute for Defence Studies and Analyses, July 2012).

Mullik, BN, *My years with Nehru 1948-1963* (New Delhi: Allied Publishers, 1972).

Nawaz, Shuja, *Crossed Swords: Pakistan: Its Army, and the Wars within* (Oxford University Press, 2008).

Panikar, KM, *India and the Indian Ocean* (Bombay,1945).

Pradhan, RD, *Debacle to Resurgence, YB Chavan, Defence Minister (1962-66)* (New Delhi: Atlantic Publishers, 2013).

Raghavan, Srinath, *War and Peace in Modern India: A Strategic History of the Nehru Years* (Ranikhet: Permanent Black, 2010).

Raina, Dhruv, *Images and Contexts: The Historiography of Science and Modernity in India* (Delhi: Oxford University Press, 2003).

Rao, PVR, *Defence Without Drift* (Bombay, 1970).

Reforming the National Security System – Recommendations of the Group of Ministers (New Delhi: Government of India, 2001).

Singh, Jasjit, *Defence from the Skies* (New Delhi: Knowledge World Publishers, 2007).

Singh, Rajneesh, *United States Reforms to its Higher Defence Organisation: Lessons for India*, Monograph No. 41 (New Delhi: Institute for Defence Studies and Analyses, July 2014).

Singh, Simon, *The Code Book* (London: Fourth Estate).

Sinha, SK, *Higher Defence Organisation in India*, USI Papers No. 7 (New Delhi: United Service Institution of India, 1980).

Sinha, SK, *Operation Rescue: Military Operations in Jammu & Kashmir 1947-49* (New Delhi: Vision Books, 1977).

Smith, Chris, *India's Ad hoc Arsenal: Direction or Drift in Defence Policy* (SIPRI, 1987).

Strachan, Hew, *The Direction of War: Contemporary Strategy in Historical Perspective* (Cambridge, UK: Cambridge University Press, 2013 Kindle Edition).

Subrahmanyam, K, *Our National Security* (New Delhi, 1972), pp. 8–9.

Subrahmanyam, K, 'Defence Policy and Analysis,' in ICSSR Survey, *A Survey of Research in Political Science*, Vol. 5: International Relations (New Delhi, 1988).

Sun Tzu, *The Art of War.*

Tanham, George, *Indian Strategic Thought: An Interpretative Essay* (New York, 1992).

Tankhel, Stephen, *Storming the World Stage: The story of the Lashkar-e-Taiba,* (Hachette, 2011).

Tertrais, Bruno, *Pakistan's nuclear programme: a net assessment* (Fondation pour la Recherche Strategique, June 2012).

The Military Balance 2014 (London: International Institute for Strategic Studies).

Zaidi, S Akbar, *Military, Civil Society and Democratization in Pakistan* (Lahore: Vanguard Books, 2011).

List of Contributors

V Balachandran was Special Secretary, Cabinet Secretariat and Member of the High-Level Committee appointed by the Government of Maharashtra to enquire into the police response to the 26/11 terror attacks. A specialist in security affairs, he is a regular contributor to *Sunday Guardian* and has authored a book, *National Security and Intelligence Management*.

Rana Banerji was Special Secretary, Cabinet Secretariat. He is currently a Distinguished Fellow at the Institute for Peace and Conflict Studies, New Delhi and Visiting Professor, Jamia Millia Islamia University, New Delhi. He has written extensively on Pakistani politics and army including detailed monographs. He has been a member of several Track II dialogues.

Air Marshal BN Gokhale has been a fighter pilot and a qualified flying instructor and has actively participated in operations in the 1971 Indo-Pak hostilities. He has been Assistant Chief of Air Staff, Air Officer Commanding-in-Chief of Training Command and Vice Chief of Air Staff. He is currently heading the Centre for Advanced Strategic Studies, Pune.

Nitin A Gokhale is an authoritative defence analyst, author, media trainer and a multi-media reporter with more than 31 years' experience across web, print and broadcast mediums. In his reporting career, he has reported the Kargil War, the Eelam War IV in Sri Lanka for three years and different insurgencies from Kashmir, Northeast and Maoist-hit areas. He has written four books on insurgency, war and demography.

Dr S Kalyanaraman is a Research Fellow at the Institute for Defence Studies and Analyses (IDSA), New Delhi. He is also a member of the Editorial Board of the *Journal of Defence Studies*, and Advisor for *The Week in Review*. He was a Visiting Fellow at the Department of War Studies, King's College London. He is currently writing a book on the evolution of India's strategy and military doctrines.

Dr Amitav Mallik is a defence technologist who was among the first in India to work on indigenous laser technology. This culminated in his creating the first Indian Laser laboratory 'Laser Science & Technology Centre' (LASTEC) in Delhi under the aegis of the Defence Research and Development Organization (DRDO). He is a technology consultant and strategic affairs analyst and continues to contribute to national security issues including defence, space, energy, and environment security.

Lt Gen (Dr) Prakash Menon (Retd) PVSM, AVSM, VSM was the Military Adviser in India's National Security Council Secretariat. He has had extensive operational experience at different levels that included Company Commander on the Siachen Glacier and Line of Control (LoC) and counter-insurgency in Kashmir. He was the Commandant of the National Defence College, New Delhi.

Dr Deba R Mohanty heads Indicia Research & Advisory, a New Delhi-based research and consulting firm on defence and strategic affairs. He is also Vice President at the Society for the Study of Peace and Conflict (SSPC). He has been a member of the national defence committee of the Federation of Indian Chamber of Commerce and Industry (FICCI), United Services Institution of India (USI), Institute for Defence Studies and Analyses (IDSA) and Confederation of Indian Industry (CII). He has authored a number of books, research papers and commentaries/opinion pieces.

Dr Shrikant Paranjpe is Professor in the Department of Defence and Strategic Studies, and Director, Yashwantrao Chavan National Centre of International Security and Defence Analysis (YCNISDA), University of Pune, Pune 411007. He was a Fulbright Fellow (Post Doctoral Research) at the George Washington University, Washington DC in 1984-5 and a Visiting Professor at Colorado College, Colorado Springs. He has published several books and papers in the area of national security, strategic studies, and South Asian security issues.

Vice Admiral Vinod Pasricha (Retd) has been a Naval Fighter on the Seahawk Aircraft and the Flag Officer Naval Aviation and Assistant Chief of the Naval Staff. He has been the Flag Officer Commanding-in-Chief of the Eastern Naval Command at Visakhapatnam and also the Flag Officer Commanding-in-Chief of the Western Naval Command at Mumbai.

Maj Gen Shashikant Pitre (Retd) was Chief of Staff of the Army Training Command and has directed operations of the Indian Peace Keeping Force in Sri Lanka. He is the Founder Chairman of HORIZON, an organization for post-conflict environ management. He is a prolific writer having published articles and books on Kashmir Imbroglio, Conflict in Sri Lanka, biography of Admiral Bhaskar Soman and the 1962 India-China conflict.

Lt Gen VR Raghavan (Retd) PVSM, UYSM, AVSM was Director General of Military Operations. He was the founder Director of the Delhi Policy Group (DPG). He led the programme on nuclear policy stewardship aimed at sharpening the nuclear debate in India for introducing restraint and responsibility in nuclear policy. Lt Gen Raghavan has authored and edited a number of books on military strategy and security.

Jayadeva Ranade was Additional Secretary, Cabinet Secretariat. Presently he is a Fellow with the Centre for Air Power Studies. He has been appointed Member of the Core Group of China of the Indian Council of World Affairs (ICWA). He is a security and intelligence expert and a China analyst. He also writes for national newspapers, magazines and leading publications, mostly on strategic and security issues relating to China and has contributed chapters on these areas to five books.

Rakesh Sood is India's former Ambassador to Nepal, Afghanistan and France and the country's first Ambassador in charge of Disarmament in Geneva. He oversaw the negotiations concerning the Comprehensive Test Ban Treaty (CTBT) and the Chemical Weapons Convention (CWC), the deliberations on the Fissile Materials Cutoff Treaty (FMCT) and also participated in the Indo-US talks on security, non-proliferation and disarmament.

INDEX